DRAMATURGY OF THE DAEMONIC

Dramaturgy of the Daemonic

*Studies in Antigeneric Theater
from Ruzante to Grimaldi*

Jackson I. Cope

THE JOHNS HOPKINS UNIVERSITY PRESS
BALTIMORE AND LONDON

The Johns Hopkins University Press, Baltimore, Maryland 21218
The Johns Hopkins Press Ltd., London

Library of Congress Cataloging in Publication Data

Cope, Jackson I.
    Dramaturgy of the daemonic.

    Includes index.
    1. European drama—History and criticism—Addresses,
    essays, lectures.   I. Title.
PN1811.C67   1984   809.2′9353   83-23886
ISBN 0-8018-3120-2

For JOHN MALCOLM WALLACE

The double wood of ancient stocks
Linked in, so thick an union locks

Contents

Introduction

Some of the following essays were written ten to twenty years ago. They seemed worth writing at the time, and they still seem to me worth distinguishing from the detritus of false starts which litter any honest scholar's backward glance over the path of his developing or abandoned passions. In origin they reflected only critical and historical recognition of this or that monument or moment of a temporarily lost yet accessible past, a past to be saved by the critic from the dispersal of Babel. But now they are reengaged with the emphases of new essays which attempt to deny the finality of their earlier isolated existence, refocusing them in the context of a thesis—or an insight, or a claim—that I did not understand they were serving when they were written.

As the title suggests, this is a book rather than a collection, but what an Italian might call only a *bozza*, a sketchbook toward a history of dramatic continuity which I would wish to write if I could read enough. And I have let the two intentions dictated by my own critical history interact here in a sort of power struggle between the voice of the thesis-maker, the potential grand historian, and the voice (often calmer because more assured by self-imposed limits) of the younger critic.

When I have found my earlier essays so self-subsistent that, in spite of their relevance to the thesis, they seemed impregnable to restatement, I have left them intact except for the excision of allusions to scholarship which time has melted down. Nor have I made any effort to replace these losses with an updating that, in a few years, might seem equally ephemeral. This group is constituted by the essays on *Dido*, *Bartholomew Fair*, and *The Constant Couple*. To them might be added the essay on Peele's *Old Wives Tale* (reprinted intact from its initial publication) had it not been written recently with an eye toward the context of this book.

Others from the earlier stages of my efforts at thought simply seemed to cry out for response from the present. They appear now as obvious parts of a story I was trying to write, but obviously partial, pieces partly right and partly misdirecting attention. These—the re-evaluation of Richard Edwardes and, in a different way, the final piece on Goldoni—I rewrote to set them more closely right, the "rewriting" signifying not only the usual censorship of some of the pompous and ceremonial gestures endemic to young scholars, but an unabashed engulfing of the original intentions and attitudes into the maw of a later view capable of cannibalizing its own origins along with everything else.

What surprises me in the more contemporary essays is a sharpened edge of urgency to the critical voice, a rhetoric unpredictable from the tone of the earlier pieces, but clearly adamant. Thesis and tone, though, seem inevitable if I listen to the voices of those from whom I have learned my larger speculative perspectives: Bakhtin, Barber, Toschi, Weimann—those who have made a commitment to disestablishing a classical, generic aesthetic supposedly separable from popular, from folk, from radically pre- and antisocietal views of the human enterprise.

I find myself persistently returning to the word *daemonic* in allusion to theatrical origins and intentions from the beginning of the sixteenth century through the beginning of the nineteenth century. Being so recurrent (even if muted, implicit for many pages on end) in what follows, permit me to sketch out this word's emergence into my sense of the development and nature of Renaissance and eighteenth-century drama.

The narrowest historical sense, that developed in time most closely to our time, is the medieval adaptation of *daemon* to the diabolic. It is relevant in a double sense incorporate in my usage. First, it is incorporate in the ambivalences toward comic chaos in later centuries; second, the most central and continuous European representative of that chaos was Harlequin, who first emerges at the head of a sooty troop of devils in a monastic account of 1091 and retains his associations with this diabolic origin not only in medieval allusions, but into the eighteenth century of Germany, of Garrick, of Goldoni, and—stepping toward a new era—of Grimaldi. It is an oft-told history relevant to my terminology and before that to a long tradition, but relegated in both to a resonance, a reminder of the darkness shining in the light of bolder and lasting implications. The diabolic sense reflects an underworld; the *daemonic* in an older etymology is paradoxically more modern than medieval, yet reflective of a middle state, that of the heroes, the Homeric demidivinities who become by extension the antiheroic, anti-hierarchic intermediary spirits who aid the intercourse and mutual interpretation of men to gods and (the tragic function) of gods to men. There is a final sense in which I use *daemonic*, however, which may account for its persistence in the vocabulary of the following essays, both as a (doubtless irritating) refrain and as an ever-present implication (which I had not understood when first writing the essays on Edwardes and Jonson, for examples). It is that of a psyche less set against hierarchy than inverted, and so incorporating into the classic literary vernaculars of Europe aspects of a continuous folk world. This is the folk world that Mikhail Bakhtin tirelessly traces through the scatalogical and appetitive rites and argots of the Middle Ages as the fusion of spirit and matter in a pre-Cartesian world turned upside-down, a world where body functions simultaneously as womb and tomb, functions as a genital grave—reciprocal functions that Bakhtin's translator awkwardly passes on as his refrain in the phrase "bodily lower stratum."[1] Bakhtin set this medieval legacy to the Renaissance against the private, class-diminished inheritance he felt was all that the eighteenth century could understand and incorporate from that Renaissance. This was a mistaken view of the later period. In all of the particular and popular senses carried by or coalesced around the word, I wish in these essays primarily to reinforce what abler critics have taught us about the daemonic element in Renaissance drama and to renew a sensitivity to its persistence throughout an eighteenth century whose drama may have often seemed to modern eyes merely societal, sentimental, or farcical.

That is the informing outline of the historical *bozza* I offer to anyone interested in reading throughout what follows. For the less patient, I offer in each essay my contribution toward the understanding of some plays that individually are strong enough to bear the burden of our endless critical discourse.

NOTE

1. Mikhail Bakhtin, *Rabelais and His World*, trans. Helene Iswolsky (1965; Cambridge, Mass., 1968).

Acknowledgments

The intellectual debts incurred by a work whose parts span many years can never be recovered by the contributors, because students, colleagues, and editors have fueled and corrected my attempts at thinking about the drama beyond the possibility of recollection. In the last category, however, I can acknowledge the public help and encouragement of those several forums in which versions of some of these chapters appeared: *Texas Studies in Literature and Language* (1961) (Chapter 2); *ELH* (1982, 1974) (Chapters 3 and 6); *English Literary Renaissance* (1974) (Chapter 4); *Renaissance Drama* (1965) (Chapter 5); *MLN* (1965) and *Eighteenth Century Studies* (1973) (Chapter 8). I am also close enough to her insistence to gratefully thank Carolyn Moser for being an alert and charitable editor.

Much of the first chapter was written through the courtesy of the Rockefeller Foundation while their guest at the Villa Serbelloni in Bellagio. Some of the translations in that chapter were corrected by my generous friend of long standing, Franco Fido. He was unable to rectify the view I take of Ruzante, which he finds wrong-headed in many respects. But without his sophisticated partisanship I would have floated without anchor. My colleague Moshe Lazar not only reviewed German translations that limped, but stimulated me to rethink Goldoni's contexts when we taught together.

A word to Jack Goellner: best editor, adversary, director I can imagine for that difficult enterprise we call a university press.

A last word to DeAnn De Luna, companion who brought this *bozza*, like life, from a past into a future.

DRAMATURGY OF THE DAEMONIC

CHAPTER 1

Lives of the Daemon Players: Ruzante to Grimaldi

Poor Arlechino took a prance
To merry England, via France;
Came just in Christmas-pudding time,
And welcomed was by Pantomime.
But Pantomime's best days are fled:
Grimaldi, Barnes, Bologna—dead!
And Harlequins have ceased to draw
The town say, "Je vous n'entends pas."

—J. R. Planché, *The New Planet;
or, Harlequin out of Place*

" 'Arlequin,' said Gherardi, 'has no marked character; he is whatever one wishes him to be.' "

—M. Willson Disher, *Clowns and Pantomimes*

I cite the two quotations used as epigraphs to this chapter as the antitext from which to begin intuiting the natural development of drama as a series of antitheses to its own self-generated norms, its genres. And since most of the following essays will be concerned with comedy, let us begin with the comedians whose personae give that genre its formal epitome of stabilized chaos, yoking extreme expressions of veracity to life and a pure theatricality which gives veracity the lie.

Gherardi made his observation at the beginning of the eighteenth century, when Harlequin had been absorbed from his folk and dramatic origins into the rococo formulae of the Parisian *comédie italienne*. Willson Disher cited it as appropriate to his historical elegy on the English pantomime two centuries later. But that elegy is also an account—erratic, erroneous, but more full than any other—of the development of Harlequin's successor, the Clown. And the Clown was the creation of a single individual who, in being able to be all things, was so uniquely himself that he transcended the ephemerality of his stage vehicles but also transcended—or devoured—the impersonator necessary to the persona. "Joey the Clown, the first of 10,000 Joeys who took their name from him; here is the genius of English fun,"[1] to quote his best biographer. But Willson Disher in a characteristically pithy litotes has observed that "the history of mirth is mainly Italian."[2] It is no accident; rather, it is metonymy for the historical relations of modern comedy that English Clown's originator was Joe Grimaldi, child of an Italian actor with a murky but long family theatrical tradition (29–42, 240–42).

That such a cross-breeding should seem appropriate if not inevitable is a function of the historical implications unabashedly offered in this excursion into the comedian's particular paradox of self-creation. It is a paradox which begins in the sixteenth century with Angelo Beolco, who, never a member of a truly professional troupe, nonetheless energized the creation of the commedia dell'arte more forcefully than any other individual. It concludes in the nineteenth century with Grimaldi's success in replacing that debilitated tradition's ghostly legacy of Harlequins and Pierrots and Pantalones with Clown. I am making juxtapositions across some centuries, then, to suggest a history not of sources but of inner forms. The following essays will sketch that history in some detail but without the pretense to that exhaustive authority which alone could justify definitive description of those forms. And this first one is appropriately about players and playwrights rather than plays.

I

Joe Grimaldi's grandfather "Iron Legs," performer at the Paris *foires* in the 1740s (and probably in London even before), once leapt so high at the Opèra Comique as to shatter a chandelier over the Turkish ambassador sitting nearby. From the early through the mid-century this Grimaldi is reported as a dancer and pantomimist in and out of England and France, reports interspersed with allusions to his wife's appearances at the London fairs and in a Drury Lane harlequinade of 1768 (240–41). Joe's father Giuseppe carried on the tradition on the continent and in England, notices of him there appearing from the late fifties.

Both the professional and personal aspects of Giuseppe merit consideration as factors in making Joe Grimaldi the man and Joey the

Clown. Giuseppe spent thirty years in England as a well-known Pantaloon in the pantomimes, largely under Garrick at Drury Lane. He was a dancer and acrobatic comedian into his sixties ("the first to make the sad pierrot into a comic one and was known as the rough and tumble pierrot," recalled a contemporary),[3] serving generally as ballet-master to the troupe. "His own appearances as a dancer were intermittent, but he continued to compose ballets, to train dancers, and to perform in pantomime" (33). A veteran stager, then, product and representative of the versatility of continental *forains*. The acrobatic background was early passed to Joe Grimaldi. When he was less than three years old, he and his infant sister were enlisted as "dancers" in one of the older Grimaldi's spectaculars (this one in the raucous atmosphere of Sadler's Wells), *The Wizard of the Silver Rocks; or, Harlequin's Release* (20–21). The child was taught by his father dancing and acrobatic routines, stage sword combat, and even "skinwork"—the playing of monkeys and small beasts chained and trained; one story tells of his father having swung Joey so vociferously at chain's length that he flew out into the arms of the audience. A tale apocryphal but appropriate. For Giuseppe Grimaldi was widely known as a cruel, unscrupulous, and neurotic old man. The *Memoirs* of Grimaldi combine with gossip about the father to paint a social background for the Clown's originator in shadings of Dickensian dark. The children were beaten often. That there is more than memory's exaggeration here is made clear by the fact that when Grimaldi was four or five, his father, briefly engaged as ballet-master over a new troupe of sixty children, so abused them that criminal charges were preferred by a number of parents, and a sordid investigation and whitewash followed; a decade earlier Garrick complained that Giuseppe Grimaldi was "the worst behaved man in the whole company and should have had a horse whip" (43–46).

Joey Grimaldi was the illegitimate son of this father and a cockney minor actress who was third in the hierarchy of wife and mistresses whom his father currently was keeping. He was a theater great born into a theatrical tradition rich in continuity from the popular playing of Italy and France. And yet Joe, in spite of his Italian heritage, became "the genius of English fun." To unknot the paradox here it is necessary, for our history of inner forms, to abandon the bell-shaped historical mode of influence/development/decline so frequently applied to post-Renaissance drama and popular entertainment. But to understand why Grimaldi's particular adaptation of those forms should have so individualized them that they became his theatrical moment's indigenous voice in (and of) England, one has to intuit what one reasonably can of the absorption of player into role. It is to watch the comic reform pain and fear into the laughter that lies like truth. And this, after all, is where comedy had its vague but indubitable origin: in all those rites of regeneration which offer a Rosetta stone to translate the kinship of meaning among the Babel of popular theatrical events practiced well into Grimaldi's time by every folk culture of Europe.

In Grimaldi's case, we must begin with the father, not as his dramatic tutor but as the psychic model, exorcised only by being used as the spirit of that grotesque theater of extreme cruelty which was regenerated from the feeble harlequinades into the Clown. A perennial regeneration, of course, which Garrick and Goldoni had managed at their moment a few decades before Grimaldi made his own stage reform. But each regeneration was different, incremental. So one begins again with Giuseppe Grimaldi.

Joe reports his father's staging of a death-bed scene, impersonating his own corpse before his children to test their reactions; and reports his own childhood shrewdness in playing the grief-stricken son in self-protection shored against the inevitable resurrection of the "corpse."[4] This is a homemade "turn," a chilling, near-spontaneous adaptation to life of those "testings" of love risen from the bier which stud the English drama from Beaumont's *Knight of the Burning Pestle* or Chapman's *Widow's Tears* through Etherege's *Love in a Tub*, Steele's *Funeral*, and beyond. It chills because of the collaboration of father and son, and because it was not a sport but reflects a morbid obsession Giuseppe impressed upon his family. Grimaldi senior's death seemed always being reported: now he had fallen into eternal perdition from the cliff at Margate; now he had eaten himself to death in Brighton. But always the resurrection. In the latter case, reported the *Morning Post*, he was "brought to life at Fulham the same day—three or four times a year he eats himself into a second sleep, and he appears as dead" (31–32). The public rumors of this sort, quite aside from the bitter animosity Giuseppe Grimaldi seems to have been capable of almost universally inspiring, reflected his private fantasies. The bridge between the personal and the public was constructed in his pantomimic performances. He created the "skeleton" scene to capitalize upon his penchant for "expiring faces"; the *Times* reported of a version: "The whole purpose of the situation [was] to enable the Clown, by means of dumbshow to give a forcible delineation of terror."[5] (Joey had early learned it at home.) Such scenes of slapstick terror were a staple of drama long before as well as long after Giuseppe Grimaldi, no doubt; and one cannot but wonder whether it was based, in part at least, upon Grimaldi's envy or emulation of Garrick's Richard III or Hamlet. But in this case of comic business the significance which transcends theater and its traditions comes from the personal neurosis reported by Joe Grimaldi in the *Memoirs* of his life:

[My father was] a most morbidly sensitive and melancholy being, and entertained a horror of death almost indescribable. He was in the habit of wandering about churchyards and burying-places for hours together, and would speculate on the diseases of which the persons had died; figure their death-beds, and wonder how many of them had been buried alive in a fit or a trance; a possibility which he shuddered to think of, and which haunted him both through life and at its close.[6]

So it did. Dying just before Joe Grimaldi was ten, Giuseppe left a last heritage of the grotesque. His will instructed Joey's older sister to have his head severed in the coffin before he was buried. She did. A surgeon cut off her father's head, "she touching the instrument at the time" (42).

Joe Grimaldi, after this grotesque paternal farewell, grew up in greenrooms and on the fringes of the stage. By thirteen he was a promising actor; by the age of eighteen he was a successful Pierrot—and married. A year later wife and offspring died during childbirth. As the *Memoirs* observe, "There always seemed some odd connexion between his good and bad fortune; no great pleasure appeared to come to him unaccompanied by some accident or mischance."[7] He became hysterical, suicidal; then he turned his passion to his work: "He became fanatical, and the daemonic energy which he released upon the stage served to build up the second personality of Joey the Clown" (85).[8] But the first personality was that of Grimaldi's anxiety-ridden son. Misfortune shockingly (or inevitably) offered Grimaldi that experience of premature entombment which his father had vividly fantasized. A theater riot at Sadler's Wells caused numerous people to be trampled to death one night in 1807. Awakened and partly informed, Grimaldi, then thirty, rushed to the theater, where his father-in-law resided. Finding the entrance jammed with crowds, and a back window unlocked, he

flung the sash and jumped in 'à la Harlequin.' There, around him, were the corpses of men, women and children, stretched out on the floor and the furniture. . . . This was a room of the dead, . . . and not a living soul but the Clown. . . . Worse still, the door was locked on the other side: he was shut up in a tomb. . . . It was nightmare terror . . . he began to shout and bang on the door, in rising hysteria. But the Hughes family, in the neighbouring room, were so terrified to hear this screaming from a room which they had locked upon the dead, that they clung together in fear . . . until someone recognized the raging, beseeching voice as that of Joe Grimaldi. (124)[9]

Never has child acted out more literally his parent's fantasies than did Joey those imaginings which the older Grimaldi had externalized in his "skeleton" scenes. And like the father, the son translated the horror to the stage, himself repeatedly incorporating the skeleton scene into his pantomimes. The terror he conveyed in these skits clearly was more daemonic than slapstick, as evidenced by an account of a Shakespearean venture: "I once saw Grimaldi, on a benefit night, give the dagger scene in *Macbeth*. It was a darkened scene introduced in a pantomime, and he was in his clown's dress. Notwithstanding which, and that he only made audible a few elocutionary sounds of some of the words, a dead silence pervaded the whole house, and I was not the only boy that trembled. Young and old seemed to vibrate with the effect upon the imagination."[10]

Joe Grimaldi, perhaps hereditarily syphilitic and, in any case, an overwrought and overextended practitioner of an emotionally and physically draining profession (he once said every bone in his body had been broken or injured in performance),[11] aged rapidly. Before he was forty he suffered an illness which made him an old man within the next half-dozen years. And it was this illness, no doubt, which created another macabre bond with his father's dark legacy when (as Hazlitt reported) premature rumours of Grimaldi's death circulated in 1815 (185).[12]

Grimaldi would, in fact, live another twenty years, twenty years of physical and emotional suffering. He became crippled and unable to play; his old friends died; his wife died; his son deserted the stage, became a heart-breaking prodigal, and died. Yet Joe Grimaldi possessed in these years the balsam of knowing that Joey the Clown was the most popular figure of the English stage, celebrated by simple and great alike. Crowds stampeded the theater for hours before his farewell benefit performance, and the players stopped the pantomime to lead the audience in hailing him when Grimaldi anonymously attended a performance at Sadler's Wells in 1837, four months before he died. Byron, Hazlitt, the king, and his fellow stagers all celebrated his talents in varied homage. Neurotic and ill-starred Joe Grimaldi was repeatedly resurrected by Joey the Clown. And, based on fact or fiction, a story told of Grimaldi by the illustrator Cruikshank has a poetic truth as an epitome of the comic's function in transcending pain and resurrecting the pleasure principle at a level so far beyond ordinary expectation as to lead us through the absurd view of daily life back to the daemonic from which comic forms and characters come.

Grimaldi and his wife quarreled over their finances so violently, Cruikshank records, that they despaired and agreed upon joint suicide by poison:

> But not taking enough, . . . the feeble dose merely kept them awake and talkative, and lying in the same room, with a slight partition between

them, sensations became unpleasant; and so they held a colloquy in their fears as follows:

'Joey, are you dead?'

'No, Mary—are you?'

'No,'

And then they altered their minds, and felt disposed to live a little longer, arose, had a good supper and something warm and comfortable as a sedative and antidote, and then jogged on a little more in unison.[13]

It is a story which brings us back to the birth of a legend, to the question of the mechanisms by which Joey the Clown came to share and overshadow the life of Joe Grimaldi.

II

Gherardi's remark that the declining Harlequin of the late seventeenth century "has no marked character; he is whatever one wishes him to be" is echoed by Lamb in describing Joseph Munden, contemporary and, in a fashion, successor to Grimaldi as England's leading clown: "He is not one, but legion. Not so much a comedian, as a company. If his name could be multiplied like his countenance, it might fill a play-bill." Richard Findlater cites this description as the antithesis to Grimaldi's Clown, who was "always the same Joey: that was the essence of his success" (163). And this Joey was a thoroughly English clown, "neither butt nor yokel, but a true John Bull" (155-56).[14] But this highly individualized Clown, of course, is highly dependent upon tradition for becoming that to which Grimaldi gave being. Moreover, it is in good part the tradition of Harlequin himself in his earlier manifestations as they were shaped from the *zanni*, the countryman alternately, simultaneously dumb and shrewd, butt *and* trickster. And this type was given impetus in the Renaissance by the "Ruzante" of Angelo Beolco, closing the circle of that popular comedy so important to the great drama of England and Italy alike, closing a grand circle of almost exactly three centuries.

In the Commonwealth the exaggerated ruff became a part of varied costumes for English clowns and fools and Merry Andrews at Bartholomew Fair and other occasional playing sites, but these were displaced at the beginning of the eighteenth century almost entirely by the personae and costumes of the commedia dell'arte figures so violently transformed otherwise by the French *forains*. Harlequin, Pantalone, Scaramouche, and Pierrot became the universal, if no longer individualized type rôles upon the international stage, their dominance persisting in the very name of the English "harlequinade" of Grimaldi's time. The London companies, however, early introduced a country clown as Pantaloon's or even Harlequin's servant; this clown was a fellow traveler to the earlier zanni, notable primarily as an acrobatic target of abuse and for the ragged nondescriptness of his costume, in contrast to those of the commedia types with whom he shared the stage.[15]

But Harlequin and the others persisted, and Grimaldi's father was best known as a Pantaloon. Then, in 1800 Joe Grimaldi ushered in the new century with a new conception of the Clown's central role. The emergence was announced with flair. Young Grimaldi persuaded the proprietor's son-in-law, Charles Dibdin, to risk innovations in the traditional Easter pantomime at Sadler's Wells. In spite of having played largely straight character roles previously at the Wells, Grimaldi made a place for himself beside the veteran primary clown, Dubois. The pantomime, *Peter Wilkins*, was to have two clowns, Gobble and Guzzle. As the latter, Joe Grimaldi was of course the drinking clown. This much had been Dibdin's conception, recalling Joe's earlier sporadic comic attempts and the power of the older Grimaldi's name. But Grimaldi himself, apparently, induced Dibdin to clothe the two clowns in extravagant colorfulness rather than in their previous nondescript buff, an extravagance of dress which surpassed even the Italianate figures, to mark the Clown as the comic center. "From that time," Dibdin claimed in his *Memoirs*, "at the Wells at least—the Costume of the Clown was completely changed, and a whimsical mixture of colours and compositions invariably studied" (81; 78–81). The next year the older Dubois left the Sadler Wells company, fully liberating Grimaldi to enhance his costume innovations with the face painting which has become each clown's mark of individual talent within tradition to this day. As Dibdin said, "The present mode of dressing Clowns and painting their faces, was invented by Mr. Grimaldi, who, in every respect, founded a *New School* for Clowns" (97). Grimaldi was a master of quick change and appeared in dozens of costumes and roles; he was a master of satiric "construction," inventing a vegetable man opponent to his own mocking "Joe Frankenstein," or a Prussian Hussar costumed in coal scuttles, candlesticks, and brass pans. But always there was the painted visage with its exaggerated brows, its red triangled cheeks peering through the disguises which, as often as not, soon fell away or were discarded to reveal the red, white, and blue jacket, the knock-kneed knickered uniform of Clown Joey beneath.

If Joey is a recognizably English clown of Grimaldi's invention, though, he is much more. The painted face that stares at one from the dozens of depictions, like the energy Joey exhibited on stage, the grotesque absurdity of his violent "turns," appears to offer us a share in the daemonic. "Clown's" face is sub- and suprahuman simultaneously, as had been the half-beast devil mask of the original Arlecchino. Like that Italian original, Joey is a thief, a glutton, a coward, and a sadist whose greed is only expressible as a total incarnation of appetite in all things: "He was a Cockney incarnation of the Saturnalian spirit; a beloved criminal free from guilt, shame, compunction or reverence for age, class or property. That was Joey" (160).[16] When we view the character in this light we can see the history of Harlequin's decline in the eighteenth-century popular theater quite differently. The Joey who replaced Harlequin was actually the resurrection of his original form and spirit as the half-man half-daemon who irrupted from the shadowy history of Germanic devils, a carrier of irrepressible irrationality and desire into the fragile forms of social restraint.

It is through this violent element that one can best view the transmutation of that neurotic and almost tragic figure Joe Grimaldi into Joey the Clown, the alchemy of suffering into the comic which, to recall Kierkegaard, "transforms as by magic the reasonable creature one calls man into a caricature." The great triumph in which the harlequinade was redefined and Grimaldi became the preeminent clown without rival was the 1806 *Harlequin and Mother Goose*, which set the pattern for a century of pantomime. Among the myriad of episodes is the capture of Pantaloon in a steel trap which sets off a gun that shoots Clown in the belly. Harlequin cuts off Clown's ear, and it is glued back. In vengeance, Clown kills Harlequin with a red-hot poker, and he is at once resurrected. As Disher reminds us, Grimaldi had the "ingenuity to produce some new thing but did not despise the old. That Italian device of a dismembered body which is joined together and revives was tried by him in a scene where Harlequin was chopped up in a cauldron, nailed limb by limb against the wall, and restored to life."[17] In the twilight of his career, under the gentle title of *Harlequin and Cinderella*, Grimaldi introduced a scene in which Clown Joey's arm is lost in a scramble of slapstick. Soon the arm reappears, skipping about the stage to taunt him. Joey chases it, catches it, stomps on it—and screams in pain. This skit was from 1820, when Grimaldi's body was already on its way to the continuous agony which by rapid stages would leave him a cripple. It is a small symbol of that way in which the fears of the man were absorbed into the renewing life-blood of old theatrical traditions. Sadistic death and inevitable resurrection had been a basic pattern of comic renewal in the *commedia scenarii*, in English comedy from *The Knight of the Burning Pestle* to Garrick's *Harlequin's Invasion*, and in the folk *Maggi* and Mummer's plays which formed much of the background of sophisticated drama in both cultures. But there was no recovery for Signor Giuseppe Grimaldi once his head had been severed in young Joey's household. And if Grimaldi emerged alive from the macabre "dead" room after the Sadler's Wells riot, it was a shattering, not a renewing experience. But who could have appreciated better than this death-shadowed man the function of all that grotesque stage violence with its predictable resurrection as the exorcising of fear and trembling? Joey the Clown and the man who became him were simply the bright face and the dark obverse of a single entity. It is good to report that on one occasion they shared the experience of renewal usually inherent only theoretically in comic form. Grimaldi played before a crowd of sailors at Islington, including a deaf-mute who had become so through sun stroke some years earlier. Grimaldi's Clown so affected him that he suddenly shouted, "What a damned funny fellow," and continued to speak. Before the almost incredulous Grimaldi could make his way to the tavern where the man was holding forth, "the news rapidly spread through the neighbourhood that Joe Grimaldi had restored speech and hearing to a deaf and dumb sailor, had given back sight to a blinded soldier, had raised a man from the dead" (133).[18]

By some such routes as those I have sketched, Harlequin became Clown, and Joe Grimaldi became Joey. But the final question remains: how and why did Joey, who arrived after decades of harlequinades and arose in that element, become the distinctively *English* Clown?

As always, one part of an answer lies in the powerful irrelevancy of large historical forces. In 1793, just at the beginning of young Joe's mature career, Napoleon's declaration of war minimized for two decades the contact between the Paris *foires* and the English theaters. The intercourse with the Continent and its players which had been a matter of course to his father's generation never was available to Grimaldi. Born in London, he spent his life without leaving the British Isles. Beyond this, of course, it was upon the skeletal type offered by the familiar contemporary country stage clod that Grimaldi built the dominant energies and colorful costume which made Joey the ever-victorious principal in the grotesque struggles with Harlequin, Pantaloon, and the other inherited figures.

But most important was the reintroduction of an English setting—of, one might say, a background of that daily life which comedy always celebrates in hyperbole. Everything was satirized in Grimaldi's skits: the interloping Prussian Hussars or the West Indian dandy Romeo Coates; Jack Tar as well as Beau Brummell and the lady "dandizettes" of Regency extravagance; Frankenstein's monster and Napoleon. But they were all current targets, interlopers and exemplars on the English scene. That was what was so revolutionary to the pantomime (and to Joey the Clown) in the 1806 premiere of *Harlequin and Mother Goose*. The pantomime opened upon an unexpected scene after all the rococo and romantic settings familiar from the Parisian borrowings of a century: an English village on a summer morning. A natural and native scene, upon which begins to unfold a familiar story: young Colinette, in love with Colin, is being forced into marriage with the wicked widower Squire Bugle. The fantasies and transformations loom in the background in the person of Mother Goose. And the wicked squire in hunting regalia reveals himself as—Joey the Clown. The transformations begin as the characters become Harlequin and Columbine, Pantaloon and the Clown. Clown dominates in a dizzy series of tricks (an inn dinner overturned; a mailbox which in a "turn" becomes a lion's head devouring the arm of thieving Clown, etc.). "The hero of the game is really the rascally Clown. Every one is on the anarchist's side. There is no end to his antics, and no particular continuity but the succession of familiar English scenes" (116).[19]

Joey became the English Clown by dwarfing the traditional cast of Italian types who peopled his harlequinades just as they had those before him, by crossing the subterranean subversiveness of the older Arlecchino with the manner and stupid shrewdness of the English country fellow, and by setting the whole in an England which gave it a local habitation and "verisimilitude" against which the extravagant triumph of life over death, the daemonic over the daily, could be played out. In this, too, Grimaldi's originality was paradoxically returning to origins. For the first great creator of a character on the modern stage was Angelo Beolco, who himself became absorbed into that comic and complex character Ruzante, whom he fashioned out of watching the Paduan countrymen react to the big wars and the big cities in which modern popular comedy was created by the dramatists of the Renaissance.

III

Luigi Riccoboni, actor and historian, said in the first history of the Italian theater that Ruzante adapted from Plautus the stylistic technique of mixing dialects, Italian, and even modern Greek in his comedies, and that "the masquerades of Carnival furnished him the dress and characters of his actors. It is Ruzante who introduced masked personages to the Italian stage."[20] This is an historical shortcut to the birth of the commedia dell'arte, a shortcut which was modernized in Maurice Sand's book of masks and has been subsequently cautioned against by serious critics. No one invented the commedia; no one introduced masks. Ruzante had no role in the earliest commedia troupes. Yet Riccoboni was right. It is not that the commedia would not have existed without Angelo Beolco/Ruzante, any more than the English clown would not have been formulated without Joe Grimaldi. It is that societies inevitably seize upon some men as epitomes of inevitable events. Beolco was one of those men. But his own achievement, the essential melding of popular past and theatrically sophisticated future, the very nature not only of Ruzante's relationship to the formation of the commedia troupes but to theater as its original forms persisted into modernity—these are the points we have missed in attempting to locate him in dramatic or social history. Riccoboni and the Italian Marxists miss the mark. The plays are neither Venetian nor Plautine ultimately, neither pre-Marxist nor pre-commedia markers of a new awareness. They are, rather, the best evidence for the difficulties of dealing with self-awareness in an art which finally defined life as dramatic form. The burden of these pages on Ruzante as dramatist-actor will be that he shared Grimaldi's talent and destiny as one who had to become a theatrical being in order to perpetuate the theatricality demanded, thirsted after, by a society in search of its past. The beginnings of the comedic tradition which the following essays examine is just this search for a paradox which Grimaldi represented at the end of its first modern stage. The daemonic essence is radical to the human state. But daemons were exorcised from the paradisiacal beginning along with man, and could not be invited back without historical baggage. Ruzante, as Beolco developed his relationship to that character, created the first truly impressive illusion of such a heavy social load. Grimaldi carried it to the end.

We can begin with the birth of Angelo Beolco, a bastard son to a Paduan professor, rector of the university's faculty of medicine and pharmacy—probably before 1496.[21] Or better, we can rebegin with the rebirth of Beolco as Ruzante, a peasant from the mainland Veneto speaking in the Paduan dialect, a version of the appetitive, hapless, and irrepressible Arlecchini who formed the mythic and structural center of the commedia dell'arte *scenarii* and their successors in the drama of Garrick and Goldoni. "Ruzante" was probably born at the estate (once harboring a theater) of Beolco's friend and patron Alvise Cornaro. Soon the little patrician playlets presented here, exercises in translation of the peasant mentality, were paralleling, but transcending, the Venetian entertainments of professional mountebanks from San Marco—Cimador, Zan Polo, and Beolco's fellow actor in the early skits Menato.[22] As in Grimaldi's case, a dramatic tradition was focusing upon a type rather than a form, in such a fashion that the type would dictate unexpected continuities once it penetrated new genres. Actor over author, or author recognizing the primacy of the actor over any notion of genre, of literary expectation: that is the history of Beolco's development into Ruzante (cf. Zorzi, xxxv).

But the genres must be established if they are to serve as stimuli and frames for antigeneric developments. This was true in one sense of the word for Grimaldi, whose Clown gained in personal definition when, with *Harlequin and Mother Goose*, he entered into unlikely juxtaposition with the English countryside, the *OED* reminding us that "genre" is "a style of painting which depicts scenes and subjects of common life." It proved true in another sense of the word when Beolco set Ruzante successively into the generic contexts most familiar to Venice and the Veneto at the beginning of the sixteenth century. Chronologically Beolco worked from smaller forms to larger ones, feeling into the formation of the character before he could trust his own and Ruzante's ability to occupy sophisticated generic territory with the double thrust of characterization and the undifferentiating energy of the perennial daemonic. In 1521 Ruzante appears in *La Pastoral* (one of those dialect comic eclogues popular in the Paduan dialect a long century before Beolco's versions) and in a dialect mock oration.[23] In another year or two came the extended development of the *mariazo*, a marriage form popular in the Veneto and as a folk ur-drama but never before developed at such length and in such complexity as in *La Betía*; Beolco returned to the expanded mariazo around 1530 in *La Fiorina*. He proceeded to the rapid development of Ruzante in two one-act plays about the peasant and the wars, "dialogues in rustic dialect," and the closely related regular play *La Moscheta*. These are Beolco's most widely known works, those most accessible to the frequent insistence upon his social conscience and realistic depiction of the horrors of war visited upon the small people who are swept into its historical whirlwind. But the hyperbolic braggart soldier is so far foregrounded in these contemporary vignettes as to go some ways toward tempering the sense of class or reportorial consciousness which has been assumed variously as Beolco's intent and focus. Finally, in 1532–33 Beolco wrote two New Comedy Plautine adaptations, *La Vaccària* and *La Piovana*, and an original romance, *L'Anconitana*. In short, his is a career which begins and ends with explicit experiment in defined genres of the most varied sort. And always Ruzante remains that developing constant whose presence reforms forms.

IV

One can begin with Zorzi's tempting geography of hunger and sexual desire with which Ruzante is separated from the usual vision of his work as precursor to the commedia dell'arte. One hears a refrain from the sociological mainstream of Goldoni criticism cast backwards three centuries when Zorzi tells us that Beolco gave historical moment to the contrast between country and city; that in Bilora (the country-man of the "Second Dialogue") he finds a paradigm: "Hunger and sex have been the impulses moving him to confront the adventures of his first urbanization" (Zorzi, xxvii–xxviii and 1380, n. 8).[24] To correct this tempting example of the sociologizing of theater, one might recall how similar are Robert Weimann's remarks upon the moment of urbaniza-tion in England which brought the countryman to the city with all his grand baggage of folk forms just at the brink of *Hamlet* and *Lear* (quoted at the beginning of Chapter 7, below); and remember that Beolco/Ruzante do, in fact, leave class and place and realism behind throughout the course of the canon by returning always to the comic magic which connects Arlecchino and Clown Joey: death and improb-able resurrection. The fatal exceptions in Ruzante's case occur when romance or reality occasionally are permitted to dominate moments of the comic pattern; they only reemphasize the sub- or suprahuman sta-tus of the character, who himself transcends generic structure.

V

The character was established in 1521 when Beolco presented the comic tour de force of a dialect dialogue for festivities on the Cornaro estate, a piece half mountebank spiel and half an aesthetic of dialect *snaturalitè*, naturalism, itself. By the next year Ruzante was ready to take his place among a group of Tuscan-speaking shepherds in a play-let known only as *La Pastoral*, which now parodies, now seems to emulate, the rarefied romantic pastorals and allegories of trouble in an arcadian paradise, even closing with a hymn to Pan ("alto rustico Idio"). But after such plot closure, Ruzante steps forth for a final *plau-dite* in dialect which broadly parodies the mass, puns and plays upon the inverted expectation in the rhetoric of the *saltimbanchi* ("San Bro-gione [Bruson], protect us from consolation and contentment"). More-over, at the beginning, before the plot is acted out, Ruzante appears as a one-man induction who relates its outlines in a parallel dream expe-rienced as he sleeps on stage.[25]

Ruzante enters with a bird-cage, bread, and wine. He sleeps and awakens to . . . death: "A'crezo . . . ch'a' sun morto" (7). He looks about, discovers his things intact; he discovers the ladies of the audi-ence and believes himself in Paradise—only in fondling himself and eating does he realise he has dreamt. Dreamed of an old shepherd mad with love for a young nymph who is struck apparently dead, discovered by a brother, and recovered by a doctor and . . . and Ruzante forgets the rest in order that the play itself, the dream's dramatic shadow (or origin), can begin, so that it can begin to act out the history of suicide on the part of the old lover Milesio, frustrated by the disdainful nymph Siringa, of the apparent death by heartbreak ("per dol sento il cor frangermi in pecto" [43]) of his devoted friend Mopso. It is only after several scenes relate this story that Ruzante appears and is disturbed at bird-hunting by a shepherd seeking to bury his dead friends. The fluid Italian verse of the shepherd is shattered by Ruzante's dialect, and the sentiments of love and friendship by appetite—that of Ruzante (we met him in the induction eating and drinking), of his father, of the folk.

Ruzante, fat and famished, wolfs down bread from the shepherd Arpino while pointing out that Mopso is not really dead and directing the stranger toward a doctor's house. Vexed savior-in-spite-of-himself, Ruzante realizes he will soon shit out the food he has gotten, when instead he could have taken the opportunity to steal the shepherd's frock had he left him for "dead." Stuffed to vomiting, he . . . eats. Henceforth the play becomes a dialect fliting between the local doctor and Ruzante except for those occasions when Mopso's friends interweave their arcadian Italian in misunderstanding the doctor's queries. Finally, the doctor goes to Mopso, assuring his friends that he can administer a potion which would resurrect a horse dead three days ("farà saltà su u caval, / se 'l fos ben stà tri dí mort e finít" [83]) or a man with the grave at his ass ("i mort co i cas al cul").[26] The last idiom draws together the pastoral and mock-pastoral plots, the sacred and profane cycles of rebirth, death, and defecation which are a natural connection between appetite and regeneration in the Renaissance folk stuff which generated Arlecchino, Ruzante, and Rabelais.[27] The doctor is an able revivalist because he has been a student of "merdesina," the pun making him an excremental expert (whose own guts are growling so that he cannot mount a mule [75]). This is a cue for Ruzante's entrance: as doctor and shepherds hover over the still-entranced Mopso, Ruzante flites with a fellow rustic, with the doctor's servant, and with the doctor himself about food, stuffing, appetite, Ruzante claiming to be so thin that his belly and anus allegedly meet—this in spite of the gorging we observe him indulging in before our eyes. But his mission is to bring the doctor to heal the gluttonous father who tyrannizes over him, whom he hates, but is come faithfully to salvage. The doctor asks only if the old man shits; Ruzante assures him positively in hyperbolic scatology (121). The remedy sent home is an equally hyperbolic suppository. Ruzante exits, Mopso revives, and Ruzante returns with a cheese to thank the doctor for this anal "arrow" which effectively killed the father and thus gave Ruzante his inheritance. Invited to the ritual offering to Pan, an offering in gratitude for Mopso's resurrection, Ruzante mistakes it for an invitation to "pan," bread. His final dramatic line before the *plaudite* is one that will echo from Arlecchino's "se magna" to Joe Grimaldi's goose and sausage stuffing acts: "I'm dying of hunger, so that I can't stand on my feet" ("A'muor da fame, ch' a' no posso star in pè" [137]). His is an appetite and a character which has stood outside the pastoral plot, has disrupted it, and yet ultimately has become the play's essence.

Arlecchino came from the shades of an older chaos to become its permanent comic voice but one passed from interpreter to interpreter through the centuries. With his creation of Ruzante, Angelo Beolco rooted this essential comic servant to disorder in a local dialect and dimension that could not be depersonalized. An actor, Beolco as Ruzante became the particularized universal which the commedia masques never became. At the end of three centuries of this comic tradition, Grimaldi would perform such an act of comic lamination again as Clown Joey.

VI

Dramatic and protodramatic genres fuse in the early history of Italian Renaissance drama. That particular fusion occurred as court and professional stages rose into prominence in tandem, both borrowing elements from folk matter which was already complicated by absorption into alternately sacred and obscene, parodic and serious, contexts in mock pastorals, *sacre rappresentazioni*, and *canti carnescialeschi*. A form which spanned popular and sophisticated contexts more freely than any other may have been the fliting *contrasto*, the bitter mock-serious debate which so often centered upon the battle of the sexes that its most popular form became a rather standard feature of nuptial celebrations known as the *mariazo*—a form nowhere more persistently practiced than in Ruzante's Veneto.[28] The status debates about marriage which were passed—to cite a significant example—from a Florentine humanist, Buonaccorso da Montemagno, into the English *Fulgens and Lucrece*[29] could be parodied for such occasions until the word became flesh in a physical mock combat which served to emphasize the inevitable chaos behind the holy but halting harmony of man and woman symbolized by marriage. Beolco explored the form on a number of occasions. *La Betía*, his earliest full-scale drama; the "due dialoghi," the most famous and popular of his "Ruzante" topical playlets; and two "regular" plays *La Moscheta* and *La Fiorina* each constitute versions of the mariazo form—versions which confirm Beolco's ceaseless energy at redefining genres.

Ruzante, like Grimaldi, is possessed of a protean sameness. If he is grossly fat in *La Pastoral*, he is grotesquely thin ("un buso d'ave" [a head like a beehive]) in *La Betía*.[30] If he is a teenage farm boy in *La Betía*, he is later a veteran of the big wars against France and a cuckolded husband of a toughened woman who lives on the criminal fringes of Venice. The character is stable, yet "within exemplary situations [undergoes] a sort of existential change which develops from comedy to comedy." (Zorzi, xxxv).[31] This is Zorzi's astute and yet inaccurate comment: the superficial changes occur as a consequence of testing dramatic rather than individual or social contexts, of setting an old natural response free to measure both its relevance and inevitability against the challenge life offers structure. It is in this sense that one can really say Beolco/Ruzante dramatically demonstrated the triumph of *snaturalitè*, naturalness, over the *"mondo roesso."* If this is a proper reading of the career, then the philological argument about the meaning of the latter Ruzantian term as a universal world or as reference to a world turned upside down loses significance: both become the same, estranged as they are from the pattern sacred to comedy and its individual avatars.

La Betía is a first formal, extended engagement with genre and multiple audience expectations. It is a five-act contrasto or perhaps mariazo which tells the triangular tale of teenage lovers: Zilio (Ruzante), Betía his inamorata, Nale his companion. But there is an older lover in the wings. And there is Bembo's mythological Cupid as a pretext for much of the parodic love action.

The fliting and parody come in the opening act, as Zilio, rejected by Betía, is sincerely comforted by Nale and mockingly comforted by the senex (Barba Scatti), whose advice comes from a distorted synopsis of *Gli Asolani*.[32] The advisers come to blows—and the senex inverts expectation by beating Bazzarello, a supernumerary juvenis introduced for the purpose. Realism and scatology escalate in the advice of Nale, who instructs Zilio in dancing, singing, wheedling, hiding in the outhouse until his beloved comes to piss. The juxtaposition of the scatological and realistic is found also at the meal they share with Barba Scatti where the discussion of love is punctuated by news and need for farting and shitting ("vuogio andar a cagare. . . . Anderè drio ste case chí" [I want to go shit. . . . I'll go back of your house here], etc.). And the plot escalates triply. The first stage is Nale's decision to turn his friend's naive failure into a more satisfactory triangular arrangement by which they will share Betía; the lusting nubile happily agrees to steal away not only with her two husbands, but with most of her mother's household goods. A hubbub ensues as mother and neighbors haul Betía home, as Zilio attacks with a pot-and-pan army adapted from the *sacre rappresentazioni*, and as Taçio the innkeeper makes peace and an offering of Betía to Zilio. But not without a staged disaster which returns the play to the nexus of death and hope: Betía's mother, Menega, faints, and her daughter despairs of everything but joining her in apparent death; Taçio loosens the corset bindings; buckets of water are thrown on both; and . . . these pseudo-dead awaken. It is a first resurrection followed by a wedding between Zilio/Ruzante and Betía which is dishonored by a condescending reenactment of folk nuptials "(il matrimonio all' osteria"; Zorzi, 1345-46, n. 271) that makes clear Betía's sexual familiarity with the Spanish and German invaders who came during the war. Nale, more innocent than the seeming innocent, advances to claim his share in the bride and is glancingly stabbed by Zilio, who terrifies Betía because she is afraid she may possess only one husband in spite of the promised two. Two plot escalations are complete, each culminating in mock deaths and real resurrections (398 ff., 438-40). Or not quite complete: Nale, wrapped in a false shroud, reappears to his wife as a supposed ghost to be questioned by the terrified woman on modes of afterlife: how one eats and all those other queries reflected in the Miltonic Adam's conversations with Raphael. Nale, in turn, teases her with damnation and tests her (in the self-cuckolding pattern of the Widow of Ephesus tales), only to elicit the admission that she has never loved him and to watch her swept off by *her* lover in the wings, the bully Meneghello. Chastened, Nale admits he has exaggerated his supposed death to test his wife, she adjusts, and Nale returns "alive" to transform the events into his supposed dream; thus he buries his knowledge of his wife's lover, draws her into the role of irenicist between himself and Zilio, and all concludes as the mariazo should, as comedy should, with life and harmony reestablished out of discord. Yet not quite; the generic expectation is not fulfilled with clear closure, because Meneghello, in an extraordinary *plaudite*, threatens to join both couples as their mutual cuckold-maker: "I cre' far i quatro continti, / e sí a sarón i çinque" (They think they will be made up of four contented ones, but instead we may be five [509]). Death and resurrection into marriage and regeneration fulfill a generic expectation that in the end is threatened by this suggested opening into an alternative future.

La Moscheta develops the generic program to the length of five acts, incorporating a variant of the testing of the Widow of Ephesus, and making explicit the triumph of the tempter in the special menage implicit at the close of *La Betía*. Menato and the soldier Tonin are suitors for Ruzante's wife Betía, the former a previous lover, the latter yet another passing soldier; Ruzante masquerades before his wife in the "scholarly" guise instigated by Menato speaking "moscheto," a Neapolitan "Italian"; the comedies of planned error continue until Ruzante's imagination again enlarges Tonin into a giant, and Menato profits by entering the house to become twinned in effect or fate with the Meneghello of *La Betía*. But the drama is no drama, the effect without affect, because the Ruzante here operates as a cog within rather than an infusing, indomitable force set against generic plotting. The alternate "prologues" (584 ff., 676 ff., 682 ff.) stress "nature" as theme but diminish the tension which Beolco usually tautens from his first accomplishment in the briefest of dramatic forms.

The "due dialoghi in lingua rustica" (labeled by a later age the *Parlamento* and the *Bilora*, respectively) are the works by Beolco which the world knows: translated, anthologized, staged. Brief and "realistic," they have been favored vehicles for actors and sociological critics, evidences of class consciousness in an early age of modernity, reflections of the wars which made the Veneto a battleground. The first (and most popular) dialogue, the *Parlamento*, presents Ruzante as a *reduce*, a veteran who volunteered for the Venetian wars against the League of Cognac. His motive was greed, but he has returned to Venice ragged and hapless, a cowardly deserter without booty, without even a weapon, having laid them down in flight from the French. Now he seeks his wife, Gnua, and meets his friend Menato. He explains to Menato how he has escaped the horrors of war á la Falstaff by way of mock deaths and resurrections: "Quante fiè criu che a' m'he fato da morto, a sí me he lagò passar per adosso cavagi?" (How many times would you believe I have played dead, and let the horses pass over me? [527]). It is an act he will have to repeat once more in Venice as Beolco's irrepressible comic cuckold. Gnua has deserted him to live with a bravo, not out of loss of love but (as she explains when they meet) out of the sheer need for survival in the chaos of war (a meeting which formalizes itself in the pattern of satiric *contrasti* in the *mariazi*).[33] Her bravo arrives, beats Ruzante mercilessly under the gaze of Menato, and leaves the latter to pick up the pieces. Ruzante astounds Menato as a precursive combination of Quixote and Falstaff. He claims a hundred men attacked him; Menato assures him it was but one. Ruzante accepts this with a jaunty acknowledgment that he had played dead as so often in battle ("me fasea da morto, mi, com a' fasea in campo" [I feigned myself dead, as I did on the battlefield] [541] because of some witch ("strigona") who used some formula to enchant him ("qualche precàntola de incantason"). Death and resurrection, the sadism associated with the clown, the greed and shameless asociality of Arlecchino—all invert the perspective upon this play taken by the historians of "realism." Menato, outraged at survival without shame (Gnua, after all, had already articulated, represented the sociologist's version, the little local mirror in which longer patterns can be briefly flashed), cries out the keys to genre and subgenre in the *mariazi*: "Now you laugh, now it appears like a joke, as though it should be like the comedies they make, even those for marriages" ("Mo a' ve la sgrignè, compare, che par che la sipia stà da befe, e che 'l sipia stò com è le comierie che se fa, o che sipiè stò a noze" [543]). Ruzante replies in the final words as victim and author laminated into the archaeologist of comedic form: "La sarae stà da riso, s' a' i ligava! [E sí aessè po dito ch' a' no ve faze pí de le comierie]." (It would have been comical if I had tied them together ["made their last testament," a pun in *legare*]! Then you would have said that was the end of comedy [543].)

Realism and death. These are periodic twins, what we mean by periods in all senses—an end to comedy as it issues into the illusionary finalities of history, ideology, time. Creating a character so particular as to seem real and local, as Grimaldi made English the Arlecchino-like Joey, Ruzante here articulated his enterprise as an independence of such finalities. Ruzante of the *Parlamento* comes into Venice as an interloper who carries older credentials. And then, in the *Bilora* he experiments again, this time erasing the origins of comedy to show the limits and *frisson* of its implications when narrowed into the personal focus inherent in the tragic genre.

The *Bilora* seems to recapitulate the relationships, the shifting domestic vectors of *La Betía*, to a point which both lulls and develops expectation. The senex Andronico, having missed sex and pleasure in general in his early life while he amassed wealth, becomes infatuated with Dina, wife of the canal boatman Bilora, and sweeps her away to Venice. Bilora doggedly hikes to the city, discovers his wife, seemingly persuades her to come home with him, she giving him money to eat and recover from the ravages of his heroic odyssey in her pursuit. An intermediary persuades old Andronico to allow Dina to decide her own fate—and she determines to remain with the old man, denying that she has ever discussed the situation with Bilora. Bilora, still the cowardly Ruzante of the *Parlamento*, talks of confronting Andronico in the role of the commedia's *miles gloriosus*, the Spanish captain: "E po a' faelerè da soldò spagnaruolo, che i sonerà pí d'oto" (And then I will make like the Spanish soldier, so I will appear to be more than eight [575]). Determining to enact the cowardly braggart, Bilora encounters Andronico and stabs him to death in a fury the seriousness of which neither anticipates, a fury originating in Dina's own playacting (an implicit imitation of Betía) when she placates Bilora with her promise to return. Her promise and the concomitant generic promise of restoration to a natural order as youth joins youth, with aged blessing, has gone generically wrong. The tragedy is complete, but completed outside the expectations of either genre, play, or players. Knife in hand, Bilora leaps upon his older rival and instantaneously becomes a soul as divided as the division between the comic promise of renewal and the tragic end of isolation. He kicks the corpse about (the protective sadism of a long tradition of clowning culminating, perhaps, in Joey) even while lamenting his action, astonished that the comic contrasto associated with the *maggi*, with marriages, with renewal, could end this time just where it always threatens a stop: debate become the image of its final conclusion, death. "Te l'hegi dito?" Bilora concludes in astonishment, "Didn't I tell you?" It is a magnificent testing of the limits of that potentially fatal play which comic form always redeems until a Bilora or Beolco steps outside of expectation just once in a long while to infuse it with tragic possibilities. But the infusion was that of the writer about the reality which could transcend forms, norms, not that of Ruzante. The title character in *Bilora* was played by Zaccaria Castegnola, not by Beolco (Zorzi, 1379). Ruzante had absorbed the actor Beolco into a mythic role from which he could not escape, as could the playwright Beolco. From this recognition Beolco arrived at what one might term a deterministic decision. Ruzante / Beolco would remerge to explore the elasticity of the more regular comic forms.

When Beolco turned again to the mariazo as ground plan in the late *Fiorina*, a five-act "regular" play written between 1528 and 1530, the results are negligible when compared to the early adventures in extending (*La Betía*) and urbanizing (*Parlamento* and *Bilora*) the mariazo in order to test and reassert its relation to radical comedic concerns. But the motifs remain: Ruzante woos Fiore, is beaten and humiliated by another lover, is saved by his father, and decides to kidnap the inamorata with his cronies (a witness inevitably conjoins the scatalogical imperative by recalling Ruzante's nickname, Scagazato, "shit-covered" [759]). The death motif returns through and is defused by the rival lover Marchiori, who, humiliated in turn, sleeps, dreams, cramps. The dream is of a cemetery, of his feet being eaten by a dream creature. But he awakens not only back into life, but into a harmony established as the older generation arranges a *pax villae* which gives Ruzante Fiore, gives Marchiori a resurrection more real than his dream awakening in the person of Ruzante's sister. It is (with *La Moscheta*) Beolco's least energetic effort, but what energy it has is reflected from the old themes which seem to have been his inevitable foci as he felt his way into the shape of folk stuff. A little shit, a little nibbling not quite to the death, and a banquet to rebegin the cycle.

VII

The *Fiorina* projects a final stage in Ruzante / Beolco's career. Beolco became a Plautine playwright, challenging the new masters of *commedia erudita*, Ariosto, Machiavelli, Bibbiena, Aretino certainly. But however the playwright's models and aspirations altered, Ruzante remained.[34] Beolco had not only made but had become molded by the characterization. He could write contemporary New Comedy, but its peculiar shape would be the reflex of this indispensable principal. It is just when Beolco attempts the most developed genre of his time that Ruzante demonstrates his ineluctable presence as a power to remind comedy of what it had been and essentially would be, not only through but long after what we label as a European Renaissance.

Two plays are direct Plautine redactions. Or almost direct. *La Vaccària* apes Plautus' *Asinaria* except for a sentimental fifth act and except for one other even more meaningful interjection which has been attributed to realism and is really a reclamation of the grotesque. This is the introduction of syphilis into the play as post-Plautine priority. Plautus' supernumerary suitor was rich and young; Beolco's is marked by the pox. It was (Sanuto's contemporary diary confirms) a new and widespread problem in Venice; but Beolco adds it to the characterization, to the distention into grotesqueness of the mother / bawd borrowed from Plautus when Beolco's figure argues the harmlessness of syphilis from its ubiquity (659–60; cf. Zorzi, 1537–38, n. 136). Ruzante, however, disappears in this play into the servant of the source, Libanus. Beolco was making adjustments toward a new form, a serious little local play, a serious sentimentality to engender an ending echoing Ariosto's Plautine adaptations. At almost this moment he had written one, perhaps two, New Comedies which would rely more upon invention than source. If one needed an origin, it might be here that one could first discern popular and classical forms merging to create that new entity which we label modern drama.

La Piovana derives not only from the *Rudens* but also, one can only assume, from Beolco's association with Ariosto when the heiress's casket demonstrates her paternity (916 ff.; Zorzi, xxiii–xxiv).[35] It is another version of *La Cassaria*: Siton is the inamorato, Tura and Maregale are the senes, there are the caustic servants, the more caustic wife, and the sighting of two girls swimming ashore from a shipwreck. There is a pimp, a church (to substitute for the Plautine shrine to Venus) wherein the pimp is revealed as a *miles gloriosus* (with a fine spice of local color, Beolco's villagers are incited with the misinformation that the intruders are Lutherans desecrating holy icons), and the usual New Comedy reconciliation of long-lost daughter and family. Thus far the formula and the basic Plautine source.

However, the servant Garbinello, this play's Ruzante figure, offers a prologue which emphasizes the newness, the originality of adaptations from older languages, drama, style (teasing with an example of old costumes withdrawn from a lost chest [889] such as that which will dictate the plot action). Then he disappears until act 4, in which he becomes identifiable as an adaptation of the title slave in Plautus' *Pseudolus.*

Surprisingly, though, it is just here, with the introduction of a contaminating figure from yet another Plautine redaction, that *La Piovana* looses itself from its classical moorings to set sail upon the popular stream of comedy upon which Beolco had originally launched Ruzante.

The situation has reached this point: girls are stolen as slaves by Slaverò the pimp; through a shipwreck, the girls are recovered by servants and father; one servant in love with one girl, the other girl beloved by the wealthy inamorato encouraged in luxury by a father unfortunately dominated by a wife. The girls recovered, are left with the alternate senex. Here Garbinello enters. With the slavers captured in the church and Tura beginning to have inklings of his not-quite-found lost daughter's identity, Garbinello persuades him to conceal them with the inamorato Siton's father, Maregale. He informs the audience of how the mother Resca has refused her son money to buy his beloved. The mother appears with money from a sale of pigs, Garbinello creates a shaggy dog story of a husband's taking new young wives in her absence to get the money, dodges in and back out of impossible troubling complications by persuading the wife to pose as a mother, attempts to involve Siton in his complications only to have the young man rush off to love and a marriage banquet in lieu of nonsensical loyalty to fiction once his dreams have come true. But old Maregale encounters Garbinello, wines and dines him from the excess joys of the wedding banquet, and persuades him to stay out of the way until the dominant older woman can be reconciled to his benevolent tricks. All this is complicated, too, by an intermittent interjection of the quarrel between servants about the identifying casket, a quarrel introduced from Plautus' *Rudens* only to become a reconciliatory vehicle among servants in *La Piovana* which allows Garbinello the final triumph of ingenuity justifying a smug *plaudite.*

But Garbinello derives from Plautus' *Pseudolus* only as one enters a masked party in disguise. In both plays this player turns to the audience to boast and protect his territory as an intermediary between drama and the society it projects, becoming a simultaneous image of stagy (or staged) prankster and nurturing source for a mimetic art (*Pseudolus*, lines 396 ff., 562 ff., 720 ff.) Yet Garbinello's final appearance as a partygoer has source if not stimulus in the close of Plautus' play. Plautus' clever slave celebrates his young master's victory, one perpetrated by the triumph of his own wit, in a party which sees him embarrass himself by an inadvertent drunkenness. He is still reeling from this drunkenness when he meets and draws into the tavern the senex, partial victim of Pseudolus' own scheming for the inamorato. It is an encounter complete with his apology and regret for having missed a sexual windfall. A slave both to drink and to society, Pseudolus has missed his final fulfillment of desire. The stage farewell of Beolco's Ruzante / Garbinello in his Renaissance redaction is quite different in its invocation of an older tone, an orgulous emphasis upon the eternal overriding triumphs of excess.

In Garbinello, Beolco is reshaping the Plautine slave into the daemonic plotter, patron of pure appetite, who antedates Garbinello through some centuries of legend and postdates him by some decades as the Arlecchino of commedia troupes.[36] His fourth act entrance is a statement of his essence. If his name translates from "Pseudolus" as the liar, the trickster, the Plautine figure had no such secure sense that he was simply, univocally, and by birth such a thing. Indeed, Garbinello's self-introduction has no rival as a description of the Renaissance daemon plotter until Jonson's Mosca glorified his own nature:[37]

> A' son Garbinello: e sí el me fo metú nome cossí, perché, dasché a' nassí, a' he sempre abú avanto de far miegio garbinele e de far trar dinari a questo e quelo, ca omo che supia stò al mondo. E i miè antessore viegi, tuti, me pare, el par del par de me pare, me messiere avo, me messier besavo, setavo, e an me messiere vintavo e trentavo, tuti, tuti ha sempre fato garbinele; e chi gi aesse torcolè, ghe ara' strocò pí tosto fuora de boca i dente ca una verité. (957)

> (I am Garbinello: and I was given this name because from birth I have had the reputation of creating deceptions and getting money from this one or that better than any man ever born. And all my ancestors—my father, the father of my father, my grandfather, my honored great-grandfather, grandfather seven generations removed, and also my grandfathers twenty and thirty times removed—all, all have always been deceivers; so that if anyone should have tortured them, he would have pulled the teeth from their mouths sooner than a truth.)

Fearing that he may be losing his natural birthright, Garbinello proceeds to concoct the complicated devices by which he bilks the mother of the money for Siton's needs, thus drawing seemingly insuperable difficulties down upon his own head. He finally extricates himself not (as he mockingly declares at the beginning of the last act) without a little help from his friends: "I must find people to help me. . . . I will seek out my neighbors' [i.e., "godmothers" '] Jokes, my neighbors' Nonsense and Idle Rumor, . . . then I will find my friends Artifice, Trick, and Stratagem" (el besogna ch'a'cate zente che

m'aie. . . . A' caterè mie comar s-cione, mie comar bufole e cape-
lete, . . . e po caterè mie compar anzinieghi e mie compar sonagi, mie
compar stregema [995]). The first stage is his decision to go to the great
wedding feast, hide himself away, and drink and eat as he can while the
old woman is reconciled with her new daughter-in-law (1015). The extravagant plotter has abetted nature's elective affinities for generational
union out of his own deceptive nature. Plautus' *Pseudolus* closes with
condescension to, apology by, the overreaching slave; Beolco's closes
with a revision of Pseudolus' drunkenness and sexual failure in which
Garbinello transcends even the wedding, which stands at the socialized
limits of comedy's endorsement of sex as a fusing drive. Garbinello
emerges from hiding with a basket of delicacies, boasting with some
obscene wordplay, upon his absoluteness for appetite:

> Orbéntena, tuti i tempi ven, chi gh'i ha asiò d'aspitare. L'è pur vegnú an
> sto tempo, ch'a' he aspietò tanto d'essere a le noze de sto puto me paron
> zovenato, per avere oto dí d'i maor piasere che se cate al mondo.
> Ché, . . . el magnar de bon è el re d'i piaseri, né no gh'è negun che'l
> passe. Perche del piasere del magnare tuti i limbri reversamen, dentro e
> de fuora, ne sente, che de gi altri piaseri el no è cossí. . . .
> In colusion el magnar è la pí bela legrazion che posse far l'omo al
> mondo. . . .
> A'no deniego zà che'l no sea bel piasere a essere noízo, mo' l besognerae a
> esser compío che la matina se poesse magnare la noíza; che cossí co' gi
> uogi e gi altri limbri de fuora via galde de quel piasere, cossí in galdesse
> an qui dentro, perché gi è da pí igi che non è qui de fuora. (1017–19)

> (Well now, the time always comes for those who are willing to wait. And
> so this time too has come: I have waited so long to attend the wedding
> celebration of this boy, of my young *padrone*, just to have eight days of
> the greatest pleasures to be found in the world. Because . . . eating well
> is the king of pleasures, nothing tops it. For all bodily members together,
> those outside and in, enjoy this pleasure of eating, which is not the case
> with any other pleasures. . . .
> (In conclusion, eating is the most beautiful joy that man can have in the
> world. . . .
> (I don't deny that it would be a lovely pleasure to be a bridegroom, but if
> it were to be completely satisfactory, it would be necessary that in the
> morning you might be able to eat the bride; so that as the eyes and the
> other outer organs enjoy that pleasure, so the inner ones might also en-
> joy, since they count for more [in man's life] than the outer ones.)

Young Siton and society set right, Garbinello / Ruzante has once
again risen to reiterate the deep structure of an inevitable occasion.
Mikhail Bakhtin discovered the Renaissance's transmutation of popular medieval icons of the serious grotesque in Rabelais. And Garbinel-

lo's fantasy of devouring the bride could scarcely be better placed in cultural psychology than by Bakhtin's description of a central aspect of this transmutation:

> The grotesque body . . . is a body in the act of becoming. It is never fin-
> ished, never completed; it is continually built, created, and builds and
> creates another body. Moreover, the body swallows the world and is itself
> swallowed by the world. . . . This is why the essential role belongs to
> those parts of the grotesque body in which it outgrows its own
> self . . . the bowels and the phallus. . . . the main events in the life of
> the grotesque body, the acts of the bodily drama, take place in this
> sphere. Eating, drinking, defecation . . . as well as copulation, preg-
> nancy, dismemberment, swallowing up by another body—all these acts
> are performed on the confines of the body and the outer world, on the
> confines of the old and new body. In all these events the beginning and
> end of life are closely linked and interwoven.[38]

Yet again, Beolco had absorbed and probed past his source to the resurrectional cycle which reforms finally all social comedy into its original shapes.

L'Anconitana has neither a known source nor a certain date; some
have argued in detail that it is from an early period of Beolco's career,
while most have grouped it at the end with the Plautine redactions.[39]
Whatever the chronology may have been, L'Anconitana is the capstone
of both Beolco's and Ruzante's career that allows us to make one final
review and revaluation of that career in the history of the development
of Renaissance drama and its interwoven popular and classical forms.

"The hour's now come," Prospero will tell Miranda as he opens
that final movement of recovery by which the loss of Milan will result
in each man's finding himself in the fullness of time. That pressure is
upon The Tempest throughout, the pressure of time realizing the hidden shape of events. So strong is it in what we have come to distinguish
as a subform of tragicomedy we label romance, that "Time" becomes
the bridging chorus in The Winter's Tale. And Prologue to L'Anconitana. "Tempo" enters, acknowledges himself as the devourer of ages,
years, months, but also—sitting with this audience through to the end
of this play, a new one set in Padua—he will retard the hours so that
they will not count against the length of the audience's life: "Arrived
at its end, you will have gained more from me than lost" (La fine per-
venuti, più da me guadagnato che perduto averete). The double appearance of Time as a self-conscious participant at the close or climax
of these two great dramatic careers is not gratuitous. It expresses the
authors' insight into (and perhaps acknowledgment of) the relationship between the form of romance and its origins.

As so frequently, Bakhtin offers a bridge from apparent coincidence to significance. In discussing the development of classic carnival forms in Rome, Paris, and Germany during the Middle Ages and into the Renaissance, focusing upon Saturnalian vestiges, he observes that "all the elements of folk merriment which constituted the second, unofficial part of holy days and legal feasts continued to exist independently; however, they had many traits in common with the carnival rituals: the election of kings and queens for a day on the feast of the Epiphany . . .and on St. Valentine's Day [for instance]. *These common elements are determined by the fact that they are all related to time, which is the true hero of every feast,* uncrowning the old and crowning the new.[40] The new, though, in recognizable attire: "Tempo" claims to have misplaced his allegorical costume, and so will sit, a Padovano among Padovani, watching a local romance unfold. (If Garbinello transcended events and social form, yet *La Piovana* had been set outside Chioggia, just where the Cornaro estate with the theater which first presented it rested.) Grimaldi's pantomimes were Christmas and Easter plays with their predestined ingredients, such as Clown; but *Harlequin and Mother Goose* was an English play, as Joey was an English clown and Ruzante a Paduan peasant originated for *carnevale* theatricals.[41] General and particular meet in the drama, which became the consequence of celebratory ritual. If Time becomes a Paduan auditor for *L'Anconitana,* in a second Prologue Ruzante (his name now reasserted) suggests the exemplary form radical to New Comedy when he claims that fear of the Turkish marauders has forced Cupid and Venus to flee Cyprus for Padua.

The plot is and is not important: it is not, because the role of Ruzante transcends and interprets it; it is important, though, because it complicates Plautine formulae with the doubling back upon a romantic New Comedy, a testing of that newer form by both the grotesque titillation inherent in persistent and multiple transvestism (a Shakespearean staple) and social satire (the Jonsonian flitings upon cosmetics from *Epicoene* and *Sejanus* are fully developed by Beolco a century earlier).

Turkish corsairs have captured Tancredi, Teodoro, and Gismondo (the last, in fact, is the boy-girl Isotta masquerading as man). To repay the merchant who ransoms them, they offer their special services to the intelligent Paduan courtesan Doralice. One dilates rhetorically upon the value of poets, one upon the value of cosmeticians, one upon the value of couturiers. So much for satire. Then complications begin as the eighty-year-old Sier Tomao hires Gismondo as servant to his wife, hoping the supposed young man will occupy her while he seduces Doralice. It is at this point in the second act that Ruzante enters to report the complications: "My padrone is enamored of Doralice, I of her chambermaid, and my mistress of that little 'turk' kidnapped by the

Turks" (El me paron è inamorò in madona Rarize, e mi in la so mas-
sarola, e la mia parona in quel turco pigiò da' Turchi [803]). The
chambermaid Bessa will become crucial, as will be seen. Meanwhile,
however, Tomao (proto-Pantalone[42]) is tricked by Ruzante into per-
forming physical and financial tricks (the former resulting in a pratfall) for Doralice so that the servants may remain together. The titular
lady from Ancona arrives in act 3, having fallen in love with transvestite Gismondo (Isotta) at first (and only) sight. Her name is Ginevra.
And the names are beginning to echo like the interchangeable characters, this itself a characteristic of New Comedy from Plautus onward
which was intensified throughout the early Renaissance. For an example, one can look ahead to that other Veneto triumph of multiple
crossed loves, Aretino's *L'Ipocrito* (1542), wherein we have Tranquillo
nominally matched with Tansilla; Prelio with Porfiria; and, with a
fine alpha to omega irony, Annetta sought by Zefiro. In Beolco's dance
of phantom and forever lovers, old and young, there are Tancredi, Teodoro, Tomao for males; Ginevra, Gismondo, and Ginevra's maid
Ghitta for females. But as Isotta is disguised as Gismondo, so the cautious Ginevra is disguised as a man in search of him. I recount the
exaggerations of sexual disguise only to make clear Ruzante's role as
ultimate agent of agreement, a role which begins to unfold in this third
act.

Ruzante tells the disguised Ginevra that Gismondo is with his master's wife, and she responds by admitting herself to be both a woman
and in love. Ruzante siezes upon the opportunity for gain: he promises,
for reward, to help Ginevra get Gismondo from Tomao's wife, neglect-
ing, however, to tell her that Gismondo is also a woman, and that his
mistress has already discovered her identity. Ruzante is, in short—even
more clearly than Garbinello of *La Piovana*—moving toward a later
version of Arlecchino, say toward that figure as epitomized in Goldoni's *Il Servitore di due padroni*. In a New Comedy setting he is
emerging as the shrewd, self-serving daemon plotter, a controller of
events much like the playwright himself, because he stands both within
and apart from the society depicted upon stage, stands beyond the ethical and other normative limits implicit in his localized dialect and
social role. A servant, then, of two masters: appetite and his own creative genius.

In act 4 he joins the two male impersonators, but refuses to dine
with them, eager to exit before they discover one another's true identity;
so Ginevra rewards him with a purse to buy—ironically—a suit of
clothes. Exultant, Ruzante gloats: "I've brought together a herd of two
cows, and three with the maid; now I don't know who will be the bull"
(A' n'he fato un s-ciapeto de do vache, e tre con la massara; a'no sè mo

chi sarà el toro [841]). But nature will have its miraculous way, and even Ruzante could not have foreseen that, each discovering the other a woman, Ginevra and Gismondo would also discover themselves to be sisters long ago parted by piracy. When Leontes rediscovers the lost one Perdita, the coincidence is so absurd that Shakespeare winks at his own plotting, or defiance of plotting, in order to let the romance form support its own message of renewal: the courtier who has heard all in *The Winter's Tale* admits that "this news, which is call'd true, is so like an old tale, that the verity of it is in strong suspicion" (5.2.27-29). The suspicion is in the court, but not in the theater. Recognizing this triumph of dramatic form over social mimesis, Beolco allows Ginevra's maid to voice the playwright's own pride in accomplishing what so many critics of the later Renaissance would insist upon as the paragon of plotting, making the preposterously improbable credible: "If someone should tell that this had happened in Padova, they would be held a liar" (Chi racontasse questo esser in Padoa intervenuto, ne saria reputato bugiardo [845]). Beolco seems to have ended all well as one does in observing the frame of wonder within which New Comedy becomes romance. And then Ruzante takes another hand, both to destroy and to heighten the significance of the affect for which the form was invented.

He tells Tomao a long pastoral story of his early love for the girl who became Doralice's maidservant Bessa (a story to which we shall return), thus making Tomao realize that Bessa is the key to rapprochement with Doralice. They quarrel and haggle, but in the end, Tomao pays a debt which will free maid and mistress to come to the country for a lovers' rendezvous. Meanwhile Ginevra is persuaded by her sister Gismondo / Isotta that they should marry Tancredi and Teodoro on the spot, which they do, the spot being Padova, "città gloriosa," which they bless with all of its inhabitants: "May the reputation of the clear spirits who reside in you remain in eternal fame. City, famous for thousands upon thousands of works, may you remain in peace" (E il nome de li chiari spirti, che in te albergano, rimanga al mondo con eterna fama. Città, per mille e mille opre famosa, rimante in pace [869-71]). Place and time seem to be bracketing the play as they should a romance, a history of losses made more fortunate in the refinding[13] of a new generation of alphabetized, indistinguishable young people marrying, generating yet a newer generation of nature's inevitable children.

But the play is not over, and it is the asocial plotter Ruzante and the senex Sier Tomao who will triumph—in another place than Padova. After the above eulogy on the city, the young lovers disappear, and Ruzante takes money to Doralice through Bessa, Tomao goes home to alibi his imminent absence to his wife, and all agree to meet on the boat that will take them to their country idyll.[44] At the penultimate moment, Tomao sends an infuriated Ruzante back to the house to gather up his nightcap, footmuffs, and other such unromantic impedimenta. Trepidatiously arrived there, Ruzante discovers with immense relief that Tomao's wife already has settled her own lover in to take advantage of the little *villegiatura*. To a din of his whining questions, Ruzante *triumphans* hurries the old man along to the boat as *L'Anconitana* closes. The final "place" of the play is, after all, not Padova but the countryside.

It would be a cynical or, at least, satiric commentary on the green fuse by which dramatic romance is grafted to its ritual origins were it not for Ruzante's fourth-act account of his early love, an account which redimensions the genre, Beolco's anti-generic conclusion, and Ruzante the rough peasant, who persists from the earliest plays on. Redimensions them in the light of the pastoral spirit through his tale of early love for Bessa. The episode begins in commedia fashion with Ruzante so treasuring a kiss upon the cheek from Bessa that in a zanni-like *lazzo* he licks his own farthest chops. Tomao interrupts and interrogates him, but Ruzante is too ecstatic to respond to the old man's impatience except in the semi-obscenities, the expletives, which belie and express his state. Then Ruzante begins the history of his love. It has been pledged long ago. When he was a young shepherd ready to abandon bestiality,[45] he began roving in the nights. Tomao, unimpressed by Ruzante's story, interrupts in terms which remind us of the figure's harlequinesque origin: "What the devil kind of story is this?" (Che diavolo de proposito sè questo? [849]). Undeterred, Ruzante continues about his ventures further and further from home until one night he saw a wolf with eyes like candles, as huge as those of asses. Tomao attempts to scream him to a halt, insisting that he wants to speak of love, not asses, and Ruzante calmly replies that he too wants to speak of love. Tomao continues his anxious counterpoint as Ruzante completes the story. He prayed, while trying to frighten the wolf; and then when he returned home, all recognized him as a poet, a player, a gamester, a playboy of the Western world. And then she saw him, appreciated him; he looked at her. Tomao's impatience heightens, and Ruzante confidently assures him that their two erotic histories will merge. He continues to recount how they, the two young lovers, had used others' holiness to promote their own, a natural resilience against the usages of society: "When I went to mass on Sundays, I planted myself near the door of the church, among the men and the women; and I pretended to say paternosters and instead said: 'I love you, I am in love with you, I desire you.' And she said the same" (Con andasea de festa a messa, a' me petava de fato a la rega, fra i gi uomeni e le femene; e mi fasea vista de dir paternuostri, e sí disea: 'A' ve vò ben a

vu, a' son inamorò in lo fato vostro de vu, a' ve vora' vu'. E ela disea
che la fasea cossí an ela [851]). Now they spoke of love: "She had a
white dress that made her seem a butterfly. And I said: 'You are really
beautiful, you please me' " (L'aéa mo una bambasina bianca, che la
parea un paveio. E mi disea: 'A' si' pur bela, a' me piasi pure'). They
dance wildly, beautifully.[46] Trouble with a rival suitor is overcome,
and Ruzante is betrothed, only to be separated by the wars. Bessa, for it
was she, escapes as a refugee and Ruzante is impressed by the Germans.
The final lyric touch is exquisitely modulated downward. Just before
their separation those years before, Ruzante had taken Bessa to a pastry
shop on a festival day (his memory stumbles over which day it may
have been in a first step back from the romantic past that has etched its
details without stopping the race of, the erasure by, time) and bought
her little round cakes (ciambelle, or, in his dialect, braçiè). When they
meet again, recognition is at once romantic and ridiculous: "She remembered the ciambelle" (La se ha recordò adesso d'i braçiè). Tomao's
response when he realizes that the love story has been pertinent to his
desire for Doralice is perfectly calculated to emphasize for the audience
the point that he misses: "Now I understand! But you could have told
me this in two words, and instead have made me lose three hours"
(Adesso intendo! Ti me 'l podevi dir in do parole, e sí ti me ha tegnuó
tre ore [857]).

What is the point? I believe it is that Beolco heightens rather than
abandons the dominance of Ruzante when he moves from the earlier
folk form of the mariazo into the classical form of Plautine comedy and
its Renaissance development as a tragicomic subgenre. The character
becomes most real when he is finally placed in the unreal countercon-
text of a genre rapidly and variously being adapted by commedia
dell'arte and commedia erudita playwrights. In a fashion, Beolco was
early and late, a participant in the history of both branches. And Ruzante the character, like Jocy the Clown, remained always a reminder of
his daemonic roots, of the violence which inevitably leads to resurrection in comedic drama and its roots. But in L'Anconitana the rough-
and-tumble has given way to a clearer and clearly analogous pattern of
our eternal loss and recovery, a pattern not to emerge again on the
European stage with such convincing grafting of the absurd and the
inevitable until, at the close of another career, Shakespeare turned to
those plays we call "romances."

Historians of Italian drama have recently come to admire the radical decision by which Beolco challenged the homogenizing linguistic
theories of Bembo and others writing on la questione della lingua. If
Bembo sought parity for the language of the Veneto with Tuscan,
Beolco emerged from the same sophisticated circle to devote his person

as actor and his diversified dramatic skills to Ruzante, the dialect voice of a people. Beolco's was not, I think, a social but an aesthetic decision. He signed his correspondence "Ruzante," and he spent his theatrical career creating a character in linguistic and formal experiments which have obscured his genius for nearly half a millenium. It was a character, if I may recall a statement I applied to Grimaldi's Joey at the beginning of this chapter, so uniquely himself that he transcended the ephemerality of his stage vehicles, but also transcended—or devoured—the impersonator necessary to the persona.

CHAPTER 2

"The Best for Comedy": Richard Edwardes' Canon Complicates the Vice

Francis Meres recognized riches at his fingers' ends, and did not often reach into history. In *Palladis Tamia* the dramatic catalogues are filled with the names of his contemporaries and juniors—Shakespeare, Jonson, Chapman—men whose greatest reputation was yet to be made. Among his nominees as "the best for Comedy," all were living but Gascoigne, Greene, and Richard Edwardes. Gascoigne's *Whole Workes* had been augmented in the third edition of 1587, a decade after his death; Greene's recent death had made him a London byword, and his plays, like Meres' own collection, were printing in 1598. But Edwardes is perhaps the most elusive figure in early Elizabethan dramatic history. In selecting him, Meres passed over the patriarchal John Heywood, in order to choose a courtier dead for more than thirty years. That this was more than personal whim is attested, of course, by Puttenham's evaluation in *The Arte of English Poesie*: "Th' Earle of Oxford and Maister Edwardes of her Maiesties Chappell do deserue the hyest price for Comedy and Enterlude."[1] Even this judgment saw print twenty years after Edwardes was dead, and it echoes more contemporary panegyrics by Turberville and Googe, who found the dramatist a peer for Plautus and Terence. There is no question of the tenacious reputation resting on only two or three plays, but none has been generally assigned to Edwardes other than *Damon and Pythias*, published under his name, and the lost romantic dramatizations of *Palamon and Arcite*.[2] Undoubtedly some of the pieces which created the persistent respect for Edwardes' talent are now either lost or hopelessly defy identification. But cumulative evidence suggests that we may attribute to Edwardes with some confidence two of the more interesting "anonymous" plays of his age. And the examination of this evidence will serve to throw into focus some of the techniques by which transitional dramatists were attempting to escape the interlude, which was their chief secular and native heritage. Edwardes' primary dramatic instrument for escape into the new was the revision of role for that oldest of English dramatic functionaries, the Vice.

Historians of the early drama have consistently coupled *Sir Clyomon* and *Common Conditions* as representatives of the Elizabethan dramatic vogue of "dragons, enchanters, armored knights, and damsels in distress who peopled the English stage for a considerable period of time."[3] Other contemporary chivalric plays adapted from the literature of romance have not survived. *Sir Clyomon* features a maiden-devouring dragon, a Forest of Strange Marvels, magicians, anonymous champions, and Alexander the Great. *Common Conditions* features "wandryng" knights, pirates, and a maiden-snatching ogre with an impregnable island.

The spirit of both plays is summed up in Sedmond's boast in *Common Conditions*: "Yet once more will i proue, / Experience showes faint harted knights wins neuer fayre ladies loue."[4] It is a proverb which the false Brian sans Foy tries to contravene in *Sir Clyomon*: "Well, yet the old prouerbe to disproue, I purpose to begin, / Which alwayes sayth, that cowardly hearts, faire Ladies neuer win."[5] If the chivalric actors share a code of love and daring, the Vices have their eyes upon other values. "Which waies so euer the winde blowes," Conditions assures his listener, "it is for my commoditie" (*Conditions*, 577). Shift admits that "such shifting knaues as I am, the ambodexter must play, / And for commoditie serue euery man, whatsoeuer the world say" (*Clyomon*, 633–34). While the word is not uncommon, "commodity" is used only once again before Shakespeare's *King John* as the key term to sum up a way of life: in Edwardes' *Damon and Pythias*.

The dialect scenes of *Common Conditions* and *Sir Clyomon* also share a trick of characterization which is never exploited in quite the same manner in other dramas of the period. Ben Jonson's late Vice in *The Divell is an Asse* recognizes that part of his traditional role is to teach devil Pug "to sweare by Gogs-nownes, like a lusty Iuuentus" (1.1.50),[6] for nothing is commoner in the early Elizabethan drama than such corrupt oaths. But only in *Common Conditions* and *Sir Clyomon* are they made the central verbal device for characterizing particular low-comedy figures.[7] After Galiarbus' children have fled Arabia at the opening of *Common Conditions*, the scene shifts to the tinkers Thrift, Drift, and Shift, whose rattle of nonsensical and abusive dialogue is punctuated at every turn by the expletory cry of "Gogs bloud," an oath shared with frenzied frequency by the members of the trio as they attack the exiled protagonists.[8] And towards the close of the play "Gogs" blood and wounds again incarnadine the dialogue of the musical pirates. In *Sir Clyomon* the Vice, Subtle Shift, and his baser relative Brian sans Foy, casually swear by "Gogs" blood and wounds at infrequent intervals, but the phrase "Gogs bones" becomes the hallmark of the old shepherd Corin, lowest figure on the comic scale. They are the first words he speaks, and—varied with an occasional "bones of my zoule"—they echo eleven times in his seventy-five lines of dialogue (1288-1476 passim). Verbal coincidences are never conclusive, but this series involves parallels not only in words but in the manner and effect of their employment. So much for the little abnormal diversions of style which so often reflect generic deflections.

Both plays, of course, are literal narratives, but Conditions in disguise can identify himself as "Master Affection," and Lamphedon responds "Master Affection, ha ye gods, now se I if it you please, / It lieth in your hands my sorrowes for to ease" (*Conditions*, 589-90). And later Conditions disguises himself as "Gravitie" (1790-96). Shift also can transmute himself into an abstraction, when he identifies himself as "knowledge," and Clamydes petitions: "O father, sith that he is knowledge, I beseech your grace set him free, / For . . . he shall waite and tend on mee" (*Clyomon*, 329-330). At other times a more genuine "Rumor" and "Providence" enter the action (*Clyomon*, 534-39, 1196-1210, 1550-73). Such a fusion of narrative levels is a period characteristic. As Doran observes, "In the early days of the Elizabethan popular drama, in the sixties and seventies, one has the impression that writers . . . when they tried to dramatize literal story . . . tended to graft on it the motivating machinery of the moral interlude."[9] The Vice almost inevitably was abstractly labeled, often presenting himself as in *Sir Clyomon*:

> *Subtill Shift* I am called, that is most plaine,
> And as it is my name, so it is my nature also,
> To play the shifting knaue wheresoeuer I go.
> (212-14)

One recalls not only Common Conditions, but an inexhaustible catalogue such as Ambidexter, Nicholas Newfangle, Hickscorner, and Haphazard. As a result, the Vice was unlikely to be successfully assimilated into the literal plot, whatever importance or impertinence his role might have in other respects. And in this matter of craftsmanship *Common Conditions* and *Sir Clyomon* are both sophisticated beyond the models of their generic origin, retaining the Vice as type while so dissolving his abstractness into the flow of plot that he emerges as person, reacting in common with his fellow players to the conflicts of the action.[10]

Both Shift and Conditions are seen as "shifting knaves," cheeky combinations of temerity and cowardice trimming to the winds of "commodity." Conditions is distinctly the more daring and the cleverer of the pair. Unscrupulously, he relates how he himself has had a hand in engineering Galiarbus' exile, half in self-interest, half as jest. Tricking robber-tinkers into hoisting him into a tree that he may hang himself, he laughs down at their perplexed attempts to recover their victim: "Backe againe or ile be so bould as pare your nails wᵗ my knife" (418). Meeting with a crew of pirates, he sees that "there is no remedy but . . . / I must needs draw, but if I fight it shalbe agaynst my will," and therefore he accosts them brazenly: "Gogs wounds defend ye, for yle take you all my selfe" (993–94, 1003). He maneuvers his boasts skilfully enough to finish by being elected their captain. He goads the lovesick Lamphedon, passing himself off as "Affection"; he stirs discord between the Duchess of Phrygia and her daughter-in-law as a means of getting himself transported to Thracia. And repeatedly he presents himself in the stereotyped guise of the cunning servant: "But in the end marke how the crafty knaves part I will play" (731). "*Conditions*? Nay double conditions is my name / That for my owne advantage suche dealynges can frame" (977–78). And echoing his own image of the winds of commodity, he gloats: "Roome for a turne coate that will turne as the wynde / Whom when a man thinks surest he knowes not where to finde" (622–23). But there is an ambivalence of motive which cuts across the type to shape it into character, for Conditions can also comment on his plans for the young lovers: "I will briyng them together sure how so euer it fauls out, / For at length it will redowne to my profit I do not doubt" (620–21). Conditions maintains this dual motive throughout. He rescues Clarisia from the tinkers when her brother has fled, he arranges for her marriage with Lamphedon, and, if he disturbs her Phrygian idyll, yet when his pirates cast Lamphedon overboard, Conditions "was in a rage yᵗ it was strange to se / And out of hand would needs fight" (1153–54). Moreover, he manages to free Clarisia from the pirates, leave her in safety, and seek out her lost Lamphedon. He weeps counterfeit tears in seeming to share Clarisia's sorrow, but he runs faithfully after Lamphedon, happily commenting: "I dare swear hee thinkes it longe till with his Lady hee bee" (1583). And if he serves as the messenger to carry poison to his masters, he has been horrified and regretful at Lomia's decision to betray them to Leostine's jealousy (1727–84).[11] The characterization is not finished, and the ambivalence at points becomes contradiction, but it is clear that Conditions is the principal manipulator of the action, whose professed dedication to "commodity" is more or less progressively undermined by his loyalty to Clarisia. Thus, unlike a Thersites, Conditions dominates the drama through his personality rather than through slapstick or nonsense jargon.

Subtle Shift is a more fully developed case. Inherent contradictions in the figure are accepted and molded into characterization by the simple but unprecedented move of making the Vice a man of remorse. At the outset he pledges himself to Sir Clyomon, but immediately deserts him to follow Sir Clamydes. To the audience, he reveals his instability on both occasions. Upon joining Clyomon's service he asserts: "And as it is my name, so it is my nature also, / To play the shifting knaue wheresoeuer I go" (213–14). Having demonstrated this quality in his desertion of Clyomon, he pauses to warn: "As the prouerbe saith, good fortune euer hapneth to the veryest knaue . . . howsoeuer my maister speed, / To shift for my selfe I am fully decreed" (351–57). Shift is soon thrown into terror again. He manages to outface Clyomon and remain loyal to Clamydes when the knights encounter, but the news that Clamydes intends to seek out a "flying serpent" in the Forest of Marvels guarded by the enchanter Brian sans Foy is too demanding a test:

> . . . to *Bryan* stright will I
> And of my maisters comming to the Forrest informe him priuily,
> So shall I win his fauour, and subtill *Shift* in the end,
> Thou shalt escape his enchantment, for he will be they frend.
> . . . for mine owne safeguard this will I do,
> And now like a subtill shifting knaue, after him ille go.
>
> (542–47)

Serving commodity and timidity, Shift does betray Clamydes into enchantment and imprisonment. Ordinarily, this would be the occasion for a clever Vice to address the audience in overweening pride at his own dexterity: we recall Ambidexter's frantic: "Ha, ha, weep! nay, laugh, with both hands to play," when Cambyses has murdered his brother. But Shift reacts with a sudden humanizing ayenbite of inwit:

> Gogs bloud what a villaine am I my maister to betray.
> Nay sure ile awake him if it be possible ere they carry him to iayle:
> Maister, what maister, awake man, what maister, ah it will not preuaile.
> Am not I worthie to be hangd, was euer seene such a deceitfull knaue?
> What villany was in me.
>
> (682–86)

Petitioning Brian sans Foy for the privilege of guarding the prison, Shift soon reappears, armed, and explains to the audience:

> Because I played the shifting knaue, to saue my selfe from harme,
> And by my procurement, my maister was brought in this charme.
> The ten days are expir'd, and this morning he shall awake,
> And now like a craftie knaue, to the prison my way will I take,
> With these same weapons, as though I would fight to set him free,

Which will giue occasion that he shall mistrust, there was no deceit in
    mee.
And hauing the charge of him, here vnder *Bryan sance foy,*
Ile open the prison doores, and make as though I did imploy
To do it by force . . .
. . . so shall they both deceiued be,
And yet vpon neither part mistrust towards me.

(854–69)

It is a knave who, for all his bluster, would be good if he could,
and his last effective appearance is inserted solely to reinforce this characterization, serving no function in the action. Through a complicated
chain of accidents, Clamydes has become the champion of one Duke
Mustantius in his struggle with the Widow Queen for possession of the
Isle of Strange Marshes. When the day of challenge arrives, the queen
has found no champion for her juster cause. Shift alone seems sensitive
to the injustice ("heres such thrusting of women as it grieueth me"),
and hints that "ant were not but that my maister the other Champion
is, / To fight for the Queene my selfe, I surely would not miss"
(1683–84). When the queen is about to lose her rights by default, sentiment topples commodity, and Shift offers himself "for halfe a doozen
blowes." But when the arbiter accepts his proffered challenge, not commodity but weakness draws it back again: "Nay soft, of sufferance com-
meth ease, though I cannot rule my tongue, ile rule my hands" (1729).
He is not done. At the trumpet's second blast, he still feels the goading
of conscience: "Faith I thinke it must be I do the deed, for none yet is
seene" (1739). At this point, Alexander the Great adjudicates the issue
harmoniously, and Shift for all practical purposes leaves the play—a
hero in heart in spite of himself.

Besides the humanization of the abstract Vice, *Common Conditions* and *Sir Clyomon* share another mode of blurring the distinction
between allegorical and literal thought. When Sedmond, a young
knight of *Common Conditions* who is in disguise, meets his own sister, also disguised, he falls in love. He reveals this love by requesting
that she listen to a long tale of a wounded deer pursued by cruel hounds
to the edge of a life-giving brook. He opens his story's significance
finally as the traditional allegory of the love hunt: "So I whose hart is
clouen in twaine through quarell fercely shot, / . . .Am faine like
deare through greedy hound from herd for to depart, / By reason of the
blinded boy that did me so subuert" (1452–55). It is a love trick which
he himself seems to have learned from Sabia, a lady who had earlier
sought his love through an allegory involving that other lovers' trope,
the storm-tossed ship. "There was a ship that chanst to sayle a thwart
the raginge sea," Sabia begins, and after having brought the ship into
haven she explicates:

The ship which I spake of before is I my selfe sir knight:
And being once inflamed alas, by *Cupids* raging flight
Was lost on waues of wrackfull woe, and all for they sweet loue.
                                        (858-60)

In *Sir Clyomon* the incident recurs: Neronis reveals her love to Clyomon through the allegory of "a ship that stormes had tossed long, amidst the mounting waues, / Where harbour none was to be had, fell Fortune so depraues" (1056-57). In explication she reveals: "Thou art the ship O worthy Knight, so shiuered found by mee" (1084). In both cases the allegory and action interlock on another level, for Clyomon has, in fact, come to Neronis through the agency of a storm-tossed ship, just as Sedmond has come to Sabia.[12]

In a number of linguistic habits, in the general pattern of adventures, in the tendency to absorb the abstract tradition of the interludes into the modern narrative of romance, in an unexpected emphasis upon complex characterization—in these respects *Common Conditions* and *Sir Clyomon* exhibit a likeness which strongly supports Fleay's suggestion of common authorship. There are differences just as significant, however, which preclude one from accepting his judgment that the author of the two plays was the "R.B." who wrote *Apius and Virginia*.[13] Yet, to counter Fleay's guess is to do homage to his sense of the sixties' energetic efforts to absorb the folk possibilities even while its dramatists reject the label and the limited function of a merely paradigmatic embedding of the Vice. It was not only in what I argue to be Edwardes' dramatic romances that revolution was appearing as more excitingly appropriate than evolution.

Quite contrary to Fleay's view, the style and meter of the classical tragedy *Apius and Virginia* seem to me patently different from that of the two romantic plays we are considering. In the latter the versification seldom falls below the minimum demands of poetry, and in such passages as the allegorical tales of love, or Shift's self-presentations, there are serious efforts to rise toward rhetorical elaboration on the one hand, and to compromise the stress of the fourteener with prose speech emphases on the other. In *Apius and Virginia* the lines fall into an extraordinary three-part structure effected by a double caesura with almost burlesque regularity:

Oh father, oh friendship, oh fatherly fauour,
Whose dulcet words, so sweetly so sauour,
On knees I beseeche thee to graunt my request,
In all things according, as lyketh thee best:
Thou knowest, O my father, if I be once spotted,
My name and my kindred, then forth wilbe blotted:[14]

If the verse is strikingly primitive, however, there is more than ample compensation in the dramatic structure.[15] The tragedy has a pure line of inevitability: illegitimate desire moves Apius to an attempt upon Virginia in open defiance of his own conscience. He drives unwaveringly toward retribution, while the tragedy of Virginia and Virginius unfolds as the dilemma of the innocent who can only choose between misery and death. But one-third of the play is over before the action begins. The opening introduces Virginius, his wife, and his daughter interweaving praises of one another and of the joy in their harmonious family idyll, ending with a song whose refrain runs:

> The trustiest treasure in earth as wee see,
> Is man, wife and children in one to agree,
> Then friendly, and kindly, let measure be mixed
> With reason, in season, where friendship is fixed.
>
> (161–64)

It is an ironic commentary upon the terrifying chaos which will so soon engulf the family, and it is an ironic commentary as well upon the unreasoning and "unkindly" passion which the once-contented *pater familias* Apius emphasizes in his first appearance. No sooner have the family left the stage than the Vice Haphazard enters with an apparent rattle of nonsense which is actually an upside-down catalogue of chaos in a world of hap, counterpointing the measured portrait of cosmic order in which Virginius had framed familial harmony. Immediately afterward, Haphazard is joined by a quarreling husband and wife, Mansipulus and Mansipula, whose Kate-and-Petruchio railing stand in counterbalance to the equally exaggerated "harmony" of Virginius' family. This thematic balance is carried into a song, whose burden is

> With thwicke thwack, with thump thump, with bobbing and bum,
> Our syde saddle shoulders shal shielde that doth come.
>
> (289–90)

It is a merry and fitting song of discord to set against Virginius' hymn to concord. But at one point in the quarrel Mansipulus and Mansipula threaten each other with a knife; and when we look back after Virginia's head has tumbled from her shoulders, we realize that both quarrel and song have been a grotesque joke, not only challenging Virginius' idyllic dream world but brutally pantomiming its violent end.

I have tried to suggest how carefully the author prepares an atmosphere of moral chiaroscuro before setting under way his tragic action. The atmosphere itself is an instrument almost of motivation, as it will later be in the hands of a Webster or a Middleton. But not quite, in this case, that function being reserved for the Vice. And it is this which sets Haphazard in clear contradistinction to Conditions or Shift. Paradoxically, Haphazard motivates the action so thoroughly as to rise above it as symbol rather than cause. This fact is consonant with the frequent weaving of allegorical characters into the narrative: Rumour, Providence, Conscience, Justice, and others.[16] Apius' first complaint is that "the forowed face of Fortunes force, my pinching paine doth moue," so that he has been brought from stability and contentment to this sudden passion in "haplesse houre" (411 ff.). But Haphazard has repeatedly laid claim to Fortune's role. His first self-presentation catalogues all men, from the "proper Gentileman" to the "creper in corners," concluding:

> By the Gods, I know not how best to deuise,
> My name or my property, well to disguise:
> A marchaunte, a May poole, a man or a mackerell:
>
> .   .   .   .
>
> Most of all these my nature doth inioy,
> Somtime I aduaunce them, somtime I destroy.
>
> (218-23)

When Apius reaches an impasse of despair in his own problem, it is Haphazard who leaps upon the stage to encourage his lust. And henceforth it is Haphazard who controls all, who suggests the plot for claiming Virginia as a slave, who dismisses Conscience and Justice so successfully that Apius in the end explicitly gives himself into Haphazard's power, crying: "Then hap as hap shall hit, / Let Conscience grope, & judgement craue" (523-24). The comic pair Mansipulus and Mansipula enter just once more, immediately after this cry by Apius seals his decision to have Virginia sequestered for his use. Again they counterpoint the tragic action, mirroring Apius' decision for treachery with accounts of their own lies to master and mistress. And again, too, their song reflects the puzzlement and despair which is about to descend upon Virginia and her family, while attributing it all to Haphazard:

> When men will seeme misdoubtfully,
>   Without an why, to call and cry,
> And fearing with temerety, its ieopardy, of libertie,
> Wee wish him take to chere his hart, Haphazard,
>   Boulde blinde bayarde.
>
> (686-90)

Again and again Haphazard announces his omnipresence, permeating the play and climaxing the tragic denouement with a bill of particulars listing his services. This ironically earns him the halter, but he is no

Mosca—indeed, no man at all. The hanging too becomes a hazard of hap, and the chaotic nature of the theater of worldly action is never better mirrored than in the gaily macabre farewell of this Vice:

> Must I needes hange, by the gods it doth spight me,
> To thinke how crabbedly this silke lace will bite me:
> Then come cosin cutpurs, come runne haste and folow me,
> Haphazard, must hange, come folow the lyverie.
>
> (1175–79)

The Vices in the three plays we have considered all represent significant advances upon their ancestors. And yet, Conditions and Subtle Shift are scarcely more different from those ancestors they are from Haphazard. "R. B." was a master dramatist, and a very different one from the author of *Common Conditions* and *Sir Clyomon and Sir Clamydes*.

However, when we turn to Edwardes' *Damon and Pythias*, we are on firmer ground for comparison. The Prologue announces:

> . . . A soden change is wrought.
> For loe, our Aucthors *Muse*, that masked in delight,
> Hath forst his Penne agaynst his kinde, no more suche sportes to write.
> Must he that lust, (right worshipful) for chaunce hath made this change,
> For that to some he seemed too muche, in yonge desires to range:
> In which, right glad to please: seying that he did offende,
> Of all he humblie pardon craues: his Pen that shall amende:
> . . . the matter to expresse,
> Which here wee shall present: is this *Damond* and *Pithias*,
> A rare ensample of Frendship true, it is no Legend lie,
> But a thinge once donne in deede as Hystories doo descrie,
> . . . doone of yore in longe time past.[17]

There are three points to note here: that Edwardes had formerly written love plays, that he considered *Damon and Pythias* a new departure because of its theme of friendship, and that he valued historical subjects over fiction even in what he called a "tragical comedy." One recalls that *Common Conditions* was allegedly "drawne out of the most famous historie of *Galiarbus* Duke of Arabia"; that the title page describes our other lovers' adventures as *The Historie of the two valiant Knights, Syr Clyomon Knight of the Golden Sheeld, sonne to the King of Denmarke And Clamydes the white Knight, sonne to the King of Suauia*; and that the latter play features not only flying serpents and enchanters, but Alexander the Great. These coincidences take on some significance when we observe that of the remaining plays listed by Harbage in the repertories for the period 1560–82, only three are cited as histories on their title pages, and only one of these credits an historical source.[18]

Beginning with the Prologue and continuing throughout the play the word "friendship" keeps the theme of *Damon and Pythias* in high relief with relentless reiteration. And the action is structured around contrasting pairs of friends. Damon and Pythias are "such men as loue one an other onely for vertue" (1021), and their demonstration of virtue is so powerful in its influence that it converts the tyrant Dionysius:

> Tirranie, flatterie, oppression, loe, hear I cast away;
> Justice, truth, loue, frindship shall be my joy:
> True friendship wyl I honour unto my liues end,
> My greatest glorie shalbe, to be counted a perfect friende.
>
> (2154-57)

As Damon comments, "If men were carefull, for Vertues sake onely / They would honour friendship, and not for commoditie" (370-71).

The other pair, Aristippus and Carisophus, illustrate false friendship. Carisophus, a vicious court parasite, fawns upon Aristippus, the philosopher-turned-courtier, but craftily assures the audience: "I wyll use his friendship to myne owne commoditie" (644). As events develop, however, Aristippus directly confronts Carisophus for this ugly piece of time-serving: "My frindship thou soughtest for thine owne commoditie, / As worldly men doo by profite measuring amitie" (1849-50), and the parasite finishes by realizing that he has overreached: "Well I see now, I my selfe haue beguylde, / In matching with that false fox in amitie: / Which hath me used to his owne commoditie" (1862-64). As I noted earlier, "commodity" had not been so precisely employed as the polar term for self-interest in contradistinction to generous loyalties since Conditions and Shift had faced the struggle of their inner oscillations.

There are other small but striking similarities between *Damon and Pythias* and *Sir Clyomon*. In the low-comedy subplot of *Damon and Pythias*, Grim the Collier is a much closer relative to the old father Corin the shepherd than to the title character in *Grim the Collier*, and his involvement with the young court pages, Will and Jack, is reminiscent of the court-and-country mingling in Corin's role as protector of Neronis in her page disguise. *Damon and Pythias* builds gradually and with considerable suspense toward the anticipated execution of Damon, but the climactic incident is transformed through a gradually evolving action which culminates in Dionysius' conversion. In *Sir Clyomon* the same slow abortive technique is pursued in building toward the repeatedly frustrated combat between Clyomon and Clamydes; as the judgment of Dionysius prevents the one, that of Alexander prevents the other. And as the two knights come to accord, Alexander summarizes: "Friendship rests, where rancor did remaine" (1851). A new note has been set: through the end "friendship" continues to ring out as the thematic keynote of the play, while Clyomon urges Clamydes' love in open defiance of his father as well as his sister.[19] This point gains added significance from Edwardes' authorship of the lost *Palamon and Arcite*,[20] which clearly demanded continued variations upon the friendship theme and may, indeed, have been suggested by Edwardes' desire to experiment with old ideas upon new materials. But the action as well as the setting must have produced something much more similar to *Sir Clyomon and Sir Clamydes* than to *Damon and Pythias*.[21]

Finally, there is the figure of Aristippus. He is an unacknowledged Vice: commentator, manipulator, vituperative satirist. He opens *Damon and Pythias* with a self-introduction worthy of Conditions and Shift. A philosopher, he argues that we should not be surprised to find him also a courtier: "Louers of Wisdom, are termed Philosophie [*sic*] / . . . I am wyse for my selfe, then tell me of troth, / Is not that great Wisdom as the world goth"? (7-12). And yet he is never quite persuaded by "commodity"; conscience and weakness struggle within him as he anatomizes the evil of Dionysius' court, the virtue of the trapped protagonists, and his own sympathies: "How so euer it be, this is the short and long, / I dare not gainsay the kynge, be it right or wrong: / I am sorry, and that is all I may or can doo in this case" (778-80).[22] This is not quite all, though. Pithias soon comes to him for aid in saving his friend. Aristippus feels that it is hopeless, but that "if any comfort be, it resteth in Eubulus, / The chiefest counsellour about kinge Dionisius" (827-28). Even as Pithias is thanking him, Aristippus catches sight of Dionysius and ignominiously steals away with a last word of advice flung over his shoulder:

> The kyng is at hand, stande close in the prease, beware: if he know
> You are friend to Damon, he wyll take you for a spie also:
> Farewell I dare not be seene with you.
>
> (837-39)

Subtle Shift had presented the spectacle of the same rip-tides of conscience, sympathy, and fear when he watched the good queen's rights being trampled.

If *Damon and Pythias* is built around the thesis that friendship creates a mystique of virtue transcending worldliness, *Common Conditions* and *Sir Clyomon* are constructed so as to emphasize the ebb and flow of the sea of fortune with a persistence which makes trope approach theme.[23] But none of the plays has the impressively tight structure of *Apius and Virginia*. *Common Conditions* is the least

satisfactory, with a confused ending and characters often moving care-
lessly out of the action never to return. But even here the author clearly
intends us to realize ironies of parallelism: both Lamphedon and Sedmond reveal their love to Clarisia through the allegory of a hunt; Sabia
and Clarisia each laments the lowly birth which is a barrier to love with
her chosen knight (although Clarisia is a king's niece!); Sedmond
points the round-robin of crossed lovers almost as neatly as Viola will:
he is loved by Sabia while he loves Clarisia, who loves Lamphedon
(1472 ff.). *Sir Clyomon and Sir Clamydes* is much clearer: each knight
is delayed by parallel misfortunes which prevent his vowed combat
with the other. There is a long ironic development of love tangles as
Clamydes is not recognized by, and Clyomon later has difficulty in
recognizing, their disguised sweethearts (a further development of the
irony by which Clyomon and his lady had earlier unwittingly crossed
paths in disguise while seeking one another). *Damon and Pythias* is
structured upon the basic contrast of the true and false friends which
runs through the course of the play, with details responsive to pattern.
For instance, low comedy is served by Jack and Will, inseparable
friends, yet always in disagreement, being pages, respectively, to Aristippus and Carisophus. When they meet Grim the Collier they trap
him into dangerous talk, echoing Carisophus' betrayal of Damon.

The touchstone of *Apius and Virginia* permits one to generalize on
the structural tendency of the entire group. *Apius* brings a number of
disparate but brilliantly contrasting elements to bear upon the central
action of Virginia's tragic appeal to judge Apius in order to raise that
action above the planes of sensation, pathos, or moralizing. For all its
ubiquity, the thematic motif of "hap" ultimately serves to create a "significant" circumambience whose tones will enhance the tragic affect of
the focal narrative. In the other series neither the verbal changes rung
upon the "fortune" and "friendship" motifs nor the parallel actions
are so clearly subordinated. Even in *Damon and Pythias* the actions
exist on nearly equal levels of interest and emphasis, resulting in a
tendency for narrative to become at times a mere vehicle for theme. In
short, they still suffer from the abstract didactic magnetism exerted
upon the early Elizabethan stage by the moral interludes, a genre still
vigorously surviving long after Edwardes' death. But when the pull of
didactic schematizing is successfully resisted in these plays, the strength
of resistance comes chiefly from the ambiguities of character in those
paradoxically humanized abstractions, the Vices.

It remains to examine chronology. Richard Edwardes was a court
poet at latest by the mid-fifties, was made Master of the Children of the
Chapel on October 27, 1561, and died on October 31, 1566. *Damon and
Pythias* was entered in the Stationers' Register in 1567–68, published
in 1571, and its presentation has been convincingly placed in Christ-

mas week of 1564.[24] *Palamon and Arcite* is known to have been first presented in September 1566, just before Edwardes' death. *Sir Clyomon and Sir Clamydes* was published in 1599, "As it hath been sundry times Acted." Various attempts have been made to date it at widely varying periods between 1570 and 1599, none of which rests on substantial ground. *Common Conditions* was entered in the Stationers' Register on July 26, 1576, as "a newe and pleasant comedie," and exists in two undated quartos. The general impression that *Sir Clyomon* belongs to a date close to 1570, in spite of its late publication, dovetails cleanly with what we have reviewed in regard to its relationships with *Damon and Pythias* and *Palamon and Arcite*. I would suggest that it preceded *Damon and Pythias* in the Edwardes canon, that he found the "friendship" motif congenial, but that the pressures implied in the Prologue to *Damon and Pythias* persuaded him to develop it in the more earnest vein of a tragicomedy, classical at least in matter. And after thus successfully demonstrating his respectability, he continued to exploit the nobler passion in *Palamon and Arcite*, but without his antecedent embarrassment at a natural taste for the worlds of Venus and Mars. There remains the problem of *Common Conditions*, published anonymously and entered as a new play several years after Edwardes' death. The evidence has suggested that it is more closely related to *Sir Clyomon* than to *Damon and Pythias*. This circumstance, taken with the much less certain organizational power exhibited in *Common Conditions*, suggests an earlier work, but one close to *Sir Clyomon* in date of composition, this latter in view of their many similarities (and here the numerous small verbal parallels are more decisive than the broader technical likeness). It may be that *Conditions* was simply Edwardes' last apprentice piece, and that his real dramatic maturation occurred between its creation and that of *Sir Clyomon*. But there are some oddities in the play which make another theory at least tenable. I feel an uncomfortable allusiveness in the long but uninformative introductory dialogue between Galiarbus and his children. Even when Conditions presents a formal speech of exposition (157–210), he leaves unanswered our curiosity about the death of Galiarbus' wife, or about Galiarbus' role in the Arabian court. And critics have been unanimous in remarking the unabashed sudden ending at the presumptive deaths of the two protagonists. Recalling the two-part *Palamon and Arcite*, it seems to me just possible that at least part of what appears to be a striking structural failure in the play is owing to our possession of only one half of a two-part drama "drawne out of the most famous historie of Galiarbus Duke of Arabia."[25]

In any case, *Common Conditions* was issued anonymously at a date when Edwardes was still well remembered as "a good wit, and a good poet, and a great player of plays."[26] And it was issued in an unsatisfactory condition. It could hardly, then, have come through the normal channels of Edwardes' literary executors, whoever they may have been, responsible for the preservation of manuscripts which eventually gave *Damon and Pythias* and *Sir Clyomon* to the presses. The former was an Oxford play, apparently entirely independent of Edwardes' function as Master of the Children of the Chapel. We know nothing of *Sir Clyomon*'s auspices except that the 1599 title page lists it as having been presented by "her Maiesties Players," an ambiguous phrase which may or may not refer to the Chapel children. The ragged publication of *Common Conditions*, however, may be explained conjecturally if we assume that it was a play for the Chapel boys. Edwardes' successor as Master of the Children was William Hunnis. Hunnis was violently attacked by Puritan critics who had been quiet during Edwardes' mastership, possibly because the new master initiated the practice of presenting open performances for profit in the early seventies. In any case, his direction of the Chapel children's performances seems to have ended in 1575 or 1576, and by January 6, 1577, his place had definitely been assumed by Richard Farrant.[27] Since *Common Conditions* was entered in July 1576, I conjecture that the manuscript had remained in possession of the Chapel Children's administrators from its preparation for a presentation given between Edwardes' assumption of the mastership in late autumn 1561 and the writing and presentation of *Sir Clyomon and Sir Clamydes*, which most probably occurred during 1564. Hunnis, his association with the Children ending in unpleasant circumstances, perhaps not unrelated to his determination to make his post pay, may have appropriated the old manuscript to turn a small gain. Certainly, the play's printing coincides strikingly with Hunnis' date of severance from the Chapel Children, and the reconstruction of events would explain why the play was sent into print without any care for its coherency, and why the still-famous name of Edwardes was not used as a sales stimulant; Hunnis would scarcely have been eager to advertise the provenience.

But even as *Common Conditions* stands, it reflects the vigorous impress of the author of *Sir Clyomon* and *Damon and Pythias*. Measured against isolated performances such as *Gammer Gurtons Needle*, these plays do not demand great critical respect. But measured as a group against the dreary moralities, translations, and slapstick which are the norm of our dramatic heritage through the sixties, they constitute a radical canon which justifies thoroughly Meres' historical entry of Richard Edwardes among those "the best for Comedy."

CHAPTER 3

Peele's *Old Wives Tale:*
Folk Stuff into Ritual Form

The romance plays I attribute to Richard Edwardes were invoked in Gummere's earliest serious commentary on George Peele's *Old Wives Tale*, and have been so repeatedly, even in one of the latest and best assessments of its burlesque qualities: "*The Old Wives Tale* bears a distinct, if pointedly exaggerated, resemblance to early Elizabethan romances such as *Clyomon and Clamides* and *Common Conditions*."[1] Such a judgment upon the relevance and distance of romance materials from Peel's text is echoed in the several serious excursions into the source materials excavated from tales and tropes labeled "folk."[2] And both backgrounds have served to obscure the structural cohesiveness of a masterpiece of plotting.

The burden of the argument here will be the justification of that claim—not a small one, perhaps, for a playwright whose distinguishing mark, in the decades when internal tests of authorship were less strict than popular, was found to be confused plotting.[3] One effect will be to make more precise the not infrequent observation that Peele's play was precursor to Beaumont's *Knight of the Burning Pestle*.

Peele's work, at first encounter, must dismay any reader who comes upon his handful of dramatic efforts from an acquaintance with Lyly or Greene, leaving Marlowe and young Shakespeare aside. Far from being a hack of Elizabeth's grub streets, Peele was a trained university wit who for several years following his graduation maintained a connection at Oxford which can best be described as that of director of dramatic entertainments at Christ Church, site of one of the finest traditional theatrical halls in the university.[4] And yet *The Arraignment of Paris* is a lagging recitative; *David and Bethsabe* an abortive confusion between thematic double plotting and the versification of scriptural story; *Edward I* a lurid compromise with early century moralities; *The*

Battle of Alcazar a truncated relic of topical chauvinism not much distant in kind or quality from Dryden's *Siege of Amboyna*. His life's historian concludes that "Peele, basically, was not a dramatist at all but a lyricist."[5]

Yet *The Old Wives Tale* abides. Remembering the professional theater man, Viguers has written a "staging" of Peele's play which sets the old wife Madge against the evil magician Sacrapant, in a reading which is demystifying: his art defies "that instrument of nature, time. His is an art of transformations that bind and impair, of unnatural stasis and paralysis."[6] A sophisticated reading, but in demystifying, demythifying, defiant of the folk impulse with which the movement as well as the details are infused. At an opposite pole is Cox's reading, which ironically invites Edwardes' older romances by way of Peele's bridge into the company of Northrop Frye's Plautine / Shakespearean form—separation, wandering, reunion: "*The Old Wives Tale* has been compared to the kind of rustic production that Shakespeare gently parodies in the tragical mirth of Pyramus and Thisbe, but Peele's play seems rather to stand midway between the likes of *Common Conditions* or *Cambises* and a sophisticated comedy like *A Midsummer Night's Dream*. *The Old Wives Tale* is not an attempt to reproduce or to satirize popular ineptitude but to adapt folk material to the conventions of popular drama. . . . Shakespeare went much further in the same direction."[7] To draw attention to this conclusion is to join issue with Peele's archaeological critics in asking to whom was the folk material directed in *The Old Wives Tale*? A university and court dramatist, Peele did not write for the "folk." Yet this play was quite possibly a provincial touring text.[8] And quite possibly not. Certainly, it was written with an awareness of change as comedy, romance, and spectacle merged in a courtly amalgam which was a new excitement and a threat to old forms and the spiritual history which informed them. There was no audience but the author and posterity.

Or, rather, the ultimate audience was Peele's view of a timeless viewer, while there was nature's plenty for the sophisticate who looked upon the folk with ironic good humor or (to remember the possibility of Peele having prepared a provincial touring vehicle for a troupe) for the folk who might recognize both some familiar elements and form in Madge's "old wives winter's tale."[9] But the plenty was brought into a coherence which employed and transcended its elements.

We begin in darkness and fear imposed by love upon the three serving men who compose the audience-within-the-play. They wander in the dark wood lost, wander because of a love tale never told: "to loose our way in the woode, without either fire or candle so vncomfortable," complains Frolic (14-16), to which Fantastic, fellow page, responds with all we ever learn about cause: "Why makes thou it so strange, seeing Cupid hath led our young master to the faire Lady?" (17–19). It is enough: love leads as in Arden or Athens into entanglements which merge this inner audience and the "tales," the tales which they will oversee with us. To cheer themselves against the night, the trio climbs into a tree to sing, a suggestion "desperately spoken . . . in the darke," says Antic, "but seeing it falles out thus, let vs rehearse the old prouerb" (25–27). This proves to be the popular tune

> Three merrie men, and three merrie men,
> And three merrie men be wee.
> I in the wood, and thou on the ground,
> And Iacke sleepes in the tree.[10]

Not a dolorous tune, this, but a prophetically gay one appropriate to the play's comic ending in love harmonies and the dawn of a new day after the darkness of the opening. Nor is it chosen at random from the popular repertoire of song at Peele's command. The figure Jack will appear in the play as a master of (only seemingly chaotic) ceremonies, much in the fashion that Merrythought will bring life out of death in *The Knight of the Burning Pestle*. For Jack is the dead man who rises to direct the restoration of order. There is no way as yet to know that the larger movement of Peele's play, which will incorporate in their parallel functions all the romantic and folk tales, has begun, that the ending is a consummation promised in the beginning. But it has begun. It is Frolic who, like Jack of the tune, would climb into the tree and who, like Jack of the tale, moans at the very beginning of events: "Neuer in all my life was I so dead slaine" (13–14). Life and death intermingle in the manner of comic dissolution and rebirth, as light immediately, if gradually, emerges in the darkness: Frolic perceives "the glymring of a Gloworme, a Candle, or a Cats eye" (40–41) which turns out to be the lantern of the first folk type of the play, Clunch the smith.

Once the pages are brought home by Clunch to the old wife Madge, she begins entertaining her guests with tales in a fashion which announces the old formulae while suggesting that the folk have forgotten a culture: "Once vppon a time there was a King or a Lord, or a Duke that had a faire daughter, the fairest that euer was; as white as snowe, and as redd as bloud" (136–39). It is a confusion that seems endorsed by the actions within the play, almost immediately out of the hands of the teller, who soon sleeps. Seven (not a casual number in this matrix of magic) stories interlace within a thousand lines. Calypha and Thelea arrive in search of their enchanted sister Delia, all children of the King of Thessaly. The magic lies less in the names than in the lack of them: if Delia is an anagram of woman which will reappear in sonnet sequences, the siblings have names only as afterthought: they are "hir two Brothers [who] went to seek hir" (154–55). As such, they can laminate tale with teller; "Soft Gammer," warns Frolic as they enter, "here some come to tell your tale for you" (160–61). They immediately encounter the (disguised) protagonist of the second tale, one remembered by Madge as an afterthought before she sleeps, that of young Erestus and his beloved Venalia. Metamorphoses occur everywhere in the mistelling and in the tale, as is appropriate to the folk stuff upon which the whole seems constructed, familiar from Bottom's dream: "O I forget: she (he I would say) turned a proper yong man to a Beare in the night, and a man in the day, and keeps by a crosse . . . and he made his Lady run mad" (154–58). Speaking in riddles which seem to invert the Lichtmetaphysik of the pages' opening terror, of the play's promise ("Blow a blast at euery flame: / For when one flame of fire goes out, / Then comes your wishes well about" [198–200]), this victim-protagonist yet promises the ultimate reinversion into the comic seasonal pattern—senex as juvenis: "All the day I sit . . . Seeming an olde and miserable man: / And yet I am in Aprill of my age" (229–32). This points to the introduction of the third, and crucial, tale: that of Sacrapant the magician whose magic is as delimited by the natural pull of mythic forces as is Madge's forgetfulness.[11] But at the play's opening he has not only exchanged his own aged body for Erestus' young one, but has imprisoned Venalia (Erestus' "true betrothed wife" [223]) in madness as well as in the enchanted wood surrounding Sacrapant's "cell."

Abruptly we have the direction *"Enter* Lampriscus *with a pot of Honny"* and the fourth narrative, the dilemma of his daughters. (Everything is rapidly becoming balanced and so, in spite of the accident of names, universalized into the world of the fairy tale, the folktale: young / old; brothers / sisters; fathers / daughters; husbands / wives—the familiar, familial polar conjunctions.) Lampriscus is Erestus' discontented neighbor; the honey is for Erestus as bear, in exchange for more riddling advice such as the questing brothers had received from Erestus as man, old man. For it is clear in some absurdly appropriate fashion that as the good young man has been victimized by the evil older magician's corporal exchange, he has also inherited the magic powers and transmuted them to good as insight and foresight.

Having survived two troublesome wives, Lampriscus is cursed with two daughters, a beautiful shrew and a sister so ugly no dowry could buy her marriage. As fire was the element with which Erestus riddled a prophecy of fulfilled desire for the brothers, water is the one he recommends for the father's quietude: "Well neighbour, nowe you haue spoke, heere me speake; send them to the Well for the water of life: there shall they finde their fortunes vnlooked for" (289–92). They shall, indeed. But first Frolic must wake Madge to check the tales: she confirms that Erestus is the bear-man and that Lampriscus is his beggar neighbor, but is surprised (and mistaken) as a masque of "harvest men" enters—surprised but certain of their obvious purpose: "Ten to one they sing a song of mowing" (304–5). This is a natural mistake (or an unnatural one, in the longer perspective offered by Peele upon such folk stuff and the form of dramatic comedy). *The Old Wives Tale* is set in the generative pattern of rebeginnings, in the "April" of Erestus' life and love in spite of the darkness, the old men, the old wife Madge herself, all apparently dominant at the opening. So the masquers "come a sowing, a sowing, / And sowe sweete fruites of loue" (309–10).

Five narratives have been initiated within three hundred lines; the sixth follows without break or rationale as Huanebango, miles gloriosus and pedant (and perhaps Gabriel Harvey), enters with "*two hand sword, and* Booby *the Clowne*" (312–13). Both are in search of a wife, in the person of the rumored enchanted beauty Venalia. They too meet Erestus and polarize into the universals with which the play is populated, into folk formulae: Huanebango refuses alms while Booby proffers them. Another prophecy is forthcoming: "He shall be deafe when thou shalt not see. . . . Thou maist have wealth to mend thy wit" (405–7). This is fulfilled by way of an interweaving back into the tale of Lampriscus' daughters and that of Sacrapant. The first part of the play has juxtaposed bits of tales which seem jagged fragments in their apparent lack of connectedness, in the implication that they are unconnectible which is raised by their dizzying succession. It is a natural inference imposed to emphasize the overpowering reordering of chaos which begins at this point. The illusion of antidrama, of formlessness, of the stuffing which marks the wandering, shaggy-dog aspect of old tales—this is quickly being reforged into the mythic form of comedy which was once ritual and became comic drama's base. It is the familiar relationship postulated in half a hundred ways between renewal and New Comedy, Shakespearean comedy, Elizabethan theater. But Peele, in a rare lamination, wrote a comedy which was also a ritual, was its own formal grandfather.

The details are the drama. Huanebango reenters like the huffing Turk of the St. George plays ("fee, fa, fum, here is the Englishman, / Conquer him that can, came for his lady bright, / To prooue himselfe a knight, / And win her loue in fight" [659–62]) and meets the mild

Booby (now Corebus). Sacrapant blasts the former's sword and the latter's sight, and, returning us to the play's black, love-instigated opening with the pages' wanderings, places a curse on Booby that he may
"wander vp & downe / In nought but darkenes and eternall night"
(680-81). No more than dozing Madge, though, does the conjuror control the tale, which begins in this case first to shape itself to the comic
form (in every sense). Lampriscus' daughters take their pitchers to the
Well of Life, where the shrew Zantippa breaks not only her own but
that of meek Celanta as well. Magic is magic, even working against its
own intentions; or, rather, nature's pattern will out. Furies lay Huanebango by the well; Zantippa returns with a new pitcher. A "Head"
(cause or creature of Erestus' prophecy rather than Sacrapant's fury)
rises from the well riddling of wealth and charity and fertility desguised
in the euphemisms of nature's grainery, of sowing and harvesting
("Faire maiden white and red, / Stroke me smoothe, and combe my
head, / And thou shalt haue some cockell bread" [788-90]). The upshot is that the beautiful fool Zantippa mates the foolish old braggart
Huanebango (who rhetorically misappropriates Erestus' fertile spring:
"as I seeme, about some twenty years, the very Aprill of mine age"
[832-34] and the sweet and ugly Celanta mates with blind and generous
Corebus to the accompaniment of a golden shower of wealth prophe-
sied by Erestus and accomplished by the "Head" which rises from the
water. She is not a mere Danaë, though, but a May Queen fulfilled in
the golden fall: "Oh see *Corebus* I haue combd a great deale of golde
into my lap, and a great deale of corne" (985-87). Of course. The poetic
justice now at work is not only of the fairy tale variety, the folk variety,
but of the natural shape which underlies these as well as Peele's sophisticated drama. Just before these marvelous ("meraviglioso": the
improbable but inevitable possibilities of nature's magic, drama's reflexive form) matings, the masquers have returned unannounced to
fulfill their pattern and usher in that sense of awe which Shakespeare
called "wonder." Now they have "women in their hands," and Fantastic, seeing, whispers "I, I, let vs sit still and let them alone" (644). The
song is inevitable, if still a promise: "Heere we come a reaping, a reaping, / To reape our haruest fruite" (647-48). Stories, patterns, suddenly coming full circle. Delia's brothers are enchanted by Sacrapant,
who himself offers an "impossible" Macbethian riddle: his power
comes from a lighted glass hidden underground, "and neuer none shall
breake this little glasse, / But she that's neither wife, widow, nor
maide. / Then cheere thy selfe, this is thy destinie, / Neuer to die, but
by a dead mans hand" (516-19). This introduces the seventh and culminating tale, that of Jack and Eumenides. The folklorists' label for its

antecedents, "the grateful dead," is inadequate for this fulcrum. It is, rather, a ritual resurrection focused upon burial, a comic epitome of the origin of comedic form in man's need for and dependence upon his role as another functionary of nature's renewal, a persona in this great pattern.

Eumenides appears seeking Delia, bearing with him that title so long associated with woods, with error, with the pages, with knight errantry: "the wandring Knight" (520). Seeking and simultaneously mourning, he invokes that natural culmination of all patterns, that personified in *The Winter's Tale* to justify marvelous activities a generation after Peele's old tale: "Tell me Time, tell me iust Time, /When shall I *Delia* see?" (522–23). Old (young) Erestus answers properly, emblem of Time as we embrace its paradox of renewal in the New Year images of the dying elder and the babe newborn (these naturalized into narrative, too, like Time, in *The Winter's Tale*). The seer's answer reflects Corebus' kindness toward bear-man and all of its harmonizing result: "Bestowe thy almes, giue more than all, / Till dead mens bones come at thy call" (535–36).

Eumenides sleeps, puzzled, as do so many characters in awaiting the fulness of Time, as—to be anthropologically structural and no more facetious than Peele himself allows with the quiet and obvious metaphors—the corn must between sowing and mowing. A little magical silence at the heart of the ritual, its natural shape.[12]

Madge the teller and the figure at the center of her tale are now both locked in sleep. But the denouement begins to unwind around the unnatural wakefulness of the dead. Corebus and a country fellow enter in harangue against two churchmen who refuse to bury generous Jack, "the frollickst frannion amongst you" (565); tale and its frame are again merging, as we recall that it was Frolic who suggested the old song of merriment on how "Iacke sleepes in the tree." Eumenides, awakened, intervenes to pay for the burial, and Madge, awakened again, assures her audience that "you shall see anon what this *Iack* will come to" (638).

But what we see immediately is the second masque of harvesters and the long wooing by the well of Lampriscus' daughters. All are reaping what they have sown. It is only after these allegorical and parabolic presentations of that theme that we reencounter Eumenides. He ritually mourns his misfortune, in keeping with the old man's prophecy that he can truly rest only when "thou repent that thou didst best" (538). *Pace* those critics who read the play as an endorsement of "charity," what Eumenides regrets is his gesture toward Jack, but his very lament incorporates a bonding to Erestus, youth, and the spring rituals: "Here pine and die wretched *Eumenides*. / Die in the spring, the Aprill of my age?" (860–61). And now Jack reappears, asking to serve as Eumenides' page, hinting at knowledge of his quest, and promising feast and lodging. Magically everything is provided, Eumenides' purse is full to overflowing, there is meat and music—and all Jack asks is to "be halfes in all you get in your iourney" (950-51). The interweaving of tales now creates a blanket reestablishment of pattern moving toward a natural and yet marvelous regeneration.

At Sacrapant's cell, to which he has brought his new master, Jack stuffs Eumenides' ears with cotton to silence the sorcerer's siren call. Then this boy ghost removes the magician's wreath and sword, and suddenly Sacrapant shrivels into age and dies like an Ur-Faust: "And now my timelesse date is come to end: / He in whose life his actions hath beene so foule, / Now in his death to hell desends his soule" (1019-21). Quickly Jack instructs Eumenides to dig up the buried light that can only be extinguished by a woman "neither maide, wife, nor widowe" (1048-49). This is Venalia, Erestus' enchanted betrothed. Upon her blowing out the light, liberty (and, paradoxically, light) is restored to all. Delia is revealed asleep, and Eumenides awakens her to love and their future with a ritual formula; all freed, Jack enters with the head of Sacrapant. Eumenides is incredulous; the conjuror was young. But Jack explains that "this Coniurer tooke the shape of the olde man that kept the crosse: and that olde man was in the likenesse of the Coniurer" (1093-96). At a horn blast by the knight, Venalia, the two brothers and Erestus all enter, freed and restored, youths all, awake and alive as natural order is reborn after the dark night of necromancy. Jack has one last *frisson* to offer the troupe that has been resurrected from unnatural suppression by the blocking senex: he demands his half-interest in Delia. Eumenides accepts his debt and "*offers to strike*" her in two, in spite of her brothers' pleas. But, in rough analogue to the Green Knight, "Iacke *staies him*" (1140). While all are being resurrected into the natural vigor of youth, Jack naturally inverts the pattern. His "disguise" has been that of a young page (as he claims, "about the age of fifteene or sixteene years" [874-75]). But his natural rest is in the grave, where he joins the folk tales' "grateful dead."

> *Iacke*: Stay Master, it is sufficient I haue tride
> your constancie: Do you now remember since
> you paid for the burying of a poore fellow.
> . . . .
> .   .   .   . thanke that good deed,
> for this good turne, and so God be with you all.
>   *Iacke leapes downe in the ground.*
>   (1141-47)

Awake and at rest, inversions reinverted, all move on as the fullness of time is accepted. Jack is buried, but he has sown the seed of the future in Eumenides and Delia, in Erestus and Venelia and all, who move in "the April of their age" on "to *Thessalie* with joyfull hearts" (1152).

The tales have been told and in the telling sealed into a single pattern. But the teller sleeps. Fantastic awakens her to the cock's crow as the dark night of the frame-tale, of the audience also, is dissipated in light's return. Madge closes the play with a miniature history of her own past, of that time when *she* had heard the tale in another April, now passing it on intact to the page: "Then you haue made an end of your tale Gammer?" "Yes faith," she replies, "When this was done I tooke a peece of bread and cheese, and came my way, and so shall you haue too before you goe, to your breakfast" (1167–70).

All is natural cycling: youth to age, dark to dawn, "an old wiues winters tale" (120) which reassures the pages about the wanderings into which their master's love affair has drawn them, which celebrates even the April of Madge's own age when she first heard it, yet lays Jack to rest when his cycle is run. It is a myriad of tales of sowing and mowing in the genre of the folk and of the popular romance which Edwardes had used on the stage before Peele.

It is appropriate to return to the question of audiences and origins raised at the beginning of this reading in Peele's complicated text, the text of a complicated figure, and to recall that it was possibly a provincial touring text, but also possibly something quite different, written as it was by a court dramatist.

Some years ago I argued that a "city" play which also seems "satiric" to many, Beaumont's *Knight of the Burning Pestle*, was, in fact, a ritual play in a serious sense.[13] Ritual I defined in part as an efficacious reenactment of past forms in the present in order to control (hence, predict) the future. I was there arguing with the late C. L. Barber's position that drama is severed from its ritual origins by its relationship to society. He argued that in ritual there is a hermetic privacy of belief which unites the participants in obviating any necessity to decide "whether the identifications involved in the ceremony are magically valid or merely expressive. But in the drama, perspective and control depend on presenting, along with the ritual gestures, an expression of a social situation out of which they grow. So the drama must control magic by reunderstanding it as imagination."[14] Barber had, of course, rediscovered a moment of particularly great intensity for that always present "tension between a magical and an empirical view of man" (221), a crucial moment which S. L. Bethell had examined in *Shakespeare and the Popular Dramatic Tradition* and which A. P. Rossiter had attempted to generalize in a too-neglected, compressed little history of early English drama. But Rossiter was on to something with which he was attempting to pull the discussion of

drama and ritual back from the great divide that Barber would so effectively articulate in such passages as that I have quoted—even, in retrospect, from Frye's seductive history of myth moving toward narrative
after it disentangled story from ritual. There is a "ritual" mode of
drama, Rossiter suggested, not necessarily religious. "In a work of art,
the RITUAL is the offering, or the hinting of an offering, of a gesture
of regard or respect for something' which goes beyond the state-of-af-
fairs or the EVENT. . . . The essence of this RITUAL aspect is that
it appeals from time to timelessness, though both the artist and his
appreciators may be quite unconscious of this, both feeling only a 'sat-
isfaction' with the performance."[15] But what if the author *did* realize
his relationship with a timeless pattern of efficacious repetition, and
thus became necessarily anonymous, even offering up as his contribution to continuity an appearance of structurelessness in order for the
patterns to reform themselves with a seeming ineluctable strength in
spite of the apparent fictional bungling of individuals attempting to
make it new? What if a playwright reversed Barber's formulaic statement that "the drama must control magic by reunderstanding it as
imagination," and revaluated imagination as the instrument of magic?
This was the experiment which Peele and Beaumont shared in creating
chaotic ritual plays plotted with a firm sweep of predestined promise
beneath the fragments of surface plots.

This double plotting (if one may invert the usual term for broader
purposes) is a reflection of the myriad forms of European folk drama
which have been gathered from Chambers and Gayley to Toschi and
Weimann into the seedground of modern drama so fecund that our
principal effort now has become the pruning of its genealogical tree.
In Mummers' plays or *Maggi*, in the French cathedrals with Boy Bish-
ops or the American minstrel skits derivative from the commedia
dell'arte, the buffoon as an *organizing* lord of apparent misrule has
been the key icon and initiator of formal reinstitution. In *The Knight
of the Burning Pestle* this role is given to the old man with eternal
aspirations, Master Merrythought. He wastes his material substance in
play, his family deserts him, his followers falter in terror at social consequences, while, as his wife complains, "he hath spent all his owne,
and mine too, and when I tell him of it, he laughes and dances, and
sings, and cryes, *A merry heart lives long-a*."[16] But it is Merrythought
who survives and revives all in a play dominated by the material, commercial values of Jacobean London—both in the larger play by Beaumont about a London grocer's family as debased audience for a
sophisticated play and that grocer's relationship to older May celebrations which have become tattered trivia in the city, and in the "inner"
play concerning Merrythought's own son, that son's apparent death

and actual comic resurrection into a natural and promising spring wedding. Death-and-resurrection is always there as the key element not only of form, not only of ancient ritual origin, but of function.

Beaumont a dozen years or so later in a city setting imitated and inverted Peele's self-abnegation as author, reorganizer of society's chaos, by mimetic appeal to an older pattern which Peele managed by displacing his authorial role upon Jack. Beaumont's Merrythought was old and generous and feckless because he did not live by the limitations of what we have come to call society. He could laugh himself to death if all else failed, because death was only a stage (as his son's resurrection parodically implied). Peele's Jack was generous ("he gaue foure score and nineteene mourning gownes to the parish when he died, and because he would not make them vp a full hundred, they would not bury him" [584–88]), was merry ("he was not worth a halfe-penny, and drunke out euery penny" [589–90], this "frollickst frannion"), and was young. And dead. But even in death he gave life (resurrection in every sense) again to the restored Delia in refusing to accept his "half" of her. He is buried only when the patterns have been worked out at last: surrogate author, spirit incarnate (or, for both, Peele and Jack, formal ghosts, one might better say, disincarnate) of paradox when that means that the womb and tomb, mowing and sowing, underlie and underline the significance of all tales.

Beaumont lived in a world more difficult, more distanced by a decade from the folk sense of Peele's audience (distanced, in part, not only by London's general growth but by that of London's theater). His play was derided by the contemporary audience, who were partially incorporated in the abuse of the grocer and his family, and it was reduced by subsequent critics to a social satire. Peele's play has been happier only in that critics have patronized the author as a happier-minded forager among the folk of his time, a literate Edwardes, albeit with the little thirty years' distance which made old stuff palatable as camp.

Both authors, different as they and their milieus were, were much closer than their critics, closer than a turn-of-the-seventeenth-century London pleb or an earlier trio of romantic court pages, to the people whose old rites shaped a sophisticated drama. Rites. Rituals, we have been taught by many less brilliant than Barber and Frye, develop into myths and individuate even more into story, into narrative, into dramatic narratives which can then be sophisticated into satire, mockery, an elitist look at what they call "folk." Well, yes. But perhaps it did not happen quite where and when we have pinpointed it by misreading the very conscious return of some Renaissance dramatists, not just to details, but to the essential structure of their popular legacy.

The courtly amateur Peele and Beaumont, the professional companion of Fletcher, Shakespeare, and Jonson, each gave a moment of their careers (and in each case it was the most permanently satisfying moment) in homage and dues-paying to the past—forming a formal bridge between their origins and their posterity which would perpetuate the oldest ritual of all, the resurrectional form of comic structure which makes community something profounder than the self's tragic cry. Just a little death and a little beginning. Again.

CHAPTER 4

Marlowe's *Dido* and the Titillating Children

Most critical commentary upon Elizabethan drama directs itself toward the play as poem rather than as production. This is properly so because we know so much about the poetic and rhetorical bent of the education received by playwrights and their auditors alike, know that it *was* a poetic drama. Boys trained "to turne the prose of the Poets into the Poets owne verse, with delight, certainty and speed, without any bodging," trained to listen to the drone against the hourglass on Sundays "in order to make a repetition of the whole Sermon without book . . . rehearsing severall parts . . . distinctly & briefly"—such were the boys trained by Shakespeare's exact contemporary John Brinsley in Leicestershire, and by many another schoolmaster less pedagogically articulate.[1] They were not so likely as our contemporaries to feel it a ludicrous assumption that the ear could catch, the mind maintain, those intricate schemes and tropes and trains of metaphor through which play becomes poem. But it is not only proper to read early plays as poems: it is, unhappily, too often necessary to read them only as poems because we know so relatively little about contemporary productions. At lucky moments staging and significance converge in strokes we cannot miss. The blind and despairing Gloucester of *Lear* cries out to the gods that he can bear no longer "and not fall / To quarrel with your great opposeless wills," enacts a farcical pratfall from the illusory cliffs of Dover in good vaudeville tradition, and so is cured of incurable despair (as Edgar comments, "Ten masts at each make not the altitude / Which thou hast perpendicularly fell: / Thy life's a miracle"). Poetry and performance converge, eye and ear, to tell us that we are once again in the presence of that great Christian myth of miracle, the Fortunate Fall.

Such triumphant moments of the playmaker's control of his media are most easily discernible when, as in this case, they fuse. That control can be as productive, however, when the theatrical *frisson* is embodied in words and scenes mirroring the psyche's pleasure in hosting conflicting systems, mutually irreverent senses of the nature of things. When this conflict emerges in the drama we, as critics, often hasten to apologize for the dramatist with the good intention of protecting the poet; better half a play than none. Such, I think, has been the case in our miscalculations about *Dido, Queen of Carthage*, Marlowe's only text written not for the public theater, but for the Queen's Children of the Chapel. Having listened too intently to the siren song of its sweet verse, we have shipwrecked its fine farce. Doing so, we have relegated what is perhaps Marlowe's best piece of total theater to the status of apprentice work.

Trollope went too far in labeling *Dido* "pretty quaint, and painful" and a "burlesque,"[2] but he moved in the right direction. Harry Levin and Clifford Leech have noted a comic element in some scenes, but only as fragmented compromise with the limitations of boy actors.[3] Don Cameron Allen alone has taken the humor seriously, and he only as it affects the play's deities: "In his poetic philosophy men are surely better than their gods and have only one mortal weakness: they lend their ears . . . to the advice and direction of the silly hulks they have themselves created."[4] The case is not, I think, quite so metaphysical. It is not its conclusions, but the play's potential for laminating conflicting sensibilities which Marlowe wishes to impose upon his audience's imagination.

The Children of the Chapel ranged in age roughly from eight to thirteen, and were, of course, chosen for their voices, not their ability as realistic "actors." Such ability could scarcely be very maturely developed even in an age of rhetorical education.[5] But with that rhetorical training, the sweet-singing boys were ideally prepared to declaim complex verse. And it is to this ability that Marlowe directed his serious adaptation (in many long passages a close translation) of Vergil. The Vergilian elements of *Dido* are much less dramatic than declamatory, and what the Queen's Children's audience heard was an expert professional declamation of parts of the best English *Aeneid* before Dryden, Marlowe's challenge to Stanyhurst, Surrey, and his other predecessors.[6]

But no matter how able verse and voices, poetic declamation was not drama in the 1580s. So Marlowe made several additions to the Vergilian narrative, the principal being a framing induction, a comic nurse, and multiple suicides at the close. All of these additions are interpolated to exploit the self-conscious theatrical situation vectored by sexually romantic love matter, a literate adult audience, and the little-boy players.

The first addition is an induction in which Jupiter is revealed dandling Ganymede upon his knee. This Ganymede is Plato's (*Laws* 1. 636c) and Lactantius' glorified catamite.[7] "Hold here, my little love! / . . . I'll hug with you an hundred times" (1.1.42–48), Jupiter cajoles, and Venus, entering upon the scene, is disgusted: "Ay, this is it! You can sit toying there / And playing with that female wanton boy,. / Whiles my Aeneas wanders on the seas" (50–52). This unexpected and broadly homosexual opening would not have failed, of course, as a joke for those friends and scandal-seekers who knew Marlowe's (at least, alleged) personal predilections. Richard Baines's note on Marlowe's beliefs reported that he had said "that St John the Evangelist was bedfellow to Christ and . . . that he vsed him as the sinners of Sodoma." Thomas Kyd was more succinct on his roommate's blasphemy: "He would report St John to be our Savior Christes *Alexis*." These were neither entirely negative nor random remarks, perhaps, because according to Baines, Marlowe felt "that all they that love not tobacco & Boyes were fooles."[8]

But this was only a private joke at best, riding upon the inevitable recognition that the boys and their masters were mirroring and mocking their own public reputations. The reflexive satire is a reflection less upon the poet and the gods than upon children's theater itself. I have said that the boys were *chosen* for the singing company; in many cases that was a euphemism for impressment or even kidnapping. Richard Edwardes, William Hunnis, and other Masters of the Chapel were given royal carte blanche by Elizabeth to search out and "take as manye well singinge children as he or his sufficient deputie shall thinke mete . . . within this our realme of England whatsoever they be."[9] Parents, guardians, or church authorities were obligated not only to surrender the boy to the Chapel Master, but to provide transportation of the child to London. The degree to which the master's privilege could be extended into flagrant arrogance is revealed in the angry litigation over the carrying off of little Thomas Clifton from Christchurch grammar school to the Blackfriars headquarters of the Chapel Children in 1600 and the subsequent taunting of father and son with threats of beating and such. That this case should have surfaced publicly is owing to the father's having been a gentleman from Norfolk with high government connections,[10] but it is unlikely to have been singular in the child companies' history. The potential for private as well as public abuse of the boys in a context which made them chattel became part of their public image.[11] Gabriel Harvey taunted Lyly as "the Vicemaster of Poules" when he was associated with the boys, and Middleton ironically informed would-be gallants later that they could "see a nest of boys able to ravish a man" at Blackfriars.[12] Stephen Gosson worried about boys who put on "the attyre, the gesture, the passions of a woman,"[13] and Phillip Stubbes found the theaters bringing mate to mate where "in their secret conclaues (couertly) they play the *Sodomits*, or worse."[14] Cocke's character of an actor asserted that "if hee marries, hee mistakes the Woman for the Boy in Womans attire. . . . But so long as he lives unmarried, hee mistakes the Boy . . . for the Woman."[15]

Before the Englishing of Vergil's poem begins, then, the metamorphosis of the boys and their master into the luxurious pagan gods provides self-conscious satire. This dimension will broaden into farce as the play develops. But it will not reduce *Dido* to travesty; rather, it will interlace farce with poetry in an atmosphere where both can survive. Indeed, it would seem that acting of serious romantic matter by little boys could *only* survive as tour de force rather than parody if a presenter occasionally winked over the performers' shoulders to indicate awareness of the suspension of disbelief imposed upon and enjoyed by the audience. A case in point is Lyly's story of unconsummated love written for the boy singers of St. Paul's in which Endymion, classical Rip Van Winkle, just before the denouement "finds means to part with his white beard and other signs of age."[16] The illusion can withstand the light of exposure only if it anticipatorily underlines the paradox which is its base: this seems the dramatic lesson of such interplay between auditor and immature actor.

Let us return to *Dido*, then, with a pertinent theatrical question: who played Jupiter? Perhaps it was the master or another adult, thus emphasizing the boys' imposed predicament.[17] Perhaps, on the other hand, it was an older boy (between eight and thirteen, inches are enhanced as rapidly as sophistication), in which case the older boy himself became publicly privy to the adults' supposedly salacious secret. In any case, this initial play upon sexual maturity and immaturity was incorporated from the induction into the body of the play by Marlowe's other additions to the Vergilian narrative.

Let us consider the frequently criticized psychology of Dido's scene of mixed emotion as she holds Cupid, supposed Ascanius, upon her lap. Venus has come upon the true Ascanius, drugged him to sleep, and carried him into the forest while metamorphosing Cupid into Ascanius' shape. Cupid's instructions from his mother are to get upon Dido's lap, "Then touch her white breast with this arrow head, / That she may dote upon Aeneas' love" (2. 1. 26-27)—a golden arrow dipped in magic love juice such as that with which Puck (upon Oberon's instructions) anointed the eyes of Titania that she might look dotingly upon Bottom the Ass. Seductively teasing, Cupid does gain Dido's lap as she is speaking with her suitor Iarbas (whose role has been expanded by Marlowe from small Vergilian hints). Then, through the magic of Venus' potion, Dido becomes a whirligig of emotion:

Dido.	O stay, Iarbas, and I'll go with thee.
Cup.	And if my mother go, I'll follow her.
Dido.	[*to Iarbas*]. Why stay'st thou here? thou art
	no love of mine.
Iar.	Iarbas, die, seeing she abandons thee!
Dido.	No, live, Iarbas; what hast thou deserv'd,
	That I should say thou art no love of mine?
	Something thou hast deserv'd—Away, I say,
	Depart from Carthage, come not in my sight!

.   .   .   .

Iar.	I go to feed the humour of my love,
	Yet not from Carthage for a thousand worlds.
Dido.	Iarbas!
Iar.	Doth Dido call me back?
Dido.	No, but I charge thee never look on me.

.   .   .   .

   . . . his loathsome sight offends mine eye,
And in my thoughts is shrin'd another love.
                               (3.1.37–57)

Such crude psychology and strident verse are not failures of either dramatic or poetic modulation; to hypothesize that is to assume sudden deafness in the ear which a few lines later could lead Marlowe to write:

I'll give thee tackling made of rivell'd gold
Wound on the barks of odoriferous trees;
Oars of massy ivory, full of holes,
Through which the waters shall delight to play;
Thy anchors shall be hew'd from crystal rocks,
Which if thou lose shall shine above the waves.
                                (3.1.115–20)

It is more reasonable to assume that what seems an unaccountably abrupt falling off upon the printed page is a deft shift of theatrical tone when the little boys must begin to talk of love. As the scene opens, Cupid sings a "pretty song," then provides some innuendos which would remind the viewer of Jupiter's homosexual toying with Ganymede: "Will Dido let me hang about her neck?" the one boy asks the other and Dido responds: "Ay, wag, and give thee leave to kiss her too" (3.1.30–31). Climbing upon her lap, Cupid produces the arrow from his sleeve and by its magic induces the improbable oscillations in Dido's attitude toward Iarbas which have been cited above. Marlowe is titillating us again with the boys' interesting limitations: instead of declaiming sentiments, he elects to have them enact a farce of love. Before our eyes one small boy crawls into the arms of another and draws a conspicuously golden arrow stealthily into view (the stage direction is built into the dialogue as the scene begins: "Now, Cupid, . . . Convey this golden arrow in thy sleeve. / Lest she imagine thou art Venus' son" [3.1.1-4]). This he periodically jabs into Dido's paps at each bewildered, wavering turn she makes back toward her old interest in Iarbas, paps either nonexistent or stuffed out and painted in parody of the life this play never intends to imitate. Any doubt of Marlowe's intentions should have been laid to rest by the repetition of Cupid's game an act later with that other boy who, in female guise as a gabbling old nurse, could challenge Salomon Pavy's alleged talent at playing old men. She scoops him into her arms and, under his influence, immediately turns lecherous: "That I might live to see this boy a man! / How prettily he laughs! Go, ye wag, / You'll be a twigger when you come to age" (4.5.18-20).

The same scene is repeated three times, a scene drawing the boys to the edge of their reputation and talents. In the Jupiter-Ganymede induction the homosexual potential of the troupe is exploited with a leer of mock acknowledgement for the scandalmongers. In the Dido-Cupid version the paradox of love's absurdity is mocked by the parody of boys playing it absurdly. In the nurse's scene with Cupid, the boy company triumphantly reclaims its reputation for charming the imagination by making us laugh at yet another boy lover because he is so obviously disqualified for love, not this time primarily because he is a boy but because he is an old woman. All three scenes are, of course, among Marlowe's additions to his Vergilian undertext. They are his answer to the challenge of making the limitations of boy players into theatrical strengths. But, beyond that, they force demands upon the audience's imagination, demands that it consciously react to that "doubleness" which is the theatrical experience: the ability to hold simultaneous consciousness of actor and role, story world and stage world, to be aware of the psyche's separate life as a fantasy in the midst of its engagement with reality.

But let us now return to look at the action with an eye on the boys' physical size rather than their sexual immaturity or precociousness, states so closely allied in this prematurely sophisticated theater. Leaving the character Jupiter aside because of the possibility that he might have been played by an adult, we find that Venus, Dido, and the nurse were all larger boys. Venus carries Ascanius on stage in her arms in order to place him in a grove; Cupid (Ascanius' double) sits in Dido's lap; the nurse carries Cupid off stage at the close of act 4. The female figures are older, larger boys thatn Ascanius and Cupid. But what of Aeneas?

The assumption that would seem most natural is that he was played by an older, larger boy, equal if not superior in size to Dido. And this assumption appears to be supported by little Ascanius when, immediately after Aeneas' initial heroic rhetoric, the son emphasizes his minority in pleading: "Father, I faint; good father, give me meat" (1.1.163). But if Ascanius is small enough to be scooped up and carried by a boy of twelve or thirteen, there is a sufficient range of potential physical size in a group of prepubescents to allow for an Aeneas large enough to play Ascanius' father yet smaller than his lover Dido. If we assume that to have been the case in the staging by the Chapel Children, certain other disturbing elements in this play cease to seem puzzling lapses.

Marlowe, as might be expected in a dramatization, expands the meeting at a cave which brings about the admission and consummation of Dido's love for Aeneas, a meeting only briefly reported by Vergil. But here Marlowe's verse again falters. Rhythms are truncated as line after line becomes independent sentence, exclamation, question. Monosyllables march across the page, false semirhymes abound internally, and schemes dominate tropes to produce flagrantly obvious conceits with which Dido attempts to reveal her love dilemma, as in "The thing that I will die before I ask, / And yet desire to have before I die" (3.4.8-9), or "And yet I'll speak, and yet I'll hold my peace; / Do shame her worst, I will disclose my grief" (26-27). But Aeneas is incapable of penetrating her messages: "What means fair Dido by this doubtful speech?" (30), "What ails my Queen, is she fall'n sick of late?" (23). Such inexplicably obtuse blunting of the climactic love scene becomes comic irony, merging staging and verse, if we project a child Aeneas being uncomprehendingly seduced by a teenage Dido. When he has freely stripped all pretensions from this boy-as-hero being bullied into improbable love by his bigger boy "queen" in skirts, Marlowe caps the farce with a closing embrace. But as he does so, he forces admiration out of fun, reinforces our awareness of the doubleness available to art when he returns to lyric rhythms graceful enough for the tongue of any Shakespearean *inamorata*:

> What more than Delian music do I hear,
> That calls my soul from forth his living seat
> To move unto the measures of delight?
> Kind clouds that sent forth such a courteous storm

As made disdain to fly to fancy's lap!
Stout love, in mine arms make thy Italy.
                              3.4.51-56

It will be a decade before the stage again will chance such stylistic juxtapositions of the lyric and the laughable, when Bottom responds to Titania's "Thou art as wise as thou art beautiful" with, "Not so, neither. But if I had wit enough to get out of this wood, I have enough to serve my turn," and invokes the reply, "I'll give thee fairies to attend on thee, / And they shall fetch thee jewels from the deep, / And sing while thou on pressed flowers dost sleep" (3.1.151-62).

The assumption that Aeneas was a smaller boy than Dido and that Marlowe was playing a double game as lyric poet and comic playwright further aids us in understanding Marlowe's addition to the Vergilian story in act 4, an addition in which the point is Aeneas' wooden helplessness in the ambience of Dido. No sooner has Aeneas declared his resolve to depart and manned his ships than he allows himself to be called back and lies about his intentions like the shuffling schoolboy which he, in fact, is: "O princely Dido, give me leave to speak; / I went to take my farewell of Achates" (4.4.17-18). Dido crowns him, dissipates his resolution, and regains his weathervane allegiance: "O Dido, patroness of all our lives, / When I leave thee, death be my punishment!" (55-56). The little hero is toyed with by the bigger queen, as she will remind us with a little irony which points back to the induction as Dido and Marlowe mock Aeneas under the Carthaginian crown he has just accepted: "Now looks Aeneas like immortal Jove: / O where is Ganymede, to hold his cup? (45-46).

The metaphoric play with Aeneas' hapless bandying among physically as well as psychically greater powers is carried into act 5. The action opens with his announced decision, induced by Dido, to establish the new Troy in an expanded Carthage, but no sooner has he finished than Hermes leads in Ascanius by the hand, emphasizing his own stature by scorning Aeneas' concern "about this little boy" (5.1.51) while Jove is anxiously desiring that he get on to Italy. Hermes scolds crossly, and Aeneas quails querulously as his deity's messenger departs in a huff: "How should I put into the raging deep / Who have no sails nor tackling for my ship?" The cause for his lack of equipment is Dido, who, after recalling him from his first attempt to leave, has "ta'en away my oars and masts, / And left me neither sail nor stern aboard" (55-61). Iarbas overhears his rival's complaint, promises to equip his ships to be rid of him, and the helpless Aeneas sadly agrees to be manipulated by god and man: "How loth I am to leave these Libyan bounds" (81).

The queen sees the new preparations and girds herself for one more seduction of the boy hero ("Dido, try thy wit" [86]), but Vergil and history have denied her, if Marlowe has not in his providing her with a fluent and lyric tongue which Aeneas can confront only with acknowledgement of his puppetlike role as a boy among men, women, and poets. All argument silenced, his last words are Marlowe's self-tribute: "In vain, my love, thou spends't thy fainting breath: / If words might move me, I were overcome" (153-54).

Then comes the close. Dido madly imagines Aeneas' return, Anna disabuses her, and Marlowe writes his psychologically soundest scene.[18] But having done so, he adds the suicides of Iarbas and Anna to that of Dido, telescoping them all within the last fifty lines of the play. This constitutes Marlowe's final departure, not only from Vergil but from tradition, it having been observed that all the other numerous Renaissance plays on the Dido story devote the entire last act to the queen's death.[19] Nothing in the first four acts has suggested a tragic tone, and Marlowe's playfulness with the dramatic limitations of the boys should have encouraged his audience until this penultimate moment to expect a denouement in the tradition which would become known as *Vergile travestée.* Such a denouement is denied as Dido throws herself upon the pyre with a dignity literally borrowed from Vergil's epic:

> Now, Dido, with these relics burn thyself,
> And make Aeneas famous through the world
> For perjury and slaughter of a queen.
>
> .   .   .   .
>
> *Litora litoribus contraria, fluctibus undas*
> *Imprecor; arma armis; pugnent ipsique nepotes:*
> Live, false Aeneas! Truest Dido dies;
> *Sic, sic iuvat ire sub umbras.*
>
> (5.1.292-313)

In this unexpected recovery of passionate seriousness, Marlowe defies anticipation by imitating the full resonances of his source. But to end upon such a reserve of lyric power would be to deny the theatrical game he has been playing with the children, and he has no intention of doing so. It is in this context that he appends the final dozen lines:

> *Enter* Anna.
> O help, Iarbas! Dido in these flames
> Hath burnt herself! Ay me, unhappy me!
> *Enter* Iarbas *running.*
> Cursed Iarbas, die to expiate
> The grief that tires upon thine inward soul!
> Dido, I come to thee: ay me, Aeneas! [*Kills himself.*]

Anna. What can my tears or cries prevail me now?
Dido is dead, Iarbas slain, Iarbas my dear love!

.   .   .   .

Now, sweet Iarbas, stay, I come to thee!

(5.1.314–28)

Having evaded the expectation of farce, Marlowe injected high feeling into the death of Dido. But, looking over the talented little boy actors' shoulders and winking at their triumph and his own, he added a fillip to that conclusion and followed up with what he had teasingly promised all along: a silly story hastily superimposed upon the realities of passionate love and death. Doing so, he prepared the mind of at least one contemporary to gather superficially incompatible forces into a play which has dogged and dodged our imaginations in its happy combination of improbabilities. I implicitly have been arguing, of course, that the mixed farce and romance of *Dido, Queen of Carthage* is Marlowe's most significant gift to Shakespeare, progenitor of that strange crossbreeding of Puck and Oberon and Theseus and Bottom's players, *A Midsummer Night's Dream.*

CHAPTER 5

Bartholomew Fair as Blasphemy

My lord of Winton told me, he told him, he was (in his long retyrement and sicknes, when he saw him, which was often) much aflickted, that hee had profain'd the scripture, in his playes; and lamented it with horror.

—Izaak Walton to John Aubrey
(*Jonson*, ed. Herford and Simpson, I, 181-182)

I

In the Macilente of *Every Man Out of His Humour*, who shares enough characteristics to be identified as a *persona* for the author Asper and for the author Jonson, the creative imagination controlling a dramatic world is embodied as a daemon plotter gone mad. The creator's poem is the satiric image of his own vileness, but once projected upon this stage of fools, that vileness is purified, the madness runs its course, and the whole is reduced to play, to the wispy breath of a theatrical impromptu, when Macilente sighs, "I could wish / They might turn wise upon it, and be sav'd now, / So heav'n were pleasd: but let them vanish, vapours" (5.11.63–65).

I make the point in order to sharpen our focus through contrast, for in *Bartholomew Fair* the created comes into independent life (as does the embedded analogue of the wooden puppet who converts the living Puritan), refusing to relinquish its autonomy into the hands of a hapless authority the ways of whose world are as mad as those of Macilente's. There is sufficient ethical questioning here to have evoked Professor Heffner's conclusion to one of the most careful examinations of the play: "All search for warrant seems as absurd as Troub-leall's. . . . Whim, animal appetite, and sordid greed have complete sway over men's actions without as well as within the fair; the fair merely provides the heightened conditions under which their disguises fall off and the elemental motivations become manifest."[1] But there is more than ethical questioning in *Bartholomew Fair*: It probes the wellsprings of religious consciousness to discover absurdity in the fullest sense of the word in both conscience and providence, in works and in grace—indeed, in all varieties of view which focus in the implicit axiom that there obtains some teleological relation between creator and creation, between God and the world. So much is this true that we might define Jonson's work as an antimorality play.

II

"Enormities," cries Adam Overdo, justice of the court of Pie-powders and hence immediate authority over the economies of the play. "Many are the yearly enormities of this Fair."[2] He is right, the word and the thing threading through the course of his disguised observation of a hubbub emanating from thieves, whores, pimps, and pudding stuffers. And there is fast approaching that fullness of time which he has awaited, the judgment day: "This is the special day for detection of those foresaid enormities" (2.1.44–45). It is the day because he has come among the children of the fair in the guise of a fool to record the scenes of sin: "Here is my black book for the purpose, this disguise the cloud that hides me" (46–47). Immediately his discoveries begin, as sharp practitioners enter threatening to betray one another in the name of the Pie-powder justice. "I am glad," observes Overdo, "to hear my name is their terror, yet" (2.2.27). It is a refrain which he repeats later to the fright of Knockem, the horse courser: "Is not my name your terror?" (5.6.11). But the justice is not yet ready to flood the revels of iniquity with the storm of his terror: "Neither is the hour of my severity yet come, to reveal myself, wherein, cloud-like, I will break out in rain and hail, lightning and thunder, upon the head of enormity" (5.2.3–6). As he once observes, ripeness is all: "I will not discover who I am till my due time; and yet still all shall be, as I said ever, in Justice' name" (3.3.39–40).

"And it came to pass on the third day in the morning, that there were thunders and lightnings, and a thick cloud upon the mount . . . so that all the people that was in the camp trembled" (Exod. 19:16). Thus begins the description of the coming of the commandments that Moses relates in the detailed reading of "the book of this law," which, replete with reminiscences of the fiery cloud of concealment, constitutes the "Fifth Book of Moses, called Deuteronomy."

As the course of human history is fulfilled in the Apocalypse of the New Testament, the imagery once more gathers into familiar conjunctions—properly, for he who here "cometh in clouds" is "Alpha and Omega, the beginning and the ending" (Rev. 1:7–8). From the cloud issues the vision of the sealed book of judgment, "for the great day of his wrath is come" (6:17) when "hail and fire mingled with blood, and they were cast upon the earth" (8:7). Clearly Justice Overdo formulates his mission of raining judgment upon Bartholomew Fair in the imagery of Jehovah's judgments, such as the one which came upon Tyre, Old Testament archetype of corrupting riches: "The merchants of Sheba and Raamah, they were thy merchants: they occupied in thy fairs with chief of all spices, and with all precious stones, and gold. . . . Thy riches, and thy fairs, thy merchandise . . . in the midst of thee, shall fall into the midst of the seas in the day of thy ruin. . . . Thou hast defiled thy sanctuaries by the multitude of thine iniquities, by the iniquity of thy traffic; therefore will I bring forth a fire from the midst of thee. . . . All they that know thee among the people shall be astonished at thee: thou shalt be a terror, and never shalt thou be any more" (Ezek. 27–28 passim). This was the type of judgment held up by Jesus before those "like unto children sitting in the markets" when he promised: "I say unto you, it shall be more tolerable for Tyre and Sidon at the day of judgment, than for you" (Matt. 11:22).

The bent for thinking in scriptural imagery constitutes a superficially improbable similarity between what one reader has tagged "the conscientious Anglican judge Overdo and the fanatical Puritan preacher Busy,"[3] for Zeal-of-the-Land also turns instinctively to Old Testament types for his justification in pulling down the gingerbread stall: "I was mov'd in spirit, to be here, this day, in this Fair, this wicked, and foul Fair . . . to protest against the abuses of it, the foul abuses of it, in regard of the afflicted saints, that are troubled, very much troubled, exceedingly troubled, with the opening of the merchandise of Babylon again." (3.6.82–87). Neither puritanical zeal nor Scripture was reserved for those outside the Establishment in 1614,[4] and it might be agreed that Overdo's near-blasphemous self-references converge with the milieu of the Purecraft-Littlewit household merely to enlarge the anti-Puritan satire and remind that zeal is as accessible to the ignorant as to the hypocritical. It might be agreed, that is, did not the others of the fair acquiesce in Adam Overdo's consciousness of a Jehovan authority, did not the action thoroughly support Troubleall's assertion that "if you have Justice Overdo's warrant, 'tis well: you are safe; that is the warrant of warrants" (4.1.18–19). And this last absolute seal of power is woven by echo as well as implication into the imagistic apotheosis of the justice when Troubleall cries out: "I mark no name, but Adam Overdo; that is the name of names; he only is the sufficient magistrate; and that name I reverence" (4.6.145-47; cf. Ephesians 1:21, Philippians 2:9).

His name *does* strike terror among the stalls, as his own minions the watchmen assert in language appropriate only for the anger of a god:

BRISTLE

He will sit upright o' the bench, an' you mark him, as a candle i' the socket, and give light to the whole court in every business.

HAGGIS

But he will burn blue, and swell like a boil (God bless us) an' he be angry.

BRISTLE

Aye, and he will be angry too, when he list, that's more: and when he is angry, be it right or wrong, he has the law on's side, ever. I mark that too.

(4.1.69-76)

Bristle's last remark embeds whimsy pretty deeply into the thunderer's nature, beyond furnishing a pointed Shakespearean allusion. It will be remembered that in the *Discoveries* Jonson observed of Shakespeare that "many times he fell into those things, could not escape laughter: As when hee said in the person of *Caesar*, one speaking to him; Caesar, thou dost me wrong. Hee replyed: Caesar did never wrong, but with just cause: and such like; which were ridiculous."[5] The passage on a law as ridiculous as it is absolute so fascinated Jonson that he tossed it to his audience as a mere tag again in the Introduction to *The Staple of News*, and its appearance as allusion in *Bartholomew Fair* leads us back to its own Induction, for there, too, Shakespeare had appeared in a motley supplied by his friend's satiric gibes.

The book-holder's articles of agreement with the audience not only serve to fuse their world with that of Jonson's fair, as Professor Horsman has demonstrated,[6] but also to initiate the movement of three themes which will eventually converge: (1) antiquated judgments, (2) legalism, and (3) puritanism—the last through the inevitable ambiguity of the repeated term "covenant."[7] It is in relation to the first of these themes that the book-holder passes ambivalent judgment upon those wits whose "virtuous and staid ignorance" shows in their constancy, from which they "will swear *Jeronimo* or *Andronicus* are the best plays yet" (Induction, 98-113). These are, of course, revenge plays in the old tradition of poetic justice rough-hewn—the justice of "eye for eye, tooth for tooth, hand for hand," the justice of the old law. *The Spanish Tragedy* was Jonson's (and everyone's) inevitable target for ridicule from *Every Man in His Humour* onward, but *Titus Andronicus* is mentioned nowhere else in his works. The reason for its appearance here is, I believe, to bridge by association the leap from the book-holder's catalogue of antiquated types to the sudden attack on Shakespeare's more recent romances: "If there be never a servant-monster i' the Fair, who can help it? he says; nor a nest of antics? He is loth to make Nature afraid in his plays, like those that beget *Tales, Tempests* and such like drolleries" (128–32). The point is that if *Titus Andronicus* is a play of just revenge, *The Winter's Tale* and *The Tempest* had closed Shakespeare's career in an aura of mercy providentially triumphant, with man's divine nature shining through his disguising passions, as Perdita shone through her peasant's weeds. From the time that Edgar told Gloucester, "Thy life's a miracle," the theme echoed, and it has become a commonplace to observe Prospero's insistence. "How came we ashore?" inquires Miranda at the opening. "By Providence divine," responds her father. And at the close Ferdinand assures all that Miranda is mortal, not goddess, "but by immortal Providence she's mine." Such cries of wonder are the proper chords with which to harmonize the ironic counterpoint of Busy's cry, "We are delivered by miracle" (4.6.160) when Troubleall frees the victims of the stocks in the course of his own providential wanderings. These cries are more than expressions of pious confidence in the gods that be, however, in plays centering upon men whose magic embodies the power of deity; for the late Shakespeare they are the symbolic tropes which broaden the implications of his plot into a restatement of the universal validity in the Christian design of man'd divine comedy. Jonson alludes to these very recent plays, then, to orient our attention to the symbolic mode of his own drama of God and man and Providence, but the pattern is of a very different design in a world wherein the staff of quasi-omnipotence is carried by Overdo rather than by Prospero.

Moreover, even in ironically warning his audience not to be "so solemnly ridiculous as to search out who was meant by the Gingerbread-woman . . . what Mirror of Magistrates is meant by the Justice" (136–149), Jonson concludes with a clue for the true "grounded judgments and understandings" as to the direction in which such allegorical spying might naturally lead. Let no one, warns the book-holder, charge "profaneness because a madman cries, 'God quit you,' or 'bless you' " (153–54).[8]

But the profanity is explicit, and persistent, throughout the last two acts, threaded as they are by Troubleall's crazed course through the mazes of the fair's intrigues. He has scarcely entered, seeking authority, when he departs with his fixed phrase: "I do only hope you have warrant, for what you do, and so, quit you, and so, multiply you" (4.1.13–15).[9] The watchmen, Dame Purecraft, Grace, Winwife, Quarlous—all who meet him are given the benediction, "quit you, and multiply you," innocuous enough until it suddenly echoes with the blasphemous turn which reinforces Overdo's own self-epithets and identifies him as the drama's deity. Frustrated, Cokes cries after a departing Troubleall, "You are a very coxcomb, do you hear?" And Troubleall returns the terrible reply: "I think I am; if Justice Overdo sign to it, I am, and so we are all; he'll quit us all, multiply us all" (4.2.107–9).

It may yet be objected with Jonson to such a politic picklock of the scene as I have played to this point that the profanity had been poured from the vessel of a madman; but to turn now to an exploration of the action as a whole will be to justify Dame Purecraft's observation: "Mad, do they call him! The world is mad in error, but he is mad in truth" (4.6.163–64).

III

Nowhere is the revolutionary dispensation of the New Testament in relation to the Old Testament history anatomized with more ringing clarity than in Paul's Epistle to the Romans: "But now we are delivered from the law . . . that we should serve in newness of spirit, and not in the oldness of the letter" (Rom. 7:6). Here are intertwined two of the dominant themes which control the action of *Bartholomew Fair*: legalism and an antiquated severity of judgment. The Induction immediately and insistently associates antiquated views with precisely the passing of judgment. The stage-keeper comes in clucking at the perverse author who would not listen to his seasoned advice: "For the whole play, will you ha' the truth on't? . . . it is like to be a very conceited scurvy one, in plain English. . . . I kept the stage in Master Tarlton's time, I thank my stars. Ho! an' that man liv'd to have play'd in *Bartholomew Fair*." Chasing this carping nostalgist from the stage, the book-holder is ambiguously satiric at the expense of one we have earlier noticed, "he that will swear *Jeronimo* or *Andronicus* are the best plays yet . . . whose judgment . . . hath stood still, these five and twenty, or thirty years." Such judgments in favor of the old plays of vengeful retribution (contrasted, we recall, with the providentially merciful romances) dovetail intrinsically, of course, into the legalistic Old Testament attitudes and language of Justice Overdo. And it is perhaps appropriate at this point to notice that where he imagines his fullness of "due time" only as "the hour of my severity," he is inverting the province of another Pauline concept and phrase, one which leads us back to the implications of Romans: "When the fulness of the time was come, God sent forth his Son, made of a woman, made under the law, to redeem them that were under the law" (Gal. 4:4-5; cf. Eph. 1:10).

The insistence upon old, superseded standards provides only a set from which attention is directed toward the ultimate implications of legálism in both secular and theological contexts. And it is in these respects that we are invited to contrast the justice, externally disguised as fool and madman, with the hypocritical puritan Busy, whose disguise is his mimicry of Overdo's genuine Old Testament conscientiousness before the "law." Quarlous' description of the Banbury brother is instructive: "A notable hypocritical vermin it is. . . . One that stands upon his face more than his faith, at all times . . . of a most lunatic conscience. . . . By his profession, he will ever be i' the state of innocence, though, and childhood; derides all antiquity; defies any other learning than inspiration" (1.3.133–143). A casuist who derides antiquity (and who, for all of his Old Testament imagery, would justify the eating of roast pig "to profess our hate and loathing of Judaism" [1.6.94–95]), Busy is a law unto himself; he claims both the authority of Overdo over the consciences of men and the innocence of Cokes. "Childhood," like the "law," is a face[10] which, looked beneath, reveals his kinship with the "children of the Fair," "sons and daughters of Smithfield" (2.6.61–64). Essence of exterior, however, legalism pursued to its issue in action succeeds in yoking Overdo for a moment of truth with his mimic Busy in the stocks, that trap which blind justice constructs as a retributive symbol for self-defeat and immobility in a world of the flesh.[11] In *Volpone* the law personified in the ambiguous justice of the *avvocatori* might seem to triumph at least over the disguises of more cunning hypocrisy; in *The Alchemist* the law of the land is bilked precisely by "Face." But in *Bartholomew Fair* neither the law nor Busy's "face" can master the seething chaos of a fair filled with fighting and beating and shouting which defies the very principle of order, even that order of self-interest imposed from beneath the disguises which served so well in Jonson's earlier comedies.

But now let us widen our focus to follow the history and value of two converging legal props—Cokes's license and Overdo's warrant[12]—for it is just these symbols which will lead us through a demonstration that law has been corrupted into the letter (false warrant), as in Shylock's bond, and that Grace is for sale because the quality of mercy is unknown in a world blinded by conscience and mad with literal authority.

"Buy any pears, fine, very fine pears," shouts the costermonger, to

Joan Trash's chorus of "Buy any ginger-bread, gilt ginger-bread," counterpointed by Nightingale's "Buy any ballads; new ballads?" (2.2., 32 ff.). This is our first introduction to Bartholomew Fair—like the fairs of Tyre, a type of commercialism.[13] The tinkle of trinkets and coins provides background music which culminates in Cokes's insistence upon buying all: "Shut up shop presently, friend. I'll buy both it and thee too, to carry down with me, and her hamper, beside. . . . What's the price, at a word, o' thy whole shop . . . ?" (3.4.138–43). But innocent silliness deepens into sin when the citizens' wives are persuaded to whore in the interest of the pig booth (4.5),[14] and then commercialism goes yet deeper, to the very bases of order, when Littlewit the proctor sells Busy into the justice of the stocks to rid himself of the Puritan's warnings, happily crying out as his opponent is dragged off, "Was not this shilling well ventur'd, Win, for our liberty?" (3.6.109). Here is justice doubly corrupted, as the legal representative has to buy true justice for the wrong reasons. But the power of money has not even yet been exhausted; it will go to the very source of authority and responsibility itself. For Overdo, the godlike magistrate of the fair, is corrupted with his world's disease. His ward is Grace, that one freest of God's gifts to man, but "he bought me, sir," Grace explains; "and now he will marry me to his wife's brother . . . or else I must pay value o' my land" (3.5.275–78).

Possession is more than nine parts of the law when Grace can be had by barter through Overdo's warrant, a point even more pressingly urged by the string of thefts and forgeries which threads the play. These begin, like the huckstering, in Edgworth's almost venial removal of Cokes's superfluous purse under the glass eyes of Overdo himself. But they soon center upon license and warrant, those dead letters of the law written, respectively, by a "Littlewit" giving Grace to a "Cokes" and an overdoer giving carte blanche to a madman. The absolute power and emptiness of the license is emphasized at once when Wasp, coming to claim it, refuses even to look at the contents: "Nay, never open, or read it to me, . . . I am no clerk, I scorn to be sav'd by my book, i' faith . . . fold it up o' your word and gi'it me; what must you ha' for't?" (1.4.5–8). The sacredness of the Word is parodied as the unread document is conveyed to Wasp in the ark of a "black box," wherein the Word can be possessed without being known, and it is only the box itself that Wasp haggles over: "You must have a mark for your thing here, and eightpence for the box; I could ha' sav'd twopence i' that, an' I had bought it myself" (1.4.21–23). When Cokes joins his guardian, the emphasis upon the sheer physical nature of the letter is reiterated as his appeals to see the license are rebuffed by Wasp's reminder that "there's nothing in't but hard words: and what would you see't for?"

and Cokes replies, "I would see the length and the breadth on't, that's all."[15] Wasp refuses, and Cokes, too, settles for the ark rather than the Word: "Then I'll see't at home, and I'll look upo' the case here" (1.5.30–40). Such innocent trust in possession is easy prey for the predators of the fair, however, and when Quarlous employs Edgworth to steal the license from Wasp, the cutpurse further develops the earlier confusion of values concerning insides and outsides: "Would you ha' the box and all, sir? or only that, that is in't? I'll get you that, and leave him the box to play with still (which will be the harder o' the two)" (3.5.254–56). Yet the cutpurse is only a tool, ironically similar to Cokes and Wasp themselves in assessing ark and law alike as mere things. Quarlous knows better the power of the letter and insists more unscrupulously upon real possession, and it is he who ultimately manages the largest theft by forging the license which has meant so little to those with a merely exterior understanding of its authority: "It is money that I want; why should I not marry the money, when 'tis offer'd me? I have a license and all, it is but razing out one name, and putting in another" (5.2.80–83).

It is Quarlous, too, disguised as Troubleall, who acquires Overdo's "warrant." Overdo, at last trying to show his mercy toward the man made mad by his unbending justice, instead gives infinite power (the warrant bearing only his signature on a page to be filled in at the possessor's will) to the thief who thus steals Grace from his very hands. In the discovery scene at the close, it is his possession of these two documents of the law which gives Quarlous absolute authority and humbles Overdo to mere "Adam, flesh and Blood." But perhaps the cruelest irony and severest comment on the world of the fair comes earlier, when Quarlous' theft of Troubleall's clothing in the interest of disguise not only gains him the warrant, but forces the madly conscientious victim himself into the vicious circle in which he too becomes a hunted thief who "has stol'n Gammer Urs'la's pan" to cover his nakedness (5.6.52 ff.).[16]

Commercialism, then, readily passes into theft and corrodes all within its ambience.[17] But what the entangled motifs of money and theft demonstrate is that authority resides in possession and is a power as arbitrary as that of the Old Testament Jehovah whose whimsical qualities echo so dangerously in Justice Overdo.

We can view the arbitrariness from its other side if we consider the state of the innocent rather than of the corrupt actors. Overdo's unscrupulous employment of his power of disposition over Grace drives his ward into exposing herself to the lottery of a blind destiny when she agrees to marry the man whose chance word "but of two, or three syllables at most" is chosen by the next passerby. Not only does this scroll of fortune ring one more change upon the terrible power of the literal word emptied of spirit, but it also compounds that horror when the arbitrator of her future turns out to be that "fine ragged prophet," the madman Troubleall (4.3). Grace is fully conscious of the absurdity of her marital lottery, yet sees an absurd choice as the only suitable mode of coping with an absurd world, arguing that it would be "levity" to pretend to choose rationally between men on a two hours' acquaintance in the fair. Cokes, on the other hand, like Overdo, is in fact what Busy pretends to be: "He will ever be i' the state of innocence . . . and childhood." His toy-shop enjoyment of the fair, as of the world, draws children into his orbit everywhere. "We walk'd London," Wasp explains, and Cokes "would name you all the signs over, as he went, aloud: and where he spied a parrot, or a monkey, there he was pitch'd, with all the little-long-coats about him" (1.4.102–14), a scene reenacted when he is surrounded by children before the puppet booth. As even the pimp Whit can discern, "He is a child i' faith, la" (5.4.218–19).[18] But Wasp, sharing Overdo's wrath and blindness, is no more able than the justice to protect his ward from the theft and cheating of the fair.

These are the two extremes, the fully perspicacious innocence of Grace and the childish innocence of Cokes, but they meet in the third victim, Troubleall. Once a minion of the law, "an officer in the court of Pie-powders," he was "put out on his place by Justice Overdo. . . . Upon which he took an idle conceit, and's run mad upon't. So that, ever since, he will do nothing but by Justice Overdo's warrant" (4.1.49–54). Justice has made Troubleall over from judge to innocent, as ignorant as Cokes and, like him, seeking no longer the substance of the law but the mere letter of the warrant. Willy-nilly the innocent—Grace with her word lottery, Cokes with his "length and breadth" conception of the license, Troubleall with his blind confidence in warrant—have been absorbed by the sterile, literal legalism of Overdo's world.

IV

Let us now perceive in more detail how action and language coalesce to make this law-maddened Troubleall into a figure of destiny at its most capricious, the very fact of whose madness makes his agency in the affairs of Grace, Cokes, Purecraft, Winwife, and Quarlous determining.

Even the indirect preparation for Troubleall's role in Dame Purecraft's life is couched in terms which make him the specter of an ambiguously conceived destiny, since the fortune-tellers have advised that the good lady "shall never have happy hour, unless she marry within

the sen'night, and when it is, it must be a madman, they say"
(1.2.30 ff.). (The fortune-tellers' advice is perhaps a simple deception,
or perhaps a diabolic oracle—for, as Littlewit says, "the devil can
equivocate, as well as a shopkeeper.") And so the idea of a providential
destiny enters, to be associated with the peripatetic Troubleall
throughout the drama. When Grace invents her lottery, it is because
"destiny has a high hand in business of this nature" (4.3.51-52), and
when the "fine ragged prophet, dropp'd down i' the nick" arrives the
next moment, crying "Heaven quit you, gentlemen," Quarlous comments, "a fortune-teller we ha' made him" (75 ff.). Winwife, later admitting that he has won Grace by "the benefit of her fortune," reassures
her that it may have seemed a blind action but that eventualities will
"make you rather to think that, in this choice, she [Fortune] had both
her eyes" (5.2.33-34). Quarlous, too, senses something divine in Troubleall, "my tatter'd soothsayer . . . who was my judge . . . to decide
whose word he has damn'd or sav'd" by awarding the gift of Grace
(4.6.42-44). They all would seem to echo in their reactions Busy's own
ejaculation when Troubleall inadvertently freed the prisoners from the
stocks: "We are delivered by miracle . . . this madness was of the
spirit" (4.6.160-61).

Troubleall, the omnipresent destiny of *Bartholomew Fair*, has
been made mad by the omnipotent Overdo because this latter Jehovah-
like figure refused him mercy in the name of justice, thus exaggerating
his agent's conscience beyond the limits of reason. There is logic in the
unreason because conscience *must* be an irrational concept when it de-
pends upon arbitrary, blind authority: a blind God must create a blind
destiny, call it Providence though men may. And Overdo's own grop-
ings toward a realization have approached this discovery when he admits that he begins "to think that, by a spice of collateral justice, Adam
Overdo deserv'd this beating; for I, the said Adam, was one cause (a by-
cause) why the purse was lost" (3.3.2-6). It is an attitude reinforced by
Nightingale's ballad, which begs all to remember that if purses are
stolen from his audience, they have been taken as well in Westminster
Hall, demanding hence, "why should the judges be free from this
curse, / More than my poor self, for cutting the purse?" (3.5.79 ff.)
From this vantage point we can see the fair's corruption as both emanating from and encroaching upon the actions of its controlling authority.

V

It is here necessary to recall that blindness is not an imported metaphor for this world's disorder, but one implanted at important junc-

tures in the very texture of *Bartholomew Fair*. We have already noticed two versions of this image of ignorance, one in Winwife's promise that Troubleall's choice has been made through a fortune with "both her eyes" (sec IV, above) and the other in Overdo's "cloud that hides me" (sec. II, above). This latter, we may remember, takes literal form as the guise of "a certain middling thing, between a fool and a madman" (2.2.147–48), more tightly binding the persons and qualities of Overdo and Troubleall. Overdo hopes that this disguise will serve to prevent others from seeing into his identity, because public officials can only "see with other men's eyes; a foolish constable, or a sleepy watch- man . . . ourselves thought little better, if not arrant fools, for believ- ing 'em. I, Adam Overdo, am resolv'd therefore to spare spy-money hereafter, and make mine own discoveries" (2.1.29–42). It is soon ap- parent, though, that the cloud effectively prevents Overdo from seeing out as well, since he immediately mistakes Knockem for a cutpurse (2.3) and then, blind to thefts performed before his very eyes, mistakes the cutpurse Edgworth for an innocent (2.4). In this, Overdo is like the minor guardian, Wasp, who will not read the license and who loses it in the course of an angry outburst of "vapouring" as arbitrary as Ov- erdo's own when he cries, "I have no reason, nor will I hear of no reason, nor will I look for no reason, and he is an ass that either knows any, or looks for't from me . . . I am not i' the right, nor never was i' the right, nor never will be i' the right, while I am in my right mind" (4.4.37–40, 60–68).

And Wasp's vision clouded in the vapours brings us to that center within the center of the fair, Ursula's pig booth. It is here that we must seek the governing metaphors, for the vapors rise from the heat of this diabolic furnace, to provide infernal counterpart to Overdo's own cloud of unknowing.

Ursula characterizes her booth and occupation by swearing that "Hell's a kind of cold cellar to't" (2.2.44), a point affirmed by the shocked Overdo, who, upon overhearing the enumeration of her cheats, cries, "This is the very womb and bed of enormity" (107). The lurid heat continues to rise, and if Busy sees that "the wares are the wares of devils" and that "the whole Fair is the shop of Satan," he focuses his intuition upon Ursula directly in scriptural phrasing: "The fleshy woman (which you call Urs'la) is above all to be avoided, having the marks upon her, of the three enemies of man: the world, as being in the Fair; the devil, as being in the Fire; and the flesh, as being her- self" (3.6.32–36).

For once Busy is justified, for it is the pig booth and its mistress from which the vapors, both in the physical sense of smoke and heat and in the metaphorical sense of the quarreling game, rise. And Ursula is not only an angry woman, but the very champion of discord, of the lust, theft, fighting, and litigation which dominate a legalistic world gone beserk. There is a strange scene near the opening which in relation to the plot appears an elaborately pointless excrescence, but in fact is richly symbolic in its iconographic details. And following closely upon Overdo's first extended characterization of himself and his role in Old Testament imagery, it serves as contrapuntal commentary upon his blindly self-righteous legalism and justice.

Winwife and Quarlous, entering the fair, are immediately hailed by Knockem, the pimp, who, hoping to strike up an opportunity for game, invites them to drink and take tobacco at the pig booth.[19] Quarlous soon berates Knockem, and Ursula's tapster tries to forestall the fast-developing conflict, pleading "for the honour of our booth, none o' your vapours here," only to be unexpectedly scolded by Ursula, who emerges waving a firebrand, angrily defending anger itself: "Why, you thin lean polecat you, an' they have a mind to be i' their vapours, must you hinder 'em? . . . Must you be drawing the air of pacification here, while I am tormented, within, i' the fire, you weasel?" (2.5.57–61). Amused, the city wits taunt her, with Knockem keeping up a wary chorus of encouragement, until Ursula rushes in shouting "Gi' me my pig-pan hither a little. I'll scald you hence, an' you will not go" (132–33). In the general confusion she drops the grease upon herself, crying out: "Curse of hell . . . I ha' scalded my leg, my leg, my leg, my leg" (151–52). This is sufficient to send Winwife and Quarlous off, and they are forgotten as the fair folk gather about, pull down Ursula's hose, and treat her leg, while commenting on it in Knockem's equine vocabulary: "Body o' me, she has the mallanders, the scratches, the crown scab, and the quitter bone, i' the tother leg" (167–68). The scene seems pointless because it is without further consequences: the gentlemen escape untouched, and when we next see Ursula, she angrily shrugs off her injury as insignificant and rushes about as energetically as before. Its importance emerges, however, if we open the mythographic compendiums with which Jonson so proudly annotated the masques. For these encyclopedias reveal that the details of this action have been selected to transmute Ursula from a mere exemplum of the angry woman into a symbol. The increasingly pointed scriptural images, I have argued, eventually permit us to see in Overdo not just another shallow justice, but the very fount of Old Testament legalism. This scene of the scalding allows us to identify the pig woman as Ate, Discordia herself.[20]

In Ripa's account, Discordia is depicted as carrying a firebrand in one hand, legal papers in the other, and with her feet encircled by clouds, since she is not only the patroness of fiery passions (and hence metaphorical blindness), but especially of litigiousness. Cartari presents the same account in detail and has a woodcut illustrating the vapors which surround her legs, adding the further observation that she always "ha le gambe torte."[21] In such accounts we can see the source of that tableau-like presentation we have just reviewed: Ursula emerging from her smoking kitchen holding high a firebrand, goading on the quarrels, scalding her own "gambe torte"—a proper mistress for Overdo's world of blind, angry justice which Haggis and Bristle center for us in their description of Overdo: "He will burn blue . . . an' he be angry. . . . and when he is angry, be it right or wrong, he has the law on's side."

Ursula, of course, has her other role as the pig woman, and while the implication of sensuality and gluttony is apparent without apparatus, it should be noticed that the pig has other, and perhaps more precisely relevant, emblematic significances. Valeriano is most apposite in making the pig a symbol of "Taverna, o luogo publico disonesto," that very pig booth of the play whence all the corruption emanates as well as gathers, reaching its climax with the whoring adventures of the citizens' wives. But Valeriano adds a further note to his discussion which ties such a public place closely into the Discordia tradition, when he shows in elaborate fashion how the Egyptians treated the pig as a symbol of blindness and therefore chaos.[22]

Now it should be easy to recognize that there is a pattern in the apparent confusion of a play dominated from first to last with flytings and slapstick battles—those of Wasp in the Littlewit home, of the head-knocking between Quarlous and Knockem, of Wasp's beating upon Overdo and Troubleall's scuffle with the watchmen, of the puppets' abrupt turn upon their maker Leatherhead, of the whore's thumping on Mistress Overdo. The vapors are the clouds of discord which rise from the passions of the pig-booth hell, and they provide disastrously effective commentary on that other cloud which enfolds the angry and arbitrary Jehovah, Justice Overdo, blinded by the smoke of battle in his ironically well-intentioned efforts to establish order in this modern Tyre through applying the letter of the law—properly considered, as the mythographers knew, as the symbolic property of Discordia herself. And it is this destructive, disordering effect of legalism which Troubleall embodies. He cannot be considered in this aspect of his dramatic function, however, apart from his counterbalance, the appropriately named Quarlous, whose efficiency gains him a dubious ascendancy in every exchange.

VI

Troubleall acts as a voice of conscience troubling all with whom he comes into contact, as well as serving in the role of destiny's agent. It is, indeed, this very conscientiousness, evoked by Overdo's justice, which has driven him mad and, as we have seen, finally draws a countering gesture of mercy from the justice himself when, overhearing the watchmen describe Overdo's angry willfulness and its effect upon Troubleall, he sighs, "I will be more tender hereafter. I see compassion may become a Justice, though it be a weakness" (4.1.77–78). But this is little, grudging, and ineffective; the only truly effective mercy which Troubleall receives emanates, in fact, from the hell booth itself when the coarse pimp Knockem forges Overdo's warrant in pure pity for the "mad child o' the Pie-powders" (4.6).[23]

Only Quarlous is entirely untroubled and unscrupulous toward this victim among victims, stripping him naked in the pig booth and assuming his clothes as a disguise (4.6.151–53; 5.1.14–15; 5.6.52–67) which he utilizes to gain Purecraft's confidence and fortune, and also thus perverting Overdo's one attempt to offer merciful restitution: the warrant, which Quarlous employs to dispose of Grace at a price. In short, he uses the appearance of mad consciousness, the "face," to gain his ends much more effectively than even Busy had used his "lunatic conscience" as a masquerade for "the state of innocence . . . and childhood" (1.3.136–41). The point is emphasized by the juxtaposition of Knockem's isolated and wholly disinterested act of mercy toward Troubleall with Quarlous' aloof, unfeeling "mercy" toward his other tool, Edgworth. When the latter, having stolen for Quarlous, invites him to share a friendly whore, Quarlous mocks Scripture in warning that he would beat his effrontery down, "if I had not already forgiven you a greater trespass" (4.6.15 ff.).

If Overdo is the Jehovah of the play, his mercy has been stolen by Quarlous in the misappropriation of the warrant, which emerges by inevitable allegory as the right to dispose of Grace. Quarlous, by name and by nature the most fully acclimatized denizen of this chaotic hell, is fast emerging as the natural challenger to the omnipotence of the bungling justice, who has inadvertently passed into his hands the only source of authority in this fair: possession. To leave matters here would have been for Jonson to deny not only law but order in any form. There is yet another aspect of the drama which reverses any such tendency and establishes the ultimate new dispensation in the symbolic universe of *Bartholomew Fair*: the order of "flesh and blood."

VII

Quarlous, of course, reveals through his manipulations that Overdo must accept frailty as he reduces this deity himself to "flesh and blood," making God into man, Overdo into Adam, in the most ironic manner. The other dramatic "conversion" is that of Overdo's hypocritical counterpart, Busy, who accepts the fair and its "enormities" precisely because the puppets—after all their perverse lasciviousness in the puppet-play within the play of "Hero and Leander"—turn out *not* to be "flesh and blood," and hence are not guilty of the traditional sins found in transvestite actors. But this inverted conversion is accomplished through mockery of the order imposed by *law*: what Busy finds that their sexlessness reveals is their "lawful" calling (5.5.14–110). The lawfulness of the sexless, sterile puppets affords comment on Overdo's earlier insistence upon law (an insistence carefully mimicked in the arguments of puppet Dionysius): what he learns in being reduced by Quarlous, what we all learn from *Bartholomew Fair*, is that law, strict justice, is more and less than flesh and blood can either abide or profit from.

Overdo learns this lesson in part by discovering the prostitution which culminates in his own wife's adventures in the pig-booth hell: the pig may be lasciviously sensual in its connotations, but the ultimate perversion of natural order is the fact that in this very center of sensuality one paradoxically discovers the transmutation of sexuality into sterile commercialism. It is an essential discord like that revealed by the lascivious puppets, who justify their bawdy playlet by revealing their wooden sterility. Intensifying the paradox which sterilizes in the name of the pig and the shilling, is the fact that Win-the-fight[24] Littlewit joins the ranks of the whores willingly, although it is her very pregnancy which was the original instrument for bringing the others of the Littlewit ambience to the fair, fearing lest she should long too passionately for roast pig and "miscarry, or hazard her first fruits" (1.6.64). In fact, fruit as the emblem of sexuality has been made a very anatomy of the desirable, fertile young Win, whom Winwife compliments as a "garden" herself, "a wife here with a strawberry-breath, cherry-lips, apricot-cheeks, and a soft velvet head, like a melicotton" (1.2.13–15).

The plot sets Win's and Littlewit's scheme to use her pregnancy, her incipient "first fruits," to lead the family to the fair in immediate juxtaposition with Cokes's insistence upon taking Grace to "my Fair: I call't my Fair, because of Bartholomew; you know my name is Bartholomew" (1.5.62–64). Wasp argues and harangues against the pastime because of Cokes's vulnerability in special sort to fruit: "If he go to the Fair, he will buy everything to a baby there. . . . Pray heaven I bring him off with one stone! And then he is such a ravener after fruit! You will not believe what a coil I had, t'other day, to compound a business between a Cather'ne-pear-woman and him" (110–16). Wasp's premonitions are more than justified when Edgworth and Nightingale employ the confidence game of spilling "Cather'ne pears," which Cokes scrambles to gather while they steal his very clothes (4.2). In the end, Cokes hurls his pears away in a pathetic pet:

I ha' paid for my pears, a rot on 'em. . . . Methinks the Fair should not
have us'd me thus, an' 'twere but for my name's sake; I would not ha'
us'd a dog o' the name, so. . . . I ha' lost myself, and my cloak and my
hat; and my fine sword, and my sister, and Numps, and Mistress Grace (a
gentlewoman that I should ha' married), and a cut-work handkerchief
she ga' me, and two purses, today. And my bargain o' hobby'horses and
ginger-bread, which grieves me worst of all. (4.2.73–86)

The juxtaposition and conclusion suggest the catalogues which de-
limit the mentality of Pope's Belinda, and this is just the point. For
Cokes, fruits are simply to be possessed and eaten, and his longing for
the fruits of marriage is no more profound than that for the toys of the
fair. Even as he is collecting his license to marry Grace, he glances up
at Win and would possess her, too: "A pretty little soul, this same
Mistres Littlewit! would I might marry her" (1.5.79–80). This trivial
possessiveness, the reduction of human relations to things to be bought
and owned, is reflected in his delighted decision to furnish out his wedding masque and banquet with the toy people and gingerbread he finds
on the stalls (3.4.93–165). Thus, like the pregnant prostitute Win Littlewit, Bartholomew Cokes, the fair's most innocent child, accepts
"face" value: sterility and the reduction of marriage to possession, of
flesh and blood to mere toys. And in his gewgaw-seeking lust Cokes
becomes the internal symbol for the larger symbolic action of the others
who seek the possession of toys in the chaos of Vanity Fair.

VIII

There remains now only to review the denouement, which brings
together the threads of imagery and of action into a coherent pattern.

Troubleall has invoked a double blessing throughout the course of
his meandering appearances—"quit ye, and multiply ye"—a blessing
which calls for mercy and fertility. It is clear, from the fair's omnipotent deity, Overdo, to its most innocent child, Cokes, that these are
precisely the least honored values. And yet, as we have seen, even in
this hell of their own invention, men and gods can turn away for a
moment from their self-seeking to feel love (and what other quality
embraces mercy and fertility in human relations?) toward one another:
Witness Overdo's or Knockem's pity for Troubleall, or Whit's gentle-
ness toward Cokes, or Winwife's decision to pass up the rich widow for
the more natural union with the young ward, Grace. All can turn aside,
that is, except Quarlous, who knows only a mocking mercy and inverts
Winwife's choice by selling the ward and marrying the widow. And it
is Quarlous who caps the paradox of possession, for, winning all, he

marries himself indissolubly to hell, to the living, sterile image of that burning chaos in which the play has been enacted. As Littlewit warned, "the devil can equivocate, as well as a shopkeeper" in prophecy, and it is this diabolic equivocation (for what is the devil but shopkeeper when the Tyrronian Fair is hell and marriage goes by shillings and pence?) which brings Quarlous and Dame Purecraft together. The instrument of destiny has been Troubleall, and if Quarlous prefers to forget it when he accepts the hypocritical widow of wealth, he once knew that Troubleall's lottery-like choice of a husband for Grace "damn'd or sav'd." He lost the lottery and compounded for the loss by selling away his right of election to Winwife, clear enough indication of his bitter triumph, tasting, like that of Satan, of the ashes of brimstone. The worst punishment, though, is that Quarlous himself has known the geography of the pit which he elects with all the aplomb of a proud victor. Ursula, we remember, in her first imagistic identification of the pig booth as hell had cried out against her destiny: "Fie upon't: who would wear out their youth and prime thus, in roasting of pigs, that had any cooler vocation? Hell's a kind of cold cellar to't, a very fine vault" (2.2.42-45). And by now we have realized how this lusty heat only burns to sterility all that enters the mouth of the passions' furnace. But this is macrocosm to what Quarlous himself had described earlier in warning Winwife away from that infernal microcosm, the aging Widow Purecraft:

> I'll be sworn, some of them, that thou art or hast been a suitor to, are so old as no chaste or married pleasure can ever become 'em: the honest instrument of procreation has, forty years since, left to belong to 'em; thou must visit 'em, as thou wouldst do a tomb, with a torch, or three handfuls of link, flaming hot, and so thou mayst hap to make 'em feel thee, and after, come to inherit according to thy inches. A sweet course for a man to waste the brand of life for, to be still raking himself a fortune in an old woman's embers. (2.3.69-78)[25]

Quarlous, in toppling Overdo as the omnipotent authority in the world of the fair, has inherited hell—the hell of a commercial, self-serving, merciless world. Jehovah, tested and found wanting by that symbolic "fleshly motion of pig" whereby "the wicked Tempter . . . broacheth flesh and blood, as it were, on the weaker side" (as Busy early attests: 1.6.13-17), is reduced to "but Adam, flesh and blood" by the new Machiavellian. Neither old nor new deity seems effective, for all their paradoxical power.

But Winwife has Grace, not bought but won, albeit with the ambiguous aid of a mad destiny, and their concord alone has transcended the chaos of the fair which is to continue at Overdo's house. It is a fitting and promising close for the great humanist skeptic's last great play. For if Overdo has learned mercy only through his discovery of the weakness of literal justice in a human cosmos, and if Quarlous has continued and intensified the old errors in a new way by embracing sterility as if it were to be possessed, then it is clear that all men, like Winwife, can obtain Grace only through the concord of flesh and blood living together to multiply in the mysterious, even mad, destiny of their union of love.

In *Every Man Out of His Humour* Jonson permitted his deity to blow away the actors as mere embodiments of the vapors of their own infernal stage. But in *Bartholomew Fair* man finally emerges from the vapors engendered by the discords of passion, of lust, and of litigation, to announce the ultimate benediction: "Quit ye, and multiply ye." In one sense, Jonson has here blasphemed the Scriptures and denied the very omnipotence of God himself. But, as he said in the Induction, it was not "profaneness," because deity has again announced his Grace through incarnation. If he has written an antimorality play, it has become an allegory of love.

CHAPTER 6

The Constant Couple:
Farquhar's Four-Plays-in-One

 George Farquhar the playwright emerged from the failure of George Farquhar the actor. He arrived in the London stage world just a few years after the great theatrical schism of 1695 had created a second war of the theaters, a war generated by the actors. One of the most prominent of these actors was Robert Wilks, and it was he who returned to Dublin from London to discover Farquhar's weakness as an actor and promise as a dramatist. He allegedly advised Farquhar

> to relinquish that Method of life [i.e., acting], and think of writing for the Stage; he told him at the same time that he would not meet with Encouragement in *Ireland*, adequate to his Merit, and therefore counselled him to go to *London* . . . . By this time Mr. *Farquhar* had prepared the *Drama* of his Comedy, call'd *Love and a Bottle*, which he shewed to Mr. *Wilks*, who approving of it, advised him to set out for *London* before the Tide was too far spent, meaning while he had any Money left to support him; he took his Counsel, and bid him adieu, and the next Day went on board a Ship bound for *West-Chester*.[1]

It has been argued convincingly that the plot which Wilks admired was a burlesque of Nathaniel Lee's heroic afflatus over much of its surface and a satire upon the conventions of Restoration comedy in its overall form.[2]

Soon Farquhar had come to know the members of Rich's company at Drury Lane, a group augmented by his friend Wilks' arrival for the season of 1698–99. It was around his own (and his audience's) knowledge of this group that Farquhar created his second play, *The Constant Couple; or, A Trip to the Jubilee*. It was an instant success, continuing the theatrical self-awareness of *Love and a Bottle* and taking up hints from the earlier play, but creating a dizzying impact for contemporary

91

theatergoers by complicating the allusive surfaces and deepening the exploration of their own dramatic taste and what that implied about social, ethical, and generic values. This was Farquhar's four-plays-in-one: a comedy of wit, a burlesque, a scandalous *roman à clef*, and a problem play focused upon the ethical paradoxes shared by the role-playing societies upon both sides of the proscenium.

I

As a comedy of sex and wit the play opens with three young men laying a bet upon the relative merits and beauty of their mistresses, a ploy familiar in one form or another at least since its early-sixteenth-century employment in *La Mandragola*. They are the niggardly hypocrite Vizard, disbanded army colonel Standard, and the Gallicized beau Sir Harry Wildair. Complications set in, however, when it becomes apparent that the three are (at first) unwittingly rivals for Lady Lurewell. And the conventional expectations are soon reversed when it is discovered that the key to the outcome is held by none of the plotting males, but by the master counter-plotter Lurewell herself, "a Lady," as the *dramatis personae* indicates, "of a jilting Temper proceeding from a resentment of her Wrongs from Men."[3]

Vizard is a parody of Restoration wits of earlier vintage. Walking in the park he opens the play reading from Hobbes and plotting love intrigues and vengeance: "May Obstinacy guard her Beauty till Wrinkles bury it, . . . Run to Lady *Lurewell's*. . . . Her Beauty is sufficient Cure for Angelica's Scorn" (93). But behind his libertine facade (itself hidden behind priggery in dealing with his rich uncle Smuggler) Vizard masks a viciousness of real consequence foreign to his models: "The Colonel my Rival too! how shall I manage? There is but one way—him and the Knight will I set a tilting, where one cuts t'other's Throat, and the Survivor's hang'd. So there will be two Rivals pretty decently disposed of. Since Honour may oblige them to play the Fool, why should not Necessity engage me to play the Knave?" (110). Wildair, on the other hand, intrigues, loves, and quarrels with a stoic complacency exaggerated beyond that of earlier stage wits: "His florid Constitution being never ruffled by misfortune, nor stinted in its pleasures, has render'd him entertaining to others, and easy to himself" (96). The description is Vizard's, but it is true—to the point of burlesque—as, for example, in Wildair's meditation upon a thrashing and humiliation he has dealt to Smuggler when he traps the old man in a boudoir:

How pleasant is resenting an Injury without Passion:
'Tis the Beauty of Revenge   .   .   .   .   .

I make the most of Life, no hour mispend,
Pleasure's the Means, and Pleasure is my End.
No Spleen, no Trouble, shall my time destroy,
Life's but a Span; I'll every Inch enjoy.

(116)

And he is equally at ease in love as in war: "Now why should I be angry that a Woman is a Woman? since Inconstancy and Falsehood are grounded in their Natures, how can they help it?" (109).

But these inheritors of tradition (along with Standard, who appears to owe a vague legacy of martial bluffness and amorous naivete to Wycherley's Manly) do not round out Lurewell's academy of aspirants: she is pursued as well by Smuggler, the merchant senex; and by Clincher, the fop-in-waiting. Her destiny is to "hate all that don't love me, and slight all that do . . . tho' a Woman swear, forswear, lie, dissemble, backbite, be proud, vain, malicious, any thing, if she secures the main Chance, she's still virtuous. That's a Maxim" (101).

Vizard carries off a coup in sending Wildair to his young cousin Angelica and her mother, Lady Darling, with a letter of marital proposal which Wildair believes to be an introduction to a brothel; this complication is enhanced by Lurewell's double play of setting Standard and Wildair into violent competition by ambiguous gestures that leave each feeling himself to be her favorite.

There is an abortive duel; there is the almost obligatory closet scene in which a wittol trapped in Lurewell's rooms escapes at a loss by exchanging clothes with a convenient servant; there are mistaken arrests—all the familiar pieces of action which were shuffled and reshuffled in the context of the sexual wars between so many dozens of Restoration couples. And, of course, the outcome is reformation through marriage. Standard is revealed as Lurewell's first lover in her youth, and happily recognizes the elective affinities which have drawn them together again. And, finally disabused of his illusion that Angelica is a whore, Wildair faces the fact that he must erase his affront to her by marriage or by a confrontation of honor with the plotting Vizard in this fasion: "Here I am brought to a very pretty Dilemma; I must commit Murder, or commit Matrimony. . . . but dam it, —Cowards dare fight, I'll marry, that's the most daring Action of the two, so my dear Cousin Angelica, have at you" (144).

Farquhar emphasizes the conventionality of character and action by enveloping his witty comedy within a network of theatrical reminders. In the first moments of the play the aptly named Vizard, anticipating sexual conquest, gloats, "That's my cue" (93). Later, Smuggler unexpectedly peers under Vizard's hypocrisy to discover him "possess'd with an Evil Spirit, he talks as prophanely, as an actor possess'd with a Poet" (135). Still later, revealed to and revealing his former apprentice-turned-fop. Smuggler reacts with the bourgeois citizen's fear of satire (first immortalized in *The Knight of the Burning Pestle*): "What Business has a Prentice at a Play-house, unless it be to hear his Master made a Cuckold, and his Mistress a Whore? 'Tis ten to one now, but some malicious Poet has my Character upon the Stage within this *Month*" (145). And Wildair is first introduced as a bridge between the stage of Drury Lane and the Hyde Park of both audience and actors: he is "the Joy of the Play-house, and the Life of the Park" (96).

If, in this first context for reading *The Constant Couple*, these little cues boast that the most traditional stuff of social comedy is being used but transcended by the author's unusual shuffling of parts, in the next they lead into a burlesque of the rival company and its leader's most famous vehicle.

II

When Thomas Betterton in 1695 successfully led the revolt of players against the wily Drury Lane patentee Christopher Rich, he succeeded in establishing the rival company at Lincoln's Inn Fields because he was unchallenged as the premier actor in London, But it was a dominance obtained through thirty-five years on the stage: Betterton was a master, but a master in an heroic tradition now running its course. The Drury Lane troupe, soon reinforced by Wilks and Farquhar, developed a different style. And in *The Constant Couple* Farquhar not only exploited Wilks's talent, but joined in the wars of the theater to spoof Betterton's own antiquated tastes and style.

The most consistently popular play of the Restoration was Lee's *The Rival Queens; or, The Death of Alexander the Great*,[4] the popularity of which was sustained toward the end of the century by Betterton's powers alone, as Cibber remembers:

> In what Raptures have I seen an audience at the furious Fustian and turgid Rants in *Nat. Lee's Alexander the Great!* . . . When these flowing Numbers came from the Mouth of a *Betterton* the Multitude no more desired Sense to them than our musical *Connoisseurs* think it essential in the celebrate Airs of an *Italian Opera*. Does not this prove that there is very near as much Enchantment in the well-govern'd Voice of an Actor as in the sweet Pipe of an Eunuch? . . . And I am of opinion that to the extraordinary Success of this very Play we may impute the Corruption of so many Actors and Tragick Writers, as were immediately misled by it.[5]

Cibber's supplementarian "Anthony, Vulgò Tony Aston" also records that, for Rich's company, Betterton's "younger Contemporary, . . .

POWEL, attempted several of *Betterton's* Parts . . . but lost his Credit; as, in *Alexander*, he maintain'd not the Dignity of a King, but *Out-Heroded* Herod."⁶ This is the George Powell who played the role of Standard in *The Constant Couple*. And it is with this orientation that we can begin to understand Farquhar's public play upon the rival theater.

It was a ploy to stimulate a shock of recognition in regular patrons which went back to the first weeks of competition. In May 1695, Betterton's company had advertised a production of *The Old Bachelor* to coincide with a *Hamlet* by Rich's players. Then, capitalizing upon Betterton's known talents in the title role, his company proposed a rival *Hamlet* at the penultimate moment: "*Powell*, who was vain enough to envy *Betterton* as his Rival, proposed to change Plays with them, . . . he would play the *Old Batchelor* himself, and mimick *Betterton* throughout the whole part."⁷

This was the tradition. Now for some specifics. A month before Drury Lane first produced Farquhar's *Love and a Bottle* they did a revival of *The Rival Queens*, undoubtedly featuring Powell. Six weeks later Betterton took up his old role of Alexander at Lincoln's Inn Fields as part of a wedding entertainment—a performance upon request of this sweeping tragedy in the small tennis-court theater which must have been ridiculed by more spectators then just the author of *A Comparison Between the Two Stages*, who said, "I have seen . . . *Alexander's Exploits* . . . all epitomized into a Raree-show, carry'd about on a Man's Head."⁸ During the closing month of 1699—which saw the first performance of *The Constant Couple*—Betterton was leading his company in such heroic tragedies as Charles Hopkins's *Friendship Improved; or, The Female Warrior* and Dennis's Euripidean adaptation *Iphigenia*. This was the aging actor's preferred genre, but a genre principally identified for over twenty years with that most famous of Betterton's roles, Alexander trapped and dying between his rival queens, faithful Statira and treacherous Roxana. In Lee's revisionist version of history, Statira takes a vow of chastity when the absent conqueror falls into the arms of captive Roxana. Returning to Babylon, Alexander is desolated at the result of his adultery and wins Statira back only to see her murdered by a vengeful Roxana, who also connives, in a political plot, to poison the slipping master of the world. Alexander's character in this vehicle alternates in tone between the closing days in the lives of Marlowe's Tamburlaine and Shakespeare's Antony. He boasts, he pleads, he drinks, he threatens—little wonder that Powell was tempted to out-Herod Betterton's Alexander. And it is upon this play that Farquhar builds his structure of burlesque in *The Constant Couple*.

Farquhar ignites the possibility for commentary upon an older dramatic mode almost immediately when Wildair begins to "mistrust some rivalship" with Standard (98) and Standard himself tells Lurewell that "emulation in Glory is transporting, but Rivals here in love intolerable" (101), introducing the usual flood of references to love and honor. But the heroic rivalry is reduced to a struggle to obtain possession of Lurewell the courtesan and the supposed whore Angelica—a struggle, literally, for possession of what Colley Cibber titled in a later, lighter parody of Lee's play, *The Rival Queans.*

Lee's penchant for heroic rhetoric (and repetitiveness) is ridiculed directly with the opening scenes of act 2 of *The Constant Couple*, in which the foppish Clincher introduces his own and Alexander's favorite oath, "O *Jupiter Ammon*" (104, 119, 132, 148)[9] and Wildair first approaches Angelica's house hopefully quoting a glorification of sexual consummation from Lee's *Sophonisba* (105). These reminders, along with a discussion of love and honor which sets the heroico-tragical dilemmas of *The Rival Queens* into the entire context of Restoration heroic drama, run throughout *The Constant Couple.* The action of the earlier play, too, is taken up, but taken up as ambivalent parody upon the sentiments of genre. *The Rival Queens* opens with a fight between Prince Lysimachus and Alexander's favorite, Hephestion, over their love rivalry for Statira's sister. They are interrupted by Alexander's eldest and most loyal soldier, who shames them into peace with the reminders of a primitivistic virtue:

> What big Ambition blows this dangerous Fire?
> A *Cupid's* Puff is it not, Woman's Breath?
> By all your Triumphs in the heat of Youth,
> When Towns were sack'd, and Beauties prostrate lay,
> When my Blood boil'd, and Nature worked me high,
> *Clytus* ne'r bow'd his Body to such shame:
> The brave will scorn the Cobweb Arts—The Souls
> Of all that whining, smiling, coz'ning Sex.[10]

Standard challenges Wildair to a duel ("You fought in *Flanders* to my knowledge" [128]), and is turned aside by a modern common sense which both echoes and updates Clytus' scorn of women:

> I tell you once more, Colonel, that I am a Baronet, and have eight thousand Pounds a Year. I can dance, sing, ride, fence, understand the Languages. Now, I can't conceive how running you through the Body should contribute one Jot more to my Gentility. But, pray, Colonel, I had forgot to ask you: what's the Quarrel?
> *Standard.* A Woman, Sir.
> *Wildair.* Then I put up my Sword. Take her.

Standard. Sir, my Honour's concern'd.
Wildair. Nay, if your Honour be concern'd with a Woman, get it out of her Hands as soon as you can. An honourable Lover is the greatest Slave in Nature; some will say, the greatest Fool. (129)

A later generation of young men has taken over the wisdom of the old: love and honor are incompatible follies. It is a situation which satirizes the posturing rhetoric of Betterton's Alexander and his legacy in lesser plays. Also, it prepares for the double parody of Angelica in act 5 of *The Constant Couple.*

At this point, Wildair, still under the impression that Angelica is a whore and her mother a bawd, returns to their house to press his passion with an escalated offer of money. Because he has been introduced as a suitor in a letter from their relative Vizard, the mother assumes that Wildair is seeking marriage and leaves him alone with Angelica. He soon disabuses Angelica, who, caught in his arms, pleads in stilted terms:

> I conjure you, Sir, by the sacred Name of Honour, by your dead Father's Name, and the fair Reputation of your Mothers Chastity, that you offer not the least Offense. . . . what wild Dream of loose Desire could prompt you to attempt this Baseness? View me well.—The Brightness of my Mind, methinks, should lighten outwards, and let you see your Mistake in my behaviour.

Then she suddenly breaks into loose blank verse:

> I think it shines with so much Innocence in my Face, [/] that it should dazzle all your vicious Thoughts: / Think not I am defenceless 'cause alone. [/] Your very self is Guard against your self: [/] I'm sure there's something generous in your Soul: [/] My Words shall search it out, [/] And Eyes shall fire it for my own defence.

Sir Harry's aside points to the tradition: "This is the first Whore in *Heroicks* that I have met." And this response points to Lee's Alexander as Harry mimics Angelica:

> Tall di dum, ti dum, tall ti didi, didum.
> A Million to one now, but this Girl is just come flush from reading the *Rival Queens*—I gad, I'll at her in her own cant.
> —*O my Statyra, O my angry dear,*
> *turn thy Eyes on me,* behold thy Beau in Buskins.

(140–41)

But at this point the burlesque merges into the third context of *The Constant Couple*, one in which regular London theatergoers might easily pierce the plot to find beneath it a living roman à clef, giving ironic doubleness to the social settlements being enacted upon the stage. In Lee's play the lines occur when Alexander first sees Statira after her vow of chastity and begins to persuade her to break it:

O my *Statira*! O my angry Dear!
Turn thine Eyes on me, I wou'd talk to them:
What shall I say to work upon thy Soul?[11]

While no cast list exists for the Drury Lane performance of *The Rival Queens* in November 1698, Statira was undoubtedly played by the same Jane Rogers who, as Angelica, is here being reminded—along with the audience—of her earlier role. We can safely infer this from the notoriety she received as Bellamira in the Drury Lane production of the anonymous *Triumphs of Virtue* at the beginning of 1697.

In this play, Antonio has squandered the patrimony of both himself and his sister Bellamira. Even so, Bellamira is honorably loved by wealthy young Perollo and lusted after by Duke Polycastro, new viceroy of Naples. Perollo is persuaded after a time to jilt Bellamira because of her poverty, and the duke takes her away into what everyone assumes is a courtesan's life. In private, however, she frustrates his expected triumph in such a fashion as to make him genuinely transcend his lust in a rhetoric not much more stilted than that of Farquhar's Angelica:

Bellamira. I fix the Bounds, where no transgressing Step
Must ever dare to enter. Hear me, Duke,
And mark the Bars I set. Touch not my chaste Bed;
Make not one loose Demand; tempt me not with a Word
Of unbecoming Sense; or on my Lips
Print but a wanton Kiss; breathe not one Sigh
That looks like begging of an amorous Pity;
But use your Visits as a Brother to a Sister.
Polycastro. This is all Cruelty.
Bellamira. No, 'Tis all Mercy:
Mercy to the whole Welfare of my Life,
The Guard and Shield of my unspotted Soul . . .

.   .   .   .
.   .   .   .   my Tongue and Heart
Breathe but one Air, and Virtue is their Soul.
Polycastro. Thou hast prevail'd; I yield the hard Conditions

.   .   .   .
Oh *Bellamira*! thou hast intirely vanquish'd;
My Soul, new-moulded, stampt it with thy own
Bright Image of Divinity, chang'd all
My sooty Love to sacred Adoration.

. . . .
And now with more than common Raptures blest,
My Love, all fragrant, as the Phoenix Nest;
I'll meet those Eyes with all that chaste Desire,
And warm in Virtue, at thy Vestal Fire.[12]

Bellamira's tactics of conversion are strikingly similar to those employed by Angelica in the first quarto of *The Constant Couple*:[13]

If my Beauty has power to raise a Flame, be sure it is a vertuous one: if
otherwise, 'tis owing to the Foulness of your own Thought, which
throwing this mean Affront upon my Honour, has alarm'd my Soul, and
fires it with a brave Disdain.
Wildair. . . . Madam, whate'er my unruly Passion did at first suggest; I
now must own you've turned my Love to Veneration, and my unman-
nerly Demands to a most humble prayer. —Your surprizing Conduct has
quench't the gross material Flame; but rais'd a subtil piercing Fire,
which flies like lambent Lightning, through my Blood, disdaining common Fuel, preys upon the nobler Part, my Soul. (361)

Bellamira has been willing to appear a whore to convert the duke;
Angelica, mistaken for a noble Magdalene, converts Wildair. But for a
contemporary audience, behind both conversions looms that of Jane
Rogers herself, announced in the Epilogue to *The Triumph of Virtue*
addressed to the ladies of London:

You shall reform the World, and wee'll reform the Stage.
But Ladies, now not for the Play alone,
I have a small Petition of my own:

. . . .
If I from those fair Eyes a Smile may find,
If possible to deserve a Grace so kind;
I'll pay this dutious Gratitude; I'll do
That which the Play has done; I'll copy You.
At your own Vertues Shrine my Vows I'll pay:
Study to live the Character I play.

The actress's vow apparently became a London *cause célèbre*; Cibber, who played her brother Antonio, remembered the event and its
upshot years later:

I have formerly known an Actress carry this Theatrical Prudery to
such a height, that she was very near keeping herself chaste by it: Her
Fondness for Virtue on the Stage made an Impression on her private Life;
and the Appearances of it actually went so far that, in an Epilogue to an
obscure Play, . . . wherein she acted a Part of impregnable Chastity, she
bespoke the Favour of the Ladies by a Protestation that in Honour of

their Goodness and Virtue she would dedicate her unblemish'd Life to their Example. . . . But alas! how weak are the strongest Works of Art when Nature besieges it? for though this good Creature so far held out her Distaste to Mankind that they could never reduce her to marry any one of 'em; yet we must own she grew, like *Ceasar*, greater by her Fall! Her first heroick Motive to a Surrender was to save the Life of a Lover who in his Despair had vow'd to destroy himself, . . . The generous Lover, in return to that first tender Obligation, gave Life to her First-born.[14]

The generous lover was Wilks, who had a long and turbulent relationship with Jane Rogers. As usual, history offers scant documentation on the origins of affairs of the heart, but Farquhar's revision of the final scene between Angelica and Wildair in a play written around his friend Wilks suggests that this one had already begun in the winter of 1699—perhaps in those weeks between the first performance in November and the following January, when the second edition came out "With a New Scene added to the part of Wildair."[15] Wildair's sudden conversion in the first edition employed Rogers's stereotype as the virtuous virgin; the scene is thoroughly transformed in the revision. Wildair, instead of being inspired by Angelica's nobility, now introduces the mocking allusions to Statira and *The Rival Queens*, then addresses this "first Whore in Heroicks" with a parody of Falstaff's catechism on honour: "Can your Vertue bespeak you a Front Row in the Boxes? No: for the players can't live upon Vertue" (141). Whereas in the early text Wildair is drawn into marriage by Angelica alone, in the later the couple are seen joined by Lady Darling, and the women gradually unfold Vizard's plot and Wildair's mistake in a rapid-fire catechism which balances his own catechism of seduction, until he cries out in self-defense: "Now dear *Roxana*, and you my fair *Statyra*, be not so very Heroick in your Styles" (143). And the whole concludes with his decision for marriage which I have cited before, "Cowards may dare fight, I'll marry, that's the most daring Action of the two," a far cry from the closing dialogue after Wildair's marriage proposal in the first edition, which climaxes with his response to Angelica's warning, "You must promise me, Sir *Harry*, to have a care of *Burgundy* henceforth": "Fear not, sweet Innocence; Your Presence, like a Guardian Angel, shall fright away all Vice" (363).

The effect has been to evoke Jane Rogers's vow of chastity, to couple it with allusion to Statira's vow of chastity (which she also breaks), and to play off against the rhetorical "heroics" of Lee the impossibility of maintaining such sentiments in the reality of everyday London. Rogers's boast was maintained only until Wilks joined Rich's company of Drury Lane players; now he is courting her stage avatar (mistakenly) as that mistress which she has (really) become. It was a nice, complicated in-joke for the many spectators who must have known the hubris of Jane Rogers's puritanical stance and its failure once Wilks determined to break it down. But the revisions here can also help us understand that Farquhar was, between the two versions, recognizing more fully that fourth and most seriously critical area of *The Constant Couple*, its analysis of the implications behind London dramatic tastes.

III

Examining the establishment of Betterton's rebels in Lincoln's Inn Fields, Cibber says, "The first Error this new Colony of Actors fell into was their inconsiderately parting with . . . Mrs. *Monfort* upon a too nice (not to say severe) Punctilio . . . which before they had acted one Play occasioned [her] Return to the Service of the Patentees."[16] Cibber was right about the seriousness of the mistake because, as he elsewhere says: "Mrs. *Montfort*, whose second Marriage gave her the name of Mrs. *Verbruggen*, was Mistress of more variety of Humour than I ever knew in any one Woman Actress. . . . Nothing, tho' ever so barren, if within the Bounds of Nature, could be flat in her Hands. . . . though I doubt it will be a vain Labor to offer you a just Likeness of Mrs. *Montfort's* Action, yet the fantastick Impression is still so strong in my Memory that I cannot help saying something, tho' fantastically, about it."[17] And this panegyric was written over thirty years after Susanna Verbruggen's death. The eccentric actor Anthony Aston did not admire her legs but did admire her style: "She was all Art, and her Acting all acquir'd, but dress'd so nice it look'd like Nature. . . . Whatever she did was not to be call'd Acting; no, no, it was what she represented: She was neither more nor less, and was the most easy Actress in the World."[18] This account of her stylistic ability to combine art and nature is pertinent because it describes not only the actress but her role as Lurewell, a role which made Mrs. Verbruggen the third pillar, along with Wilks and Farquhar, of the dramatic London mirror world in *The Constant Couple*.

Midway in the action Captain Standard—enmeshed in Lurewell's labyrinth of vengeful scheming against men—accuses her of lying, and she responds with the most important of the theatrical allusions in the play: "Hold, Sir, You have got the Play-house Cant upon your Tongue; and think that Wit may privilege your Railing: But I must tell you, Sir, that what is Satyr upon the Stage, is ill Manners here." Standard's answer cuts to the heart of Farquhar's vision: "What is feign'd upon the Stage, is here in Reality. Real Falsehood" (123). It is the young, provincial author's comment upon the society into which he had come through Wilks's encouragment: a society that might watch Wildair follow so many stage beaux into risking the matrimonial noose with Angelica, all the time aware that Wilks would offer Jane Rogers only the dubious gift of "her First-born." It was the society for which Etherege spoke when, writing from Ratisbon to comfort a friend who had been unable to seduce Susanna Verbruggen, he said: "The best fortune I have had here has been a player, something handsomer, and as much a jilt, as Mrs. Barry . . . few foul their fingers with touching of a Cunt that does not belong to a Countess."[19] It was also the society into which Lurewell had entered, a young provincial who, emulating the ideals of love and honour promulgated on the stage of *The Rival Queens* or *The Conquest of Granada*, had found herself reduced to the duplicity in sexual war implicit in her assumed name (in truth she is "Manly").[20]

"Love" and "honour" are words which are sprinkled wholesale in the dialogue whenever Standard appears, an effect natural to Powell, a failed Alexander in Lee's heroics, and to the stage colonel who has just been disbanded after the peace of Ryswick. These are anachronistic ideals in a world where sex presents the only battlefield, as Wildair persuades him when refusing to duel over Lurewell. It is not a response from a fop, but from a man Standard admires for his reputation in the wars. Shaken, Standard presses, "Sir, my Honour's concern'd," and Wildair forces him to confront the reality of life in modern London: "Nay, if your Honour be concern'd with a Woman, get it out of her Hands as soon as you can. An honourable Lover is the greatest Slave in Nature" (129).

Yet it is a truth for both sexes, as people try to survive without cynicism in the world of wits. Lurewell's maid raises the issue as she watches her mistress torment the several suitors: "Meethinks Madam, the Injuries you have suffer'd by Men must be very great, to raise such heavy Resentments against the whole Sex" (126). This elicits Lurewell's history of early seductions. Some anonymous students, through a prank, came to her father's country estate when she was fifteen and one seduced her: "What Wit had Innocence like mine? . . . I gave him a Ring with this Motto, *Love and Honour*, then we parted." Her father dead, Lurewell became a wealthy target and a deadly mankiller, armed with money and beauty against the male: "My Love for this single Dissembler turn'd to a hatred of the whole Sex, and resolving to divert my Melancholy . . . I have done some Execution: Here I will play my last scene; then retire to my Country-house, live solitary, and die a penitent" (127).

Lurewell knowingly and Angelica innocently have played the scene well: even while mocking the old principles of love and honour,

Sir Harry succumbs to them. And this seems to me both the dramatic and ideational point of Farquhar's revision. In the first version, the last-act encounter between Wildair and Angelica converts Wildair into a suddenly heroic Standard without Angelica's embodying any of the experience which complicates Lurewell's efforts to live by heroic ideals in a comic society. Both Wildair's complacent cynicism and the mockery of Betterton's antiquated vehicle *The Rival Queens* are lost. But between the two versions Farquhar recognized that the critique of socio-theatrical posturing was the real center of his play. Lurewell and Standard emerged as more important than the first, Fletcherian conception of Wildair and Angelica, causing Farquhar to rewrite the immensely popular role of Wildair in subordination to Lurewell's dilemma of being, willy nilly, a heroine from heroic drama trapped in Wildair's witty world, one less comic in the salon than on the stage. This meant relieving Wildair of his conversion by the *ingénue* Angelica and making him sustain the role of trapped *roué* which carried over into the sequel to this immensely popular play, *Sir Harry Wildair*.[21]

Between Standard and Lurewell, Farquhar developed parallels which might be called structural imperatives. Standard's youthful treatment of the girl has occasioned the staged role of misanthropic courtesan which draws her maid's dismayed reaction: "Methinks, Madam, the Injuries you have suffer'd by Man must be very great, to raise such heavy Resentments against the whole Sex." But Wildair is no less surprised by the misogyny of Standard: " 'Tis unpardonable to charge the Failings of a single Woman upon the whole Sex." Oblivious to his own irony, Standard attributes this stance to the cynicism of the Lurewell he himself unwittingly created with his desertion of the young Manly heiress years before: "I have found one whose pride's above yielding to a Prince. And if Lying, Dissembling, Perjury and Falsehood, be no Breaches in Woman's Honour, she's as innocent as Infancy" (146). Only moments later, in the discovery scene, Standard confronts Lurewell herself with these charges, and she accepts them as the way of the world: "Dissembling to the prejudice of Men is virtue; and every Look, or Sigh, or Smile, or Tear that can deceive is Meritorious" (149). Then the inscribed betrothal ring appears, and Lurewell challenges him: "If you have Love and Honour in Your soul, 'tis then most justly yours." Recognizing his lost love, Standard tells a story of past mistakes "to discharge my self from the stain of Dishonour" (150). Lurewell drops the mask of witty plotter under which she has fought the battle of the sexes: "If I can satisfie you in my past Conduct, and the reasons that engag'd me to deceive all Men, I shall expect the honourable performance of your Promise." And Standard finds that the ideal of honour is not, finally, to be sought on the battlefields of the

Low Countries, or on those of Alexander or Almanzor, where the Restoration theater audience sought them: "Not Fame nor Glory e'er shall part us more. My Honour can be no where more concern'd than here" (150).

It is a sentimental conclusion, but an earned one, tempered in the other perspectives of the play. Farquhar would go on to write *Sir Harry Wildair*, a sequel having the same relation to *The Constant Couple* as *The Relapse* had to *Love's Last Shift*, because in London, as he soon found when tricked into a desperate marriage, duplicity *is* the way of the world, on stage, beyond, or behind it. As an astonishingly able playwright for one just past twenty, he acknowledged the fact in the teasing presentation of Wilks's conquest of Jane Rogers, in the creation of "complacent" Wildair and in the revision of Wildair's conversion. But Farquhar went beyond this to scoff the sentimental posturings of Lee's Alexander off the stage, and return the wedding of love and honor to quotidian London society in the mirror-world of Drury Lane.

CHAPTER 7

Harlequin's Reinvasion: Garrick, Goldoni, and the Germans

I

I want to recollect some information into new formations, little constellations of relevance reflecting one upon another, "lasting and yet constantly moving, ideal spaces with which the practicing writer has to come to terms," as Claudio Guillen put it.[1]

First some historical truisms. The commedia dell'arte constituted the modern bridge between drama and the crossbreeding elements of folk and quasimagical practices from which it emerged in the Renaissance. In the Renaissance (and I suspect this is inevitable with a form which demands a continuous allegiance from a large audience), the developed drama lived in tandem with its own heritage, grandparent and child in vivid competition or symbiosis or both as they appealed to the imagination of a people. This is the essential focus from which Robert Weimann developed his study of popular forms in Shakespeare, seductively synthesizing old facts about a new theater:

> Bankside on the south bank, where the late Rose, Swan, and Globe theaters were built, was also closely connected with the sports and pastimes of old London. Well before the theaters were built people congregated there to watch bear-baiting, bull fights. . . . In fact, there is some evidence that elements of the May games and Morris and Sword dances lived on in the growing city. . . . If there was any place in London where the older popular miming culture, the lay drama and the Robin Hood plays were vividly remembered, it was in Finsbury Fields and Bankside. It was the common people who met there. . . . while growing capitalism . . . had *not yet* become a way of life for the masses, the new economy and corresponding social changes had already created conditions whereby a permanent public theater independent of the controlling influence of clergy and conservative guilds, could develop.[2]

These are the remarks of a Marxist critic viewing the emergence of a professional theater out of popular celebrations and rituals. But they are the remarks, too, of a critic not much interested in Italy. If he had been, Weimann would have found himself and all earlier dramatic critics of the English Renaissance (even C. L. Barber) made timid by the straightforward claims of Paolo Toschi, that Italian folklorist who, culminating nearly a half-century of study, wrote in *Le origini del teatro italiano* that all the forms of modern drama from the Renaissance are traceable to structures and characters indispensable to a catalogue of predramatic folk celebrations in Italy. The claim is breathtaking and yet developed over a lifetime of monographs and capsulated in 750 pages of documentation: "One is dealing with twenty-odd nearly dramatic forms, in the totality of which, either through sacred or profane festivities, ritual spectacles are articulated continuously throughout annual cycles. And one may say that every ritual of any importance has led to a true dramatic form; ritual has been, then, also for us the cradle of theater in every one of its features."[3]

Among those festival ur-forms are the ritual deaths and decapitations, the chaos created by the *buffoni* who run between audience and players in the *Maggi*,[4] the resurrections consequent upon these which seem in so many details indistinguishable from the mummers' plays of St. George and the Turks and the Doctor in England. And the *buffone*'s legacy to the commedia and to the drama becomes, of course, Arlecchino, whose history as a Teutonic devil become the half-animal of the *maschere* leads into the politely absurd comedies of Arlequin, with Vulcan, in the Elysian Fields, with the Great Sultan, and such scenarii in Gherardi's collection from the Parisian theater at the end of the seventeenth century.[5] A daemon domesticated, the popular original made absurdly polite. It is a history we know in detail. Without lingering over it, let us project the psychological set of these remarks by historians of the Renaissance forward, redeeming the eighteenth century as itself an age of dramatic renaissance, redeeming the constellation from the blinding effect of individual stars.

To do so, we must confront another truism: that England, Spain, and most lately France had passed their golden age when Italian drama came into its glory in the person and plays of Carlo Goldoni. Nevertheless, the distance in theatrical quality between eighteenth-century Italy and England is reduced when we are reminded that a minor playwright, David Garrick, Goldoni's contemporary, is the major actor and theatrical entrepreneur in the history of the English stage. This coincidence seems to become serendipitous when one reads through Stone and Kahrl's exhaustive biography of Garrick and his international network of relations, reads through Garrick's own letters, and discovers no mention of Goldoni. There is even the patronizing on Garrick's part implicit in Elizabeth Griffith's prefatory advertisement to her play *The Times*, an adaptation of Goldoni's French farce published in 1780. The tone is that of one updating an ancient bagatelle: "The first idea of this piece was hinted to me by my ever-respected and lamented friend Mr. Garrick, who mentioned Goldoni's *Bourru Bienfaisant*, as a sketch that, if adapted to our times and manners, might be rendered pleasing to an English audience."[6] The fact is that Garrick had just died and Goldoni would continue to write for another decade. The ignorance was mutual, though. In Ortolani's great edition of Goldoni there is recorded a single reference to Garrick, a bit of second-hand and dubious lip-service in the *Memoirs*: "Our century," Goldoni asserts, "has produced three great comedians [Comediéns]: Garrick in England, Preville in France, Sacchi in Italy."[7]

My observations will not explain but will observe the inevitable ways in which Garrick and Goldoni were restoring the vitality of an older popular tradition to a stage which seemed to have been reduced or advanced to a mirror of society, a comedy of manners, of sentiment, of local color. I wish to turn an eighteenth-century shibboleth against itself and to suggest that each was restoring the theater's original genius in contexts which seemed to militate against it.

We can begin among the folk at London's popular Bartholomew Fair at the beginning of the eighteenth century. And in doing so, we raise the suggestion that while Weimann brilliantly explains the age of Shakespeare as a moment when folk and professional forms interacted, he may be mistaken in treating that moment as though it were unique. This allows us to instructively reconstruct the setting for Elkanah Settle's 1703 *Siege of Troy*, the most famous and enduring of the fair plays so numerous throughout the century.

Elkanah Settle *was* a London poet, the fact which sealed his name to enduring ridicule in the mock *translatio* of Pope's *Dunciad*. He was the last titular incumbent of the post of city poet to the Lord Mayor, the poet of Ludstown as well as of Troy-Novant. Acknowledging Brute as the conqueror-founder, Settle wrote of Cassandra and Paris in his operetta the *Virgin Prophetess* and in his Bartholomew Fair droll at the booth of Mrs. Mynns. But Bartholomew Fair was held cheek-by-jowl in place and spirit to more rooted mythic origins than classical tradition could encompass. As the anonymous author of the *New History of the Trojan Wars* soon printed with the text of Settle's *Siege of Troy* explains, Brute defeated Albion's giants and "founded a City, which he called *Troy-novant* . . . and the building a Palace where *Guild-Hall* stands, caused the two Giants (Albion's brothers Gog and Magog) to be chained to the Gate of it, . . . In Memory of which, it is held, that their Effigies, after their Death, were set up as they now appear in *Guild-Hall*."[8] It is a version of interaction between "effigy" and living actors of history which Ben Jonson had glorified with the puppets of *Bartholomew Fair*—a play usually presented at fair time by the patent theaters to seal a truce upon their closing for the duration of the annual great event.

We know that Settle played a dragon in a green leather suit at Bartholomew Fair toward the close of his life, but the pathos often associated with that fact should be set in perspective by recalling that at Drury Lane in 1701 the highly popular team of lovers Robert Wilks and Jane Rogers broke through their usual distrust of tragedy[9] to star in Settle's *Virgin Prophetess*, an operetta with elaborate music and more elaborate effects, such as a chariot drawn by white elephants and a twenty-foot-high Trojan horse.[10] While the *Siege of Troy* at Bartholomew Fair was so thoroughly reoriented away from the focus of the *Virgin Prophetess* upon Cassandra and her brother (played by Rogers and Wilks) that the plots have little in common but the background story, the elaborate machinery and effects of Settle's earlier play were not only carried over but enhanced for the fair. At the fair, at least, the elephants (augmented by painted but substantial houses over flats) seem to have been real (it was a beast both common yet exotic enough to have its appearance at May Fair remarked upon as William Penkethman spoke a prologue from atop one in 1704).[11] Such interaction between men, beasts, and machines was common enough, but never had the fairs attempted so elaborate a transcendence of the patent theaters' spectacular effects. Evidence is in the printing and frequent reprinting of *The Siege of Troy*, described as "a dramatic performance presented in Mrs. Mynn's booth, . . . Containing a description of all the scenes, machines and movements, with the whole decoration of the play." There were "Paris and Helen fronting the audience, riding in a triumphant chariot, drawn by two white elephants, mounted by two pages in embroider'd liveries. The side wings are ten elephants more, bearing on their backs open castles fill'd with ten persons richly dressed"; in a wood outside Troy spectators saw "the Trojan Horse, being a figure of that magnitude that 'tis 17 foot high to the top of his back, the whole figure magnificently adorned"; there was a Temple of Diana whose golden statues turned black in an instant at the wave of Cassandra's wand; and Troy, of course, was burned before one's eyes, such fires being a major spectacular effect from at least the experiments of Bernini in mid-seventeenth-century Rome.

The piece was perennially revived at Bartholomew and Southwark fairs from 1715 through 1747 (when, in the sunset of fair playing, Settle's droll was renewed simultaneously at both), and always with boasts about the enhancement of the spectacle: "The whole Paintings heightened with those New Enrichments and Gilding, as to make it very much superior even to its first Original" (1716).[12]

The difference between *The Siege of Troy* and Settle's earlier Trojan play lay precisely in the difference of setting. Transferring Troy's fall from the theater to the fair, Settle had translated (in the sense that Pope feared) his spectacle from a classical operetta, a musical experiment with Gottfried Finger,[13] into a living myth, a history for the citizens of Lud-Town, who watched it under the eyes of ancient Albion's modern totems, the giants Gog and Magog, flanking the entrance into the nearby Guild-Hall where the Lord Mayor's banquets were held and parading the streets annually in the Lord Mayor's processions of triumph, customarily prepared by Settle. One supposes, even, that the fact of new permanent effigies of the giants having been installed in the year of Settle's original presentation of the *Siege* enhanced the public sense of their symbolic guardianship.[14] But it was not merely the physical setting of Britain's mythic bond to a preclassical past which made a Trojan play on the plebs' own ground at Smithfield an experience more immediate, more "popular" in every sense of the word than Settle's classical operetta. It was the introduction of the people themselves into this ancient history in the persons of Captain Bristle, his wife, her seducer, and a crowd of other Anglicized Trojans caught up in the triumph and fall of their city.

We have been told often enough of the concerns of Restoration prologues: at the least provocative, they eulogize and gossip about author, actors, or patron; at the best they are in the Jonsonian-Terentian tradition of literary criticism in defense of the author couched in tropes of cooking, sailing, coaching, and such. But Settle, without prologue, draws us back into the Plautine tradition which makes the legerdemain of places incorporated into later places more mythic than metaphoric. He sees, that is, as few of his contemporaries saw, what had been achieved when Plautus' prologues ringed Athens or Hellenic Sicily into a little room in Rome; when Dovizi da Bibbiena brought a Roman play to Urbino (just before assuming his political duties in Rome) and used the interaction of setting and history for a commentary in his "argument" upon both his artistic magic and the depressing course of Roman history. "Don't imagine that [the characters] have come here to Urbino from Rome so quickly by witchcraft; this stage *is* Rome, which, in its glory, contained many cities, towns, and rivers, but now, you see, is so reduced that it fits comfortably into our own city."[15]

Well, Settle had no such melancholy a vision. The popular *Siege of Troy* was a city classic, a play much less about the diminution of the classical world than about its rebirth and resurrection in London. The second Troy was more youthful and more hopeful than the first. But, Settle's play suggested, so it should be. It incorporated not only the spirit of ancient princes but their perennial support in the people. It is these, the citizens, who make a city. At the close of his play, Settle brings the classical heritage of Troy together with a long and ebullient English context. The Trojans are native to Troy-Novant, to the booths of Bartholomew Fair. The princes call them the "mob," but they (and Settle) wink at their inevitable survival as the city is translated from one place to another only to resettle old vitalities. As Troy burns, the plebs flee into the salvation of fresh English dialogue, that reassurance which had run through the people's dramatic dealings with the ancientry since Bottom had awakened outside Athens. It centers on one Ralph Horsenail the Farrier. "He poor fellow, had his head cut off." "His head cut off," cries Captain Tom, "how did the poor fellow look?" His informant allays alarm: "The poor fellow was a little dasht at it, but . . . had the good fortune to catch his head before it fell, and is bringing it under his arm . . . to desire his good friend Captain Bristle to lend him an awl and a cobbler's end to stitch it on again" (8). It is an old trope which Peele knew as a magic (and comic) gesture of renewal. Harlequin had invaded Shakespeare's country from the popular plays and players of Italy and the Italianized French *foires*, of course. So English, nonetheless, this beheading, so much an echo of the Mummers' St. George combats.

Settle was aware, at some level, of this trope of death and resurrection and its rightness just here at the penultimate moment of his classical spectacular. It brought everything back home where it would end, to *The Siege of Troy* and its promise of a future which had become Troy-Novant's, London's, present.

The style becomes ironic, easy. Swallows have fallen down a chimney, reports one Trojan, into the porridge pot, spoiling the broth. "Oh," cries the Captain, "Wondrous! The tale of Troy to a tittle. Down fell the nest of swallows. Down falls the city of Troy. . . . And where was this fall but in the chimney, all in fire and smoak. Troy, Troy again exactly. . . . Ah Neighbour, hadst thou been an honest man and told the King this prodigious warning-piece, it had been enough to have opened his eyes . . . and have saved the town and all our lives" (8). Prodigies and predictions—all the holiday stuff of Bartholomew Fair. And many a farmer and farrier may have nodded in tragic approval, forgetting that they were born and still stood on the firm ground of New Troy.

In a moment they would be reminded. Menelaus rushes in to stop the carnage. Turning to the Trojan plebs he says: "Here I have finished my revenge. . . . Go and rebuild your Troy." The captain turns, speaking to an ancient Greek in the eternal optimism through which a fire becomes a phoenix: "Pray tell your king from me he is a very Civil gentleman . . . to bid us build our town again. Strike up fiddles, we will give him a song and dance at parting" (8). It was the old way of resurrection, a heritage from his folk past which restored Ralph Horse-nail's head, a heritage from both the Italian Brute and Albion's guardian brothers at Guild-Hall which restored Troy in the renewed setting of a sceptered isle. A celebration perennial, if never quite so well commemorated before in Bartholomew's fair.

But now let us leap the history of the dominance that such spectacles—the drolls and pantomimes of the fairs, the quondam "afterpieces"—came to gain in the patent theaters, recalling only that in 1741 David Garrick, Lincoln's Inn law student, made his London acting debut at Goodman's Fields as Harlequin in *Harlequin Student, or, The Fall of Pantomime*, a musical which was hypocritically critical of pantomime as a debasement of the native tradition warbled by Shakespeare.[16]

It was a bit of prelude music which Garrick remembered and elaborated. Taking over Drury Lane a half dozen years later, Garrick held out against the pantomimes—especially the Covent Garden competition of John Rich, "Lun," whose Harlequinades were the town's favorites. Then in 1759 Garrick invaded Rich's territory and stole Harlequin for a tradition-breaking speaking part in his own *Harlequin's Invasion; or, A Christmas Gambol*.[17] Like the early *Harlequin Student*, this little playlet set Harlequin against Shakespeare, portraying the former as a foreign invader of the native land—even as Settle had shown Greeks invading the sacred native ground of Troy-cum-Troy-Novant. Garrick's method would also be analogous to Settle's: English folk—tailors and blacksmiths and their shrews—would mingle with the historical and fairy troupes of Shakespeare's *dramatis personae* and with the French invader Harlequin. And even the vehicle of resurrection and reconciliation would be the same trope Settle had used, the old folk topos of the decapitation repaired. But now the setting would be a recovery of voice for a dramatic tradition which had gone mute and debased through those very afterpieces of which *Harlequin's Invasion* was both corrective and example. Settle's rationale for Ralph Horsenail's recovery of his head was a mere tailor's metaphor embedded in the implicit richness of English folk custom and drama. Garrick made his tailor victim rather than master, and made the rationale for his resurrection a reminder to the mid-eighteenth-century theater of its origins, restoring his decapitated victim through the magic worked by a diabolic Harlequin whose energies make him the protagonist of the alleged history of his own demise.

The story is short but complex. Word of Harlequin's coming has been sent ahead by trumpet and drum among country people. Snip the tailor's wife sends him off expressly "to fetch me this outlandish man's head, or take care of your own."[18] Harlequin, in the traditional half-animal black mask, sits in a tree and presides over the beheading of Snip himself by two countrymen. He metamorphoses himself into Snip headless and holds a comic session of terror over the country folk amidst a chorus of diabolic allusion beginning with simple Simon's first reaction to Harlequin: "So, so! So talk of the devil and here's one of his imps" (207). Exactly so, in Garrick's insistence that his is the *original* Harlequin, a daemon unsophisticated by the Parisian absurdities of a debased *comédie italienne*. Resurrection specialist, Harlequin tells Simon that he will "step into the cave, stitch the tailor a new head on, and then you shall go to town with me and see my pranks there" (212). Simon, exiting, cries on the run: "No more devil's dances for Simon. He must be Old Nick himself for sartain, and I am dealing with him" (212). Harlequin, hauled before the justices of peace, invokes another trope from the underworld which spans the distances between the commedia dell'arte scenarii of Flaminio Scala to John Smith's mid-nineteenth-century blackface minstrel skit, "The Quack Doctor":[19] the demonic doctor as dentist. "I hear," says the first Justice, "that you cut off peoples' heads." "Yes," responds Harlequin, "to cure the toothache" (213). To no avail, this excuse. Harlequin goes to prison. But so apparently caught up in the social nets of King Shakespeare's (or post-Shakespeare's) England, Harlequin evokes the people's sympathy (or recognition as a double figure of death and resurrection at once) in the persons of Mrs. and Mr. Snip, now reconciled as well as restored. She cries out upon hearing of Harlequin's capture, "Poor soul! Pour [sic] soul!" and Snip, seeing the creature, responds: "May I never handle needle again, if this is not the blackamoor gentleman that sowed my head on" (223). Confusion ensues with quick scene changes as, rushing to capture Harlequin, the jailors find they are literally "raising the Devil here." But Mercury, little deus ex machina, descends to reveal Harlequin as a false French friar, and as the last songs praise the Bard's genius, "Shakespeare rises: Harlequin sinks." Well, perhaps; but only as social gesture and dramatic afterthought.

Garrick's playlet, in fact, might better have been titled *Harlequin's Reinvasion* or *Harlequin's Return*. Once again the spirit of the commedia dell'arte was being embodied. Harlequin was bursting through all the scenic transparencies, the topical French dialect, the pre-Stratford Jubilee bardolatry to speak in his first person to the people about the daemonic bond which had always been implicit in their contract to suspend disbelief in drama in order that it might reinvent its double, as Artaud would say, in the underground of their psyches whence Harlequin had come.

It was not only a repetition but an overlapping back in a spiral movement which requires us to reexamine Weimann's Marxist reading of Shakespeare's unique moment between older folkways and capitalism's emergence. Settle's Bartholomew Fair setting had been on the edge of London, at a convergence of country vacationers and merchandisers with the London tourists who are recorded as slumming at the fair from Ben Jonson's play to Tom Brown's newsletters. But Garrick wrote for London's most established theater and for an audience whose social status he shared and whose taste he tutored. That taste was for Shakespeare, a phenomenon emerging (in Weimann's terms) from a Bankside melding not unlike that more ephemerally, annually, found in Bartholomew Fair. This was Shakespeare who had been apotheosised almost single-handedly by Garrick from old dramatist into an institution as divine as any in the English Demi-Paradise which his own characters had described. Yet the structural thrust of *Harlequin's Invasion* is to reestablish the presence of that primal Shakespearean energy of Harlequin the murky folk daemon and the irrational rites of resurrection of which Horsenail and Snip are victims and beneficiaries, and moreover, to reestablish them in the West End, in the theater of the comedy of manners and societal satire.

In this look at playlets written, respectively, for a popular and for a sophisticated audience in the first half of the eighteenth century, I have implied that they combine to tell us a good deal about the informing instincts of English drama in an age which saw its renaissance or a continuation of the Renaissance tradition. That the theater of these years is generally remarked upon as a creature of decline or, at best, of transition suggests that dramatic history has been distorted rather than refined by sociological and generic studies, distorted so severely as to make us miss the metahistorical paradigms of modern drama given shape in that nebulous but credible era we call beginnings—in Toschi's folk forms, perhaps. And I am tempted to one more suggestion: that we might more easily discern the brightness of the century's dramatic constellation if we focus simultaneously upon the two great theater men of the age—Garrick and Goldoni—lights who when viewed together provide that parallax which reilluminates the whole dramatic cosmos.

Or, paradoxically, perhaps we can see better yet if we complicate matters with a third dimension, with another only apparently irrelevant focal point, before we think about Goldoni. I refer to the theater in eighteenth-century Germany, that last entrant into the renewal of drama in Europe. This was the culture in which popular and erudite drama were most thoroughly and theoretically discussed while Garrick felt himself merely surrendering to a commercial necessity, while Goldoni discovered his tradition only as a reflection distorted in the mirror of a Gozzi.

The theory was necessary because the self-consciousness of German drama was retarded by nearly two centuries after the Renaissance, and of course, when it arrived, it expressed itself with the usual excitement of youth. The alliance of the actress Caroline Neuber and the brilliant (if derivative) playwright-critic Johann Cristoph Gottsched is an often retold tale, but one told as if of a by-water and of the beginning of a national drama which gave us Schiller and Goethe. Let us retell it as a German articulation of Harlequin's role in drama—not as character but as essence. Or antithesis, threat to the essential enterprise. Being fresh, the German critics exercised themselves to be more explicit and articulate about this principal heritage than Garrick or Goldoni and his contemporaries bothered to do.

II

Impressed by Scipione Maffei's reformed theater in Verona, Gottsched the academic persuaded Frau Neuber to organize a troupe which would restore tragedy upon the German stage (his own *Der sterbende Cato* constituting a touchstone) and reform the public's taste for Harlekin and his ethnic offspring Hans Wurst in the mixed *Hauptund Staatsactionem* and the farcical *Nachspiele*—versions of the commedia dell'arte scenarii crossing with the Parisian farces of the comédie italienne and the *foires*. The actress signaled the opening of hostilities in this phase of the theatrical wars at Leipzig with a booth play in which Harlekin is tried and found guilty by a court of taste.[20] Gottsched in this same year (1737) had written out the detailed grounds of this challenge in his chapter on the history and state of comedy in *Versuch einer critischen Dichtkunst* (Essay on critical poetics). Here, in what is essentially an extended history of ancient and modern drama judged in the light of Horace—a Horation "commentary" even, in the same sense that Castelvetro had expanded Aristotle's *Poetics* into hundreds of prescriptive pages—Gottsched turned to the Italian Francophobic tradition represented by Maffei, Muratori, and the (self-) reformed Luigi Riccoboni. "Pragmatically one must say that Italian theater for several centuries [since Terence] has not brought forth many sophisticated triumphs. . . . Harlequin and Scaramouche are the inevitable principals on their stage . . . who perform only absurd tricks [*lazzi*]."[21]

Gottsched goes on to cite absurdities we have already documented, such as "Arlequin Empereur dans la lune" and "Arlequin aux Champs Elisees" from Gherardi's collection drawn from the *theatre italien*. He finds the English theater scarcely less irregular (although he knows of Jonson and Dryden as classicists), but returns to a regional attack, finding German comedy predominantly an unintelligent outgrowth of Italian comedy, inheriting the usual parasites, gluttons, and stagy peasants borrowed directly from Roman comedy or more probably from Josef Anton Stranitzky's *Ollapatrida des durchgetriebenen Fuchsmundi*. This latter collection of dialogues or playlets was a Germanized adaptation of Gherardi's *Recueil* into which Hans Wurst had been introduced, supplementing or replacing Harlequin and other clowns.[22] The result is often regrettable in both an aesthetic and a social sense, the former in the same way "as, for example, the Italians' Harlequin farces: but there it is not really depraved."[23] Gottsched goes on to ridicule the Italianate tradition which has invaded the Continent, including Germany: "The odd presentation of a foolish person on stage is enough to make him laughable. . . . the provocation for laughter is not in the matter, but in the foolish clothes, words, and gestures . . . one has Harlequin and Scaramouche [who] . . . through the multi-colored jacket, marvelous postures, and horrible grimaces raise laughter among the people."[24]

In the prescriptive conclusion, Gottsched insists before Goldoni upon the exile of the masks (358) and rhetorically marvels at the inexplicable tradition even in modern comedy of allowing Harlequin to wear a comic costume which is unrelated to any social or dramatic role. But these oddities are the Italians' debased legacy to France, and Germany must create a new national drama (Hans Wurst and Pickelhering must also go, being only adaptations) which is not a mere translation of or derivation from French folly.

Despite Gottsched's arguments and Frau Neuber's stage regency over a decade before Goldoni's *Il Servitore* or Garrick's account of his "invasion," Harlequin refused to decamp even from the new German drama. In 1761 Justus Moeser would give him perhaps his strangest role in the course of a long dramatic history: that of monologuist in theoretical defense of the irrational—of what the Renaissance called the "marvelous" and what I have labeled the "daemonic"—as the quintessential element in comedy. It was, of course, a pretrial of the critique of Gottsched, Neuber, and their anti-popular reaction that Lessing would develop in his *Hamburgische Dramaturgie*.[25] But Moeser's was a singularly perceptive trial and defense of what was a resurgence in European drama. Moeser gave his monologue not only the form of the medicine-man montebank spiel from which the comedia dell'arte troupes had developed, but captured both the essence and the objection to Harlequin in his subtitle: *Harlequin; or, A Defense of the Comic Grotesque*.[26]

Harlequin begins by warning that it would be a foolish work to try to count up his whole family, so numerous and ancient as it is, traceable perhaps to Bergamo, or perhaps to the entirety of the world itself (it was the reminder that Lessing picked up for his own development). It is, besides, a family which can claim royal patronage (and here [8-9] he cites Riccoboni's *Histoire du theatre italien*).[27] In spite of learned criticisms, the fact is that Harlequin is to be found in all the comic arts, to be found represented by poets, painters, players, and dancers. So he can no more be considered an aesthetic excrescence than the comic grotesquery found in Cervantes, Fielding, Scarron, et alii (20-21). But then Harlequin directly confronts the central issue implicit in all the eighteenth-century debates about farce, Harlequin, and the harlequinades: unnaturalness. As a first battleground, Moeser chooses the operetta, that most popular of mixed genres, the very mixture of which reflects the nature of Harlequin. Far from pretending to mimesis in the common sense, this genre reflects the imagination: "Opera is a representation of a possible world" (Die Oper ist eine Vorstellung aus einer moeglichen Welt) and "the opera stage is the realm of chimaeras" (die Opernbuehne ist das Reich der Chimaeren [24]). This leads into a review of the absurdities to be found in other genres (and Moeser lets the absurd shift repeatedly between the denigrative sense of the earlier critics and something approximating the modern sense of absurdist ontology), as preparation for Harlequin's rhetorical question as to why he alone should be suspect ("warum es mir allein verdacht werden wolle" [30]) for choosing the art of giving pleasure to others. From music, dance, painting, we do not ask for moral didacticism; we ask pleasure. Why then should only theater be bound to teaching rather than giving pleasure (29-30)?

Yet, even while making this plea for fairness, Moeser's Harlequin claims that in his own way he does contribute to moral amelioration (43-44). It is the way of exaggeration, of the grotesque. Certainly, Moeser acknowledges, "the taste for the distorted, or the so-called 'baroque taste,' . . . does not belong in the temple and to lasting works destined for eternal life" (der GESCHMACK DES SCHIEFEN, oder der sogennante "gout baroc," ist gewiss sonderbar schoen, gehoert aber nicht in Tempel und andre dauerhafte Werke, welche die Ewigkeit erreichen sollen [53]). Remembering the French caricaturist's illustrations of commedia dell'arte players, Moeser concludes that although "the figures of Calot [sic] do not hang near Michelangelo's *Last Judgment*, they are admired nonetheless" (die Figuran von CALOT, hangen zwar nicht bei einem Juengstengerichte von MICHEL ANGELO, sie werden aber doch bewundert [54]). The source of this admiration is Harlequin's ability to make kings, philosophers, poets, and all laughable without bitterness, ridicule being used only as a radical principle of pleasure-giving; it is his family secret: in all his training for a manner, for self-expression, he has maintained himself as a pristine fool.[28] And in modern times, he has become the servant-fool who, although in livery, is now commonly the "controlleur" (62), the daemon plotter (a term I import as a quite appropriate epitome of Harlequin's self-appraisal in Moeser's treatise). It is a generic domestication of a surrealistic or suprarealistic tradition. In preparation for his conclusion, Moeser at this point stylistically intertwines and inverts oxymoronic adjectives and nouns: Harlequin's apparent stupidity ("scheinbaren Dummheit") is the source of his audience's pleasure; and, as he generalizes, dumb cunning ("die dumme List"), or the illusion of it, is the most comic representation of all the essential idea of the comic (62). Illusion is, indeed, at the root of comedy—the sort of illusion involved in the mistaking of a person's inner nature by his outward appearance, as in Harlequin's own folly or Scaramouche's inverted cowardice (63). The harlequinade, then, is a mysterious mixture, without unity of action or tone in the critical sense, but possessing a unity of intention ("Absicht"). It is drawn together, in fact, only around Harlequin, who is himself a grotesque center, with no two limbs matching (as is the case with all such offspring of Hans Wurst) (64–66, 69). He, as principal and principle, always exhibits himself in the best places; from him the other players take their cues; through him the whole takes life (74).[29] This metaphoric sense of what Weimann has called *Figurenposition* caps a history of how even the great moderns Moliere and Goldoni have found the necessity of incorporating Harlequin into burst genres, and leads into a review of medieval folk rites and literary practices of the grotesque. The conclusion is a paradox which universalizes Harlequin's "scheinbaren Dummheit" and "dumme List" as the expression of man's ultimate nature as a divided being who exists just beyond the natural, just beyond the rational. The greatest truth is this, explains Moeser's Harlequin: "Each man is interchangeably witty and foolish" (Jeder Mensch wechselweise klug und naerrisch ist [94–5]). In the German defense, Harlequin has become the expression of man's doubleness, of his necessary ability to divide himself into a social and a disguised, appetitive being—a conclusion, to readapt Moeser's terms, which makes society no less grotesque than man himself. It was an old comic realization, one that became the metaphoric principle around which Carlo Goldoni constructed the masterpiece which would attain such immediate and lasting popularity in Germany as elsewhere, *Il Servitore di due padroni*.[30]

Garrick and Goldoni. Not sources of sustenance to one another, but key exemplars of the fact that the eighteenth century was an age of great theatrical geniuses not *merely* original, because they built the new upon the old paradigmatic structure of comedy as metaphor for the psyche. They revived that function against all odds, in theaters which had become mirrors of society, of local society, of parochial allusion in London and Venice. Both men were on the make in the theater and in the town, and yet they understood that what one drew from such quotidian stuff for the stage was only vehicle for drama's inevitable tenor, its sense of the split, doubling nature of the self.

III

The same Antonio Sacchi whom Goldoni pairs with Garrick among actors of the age came to Goldoni in 1745, when the playwright was a burgeoning lawyer, with a request and a suggestion of topic for a scenario written to be played *a soggetto*: "What a temptation for me! Sacchi was an excellent actor, comedy had always been my passion. I felt the ancient taste reborn in me, the same fire, the same enthusiasm. The subject which he proposed to me was *The Servant of Two Masters*."[31] Thus concludes the forty-ninth chapter of Goldoni's *Mémoires*. Goldoni provided this scenario for Sacchi, widely known as Truffaldino, the great Arlecchino type of his time. A few years later (probably in 1753),[32] this sketch became what we today know as *Il Servitore di due padroni* when Goldoni expanded it into a full-length script. It retained in every sense the traces of its origins in the commedia and in that phenomenon's origins, even as had Garrick's gambol of Harlequin's invasion. And the point was, as it had been with Settle, with Garrick, positive. But more complicated. That is a claim which will bring us eventually to Scripture, but only when we have looked at society, or social drama in the making.

I rehearse elements from the plot as structure and as story to indicate the social and romantic complexities of surface which overlay the dramatic deep structure which this play shares with the English playlets we have looked at. First, it is set in a contemporary Venice, the action compressed into a single day, which results in a dizzying intensification, a vertigo of narrowly missed cues and premature discoveries.

The *vecchi* of Goldoni's play are commedia figures: Pantalone and the *Dottore*. Their children can marry because one Federigo Rasponi, a Turinese, commercially betrothed to Pantalone's daughter, has been killed in a duel. As usual in Goldoni's Venetian plays, the vecchi talk of little but dowry exchanges, but in the most circumlocutory of terms. One speaks of money on the Rialto; one displays a merely metaphoric generosity bordering on carelessness in the drawing room. But the young inamorati are modern paradoxes, romantic but devoted to the main chance first, and cold to the edge of terrifying. Rasponi, whose death has been fortuitous for the Venetian lovers, was in fact killed by his sister's lover Florindo because of his attempts to forestall the match. The girl, Beatrice, journeys to Venice disguised as her own deceased brother and presents herself before Pantalone where, she explains to her maid, "Faremo il saldo di nostri conti, riscuoterò il denaro, e potrò soccorrere anche Florindo, se ne avrà di bisogno" (We'll settle our accounts, I will receive the money, and I'll be able to help Florindo if he should have any need [2:23]). Beatrice, then, as Federigo revived, becomes the first doubling and first resurrection. It is a romantic quest more commercial than comic; as she sighs, in continuing this account, "Guardate dove conduce amore" (Look where love leads us). Florindo has also fled to Venice after his crime. Both lovers take up residence at the inn of Brighella, the commedia's jovial older scamp-of-the-people who immediately recognizes and becomes the confidante of the disguised Beatrice because she knows he will wink at her con game. So much for modern times in Venice. And into them enters Truffaldino, an Arlecchino from a daemonic past in which he represented pure ego as appetite, a past whose presence will reveal the appetitive nature of the present, dramatic continuities uncovering the continuity beneath the forms of society. And Mammon's true dimensions are recovered from the petit point of bourgeoise commercial amenities. To recall Weimann's formula for the Shakespearean moment is to revise it in the light of the eighteenth-century dramatist's accomplishment: working in and with the capitalist stuff that had not yet descended upon the English folk on Bankside, Goldoni returned it to its folk roots in the daemonic side of the psyche which is appetite. "Se magna." One eats— the others, in the inevitable phrase of Goldoni's Arlecchini who cavort among the gamblers and bankrupts of Venice.

But back to Truffaldino. "Son servitor del me padron" (I am the servant of my master [15]). This is his self-identification to Pantalone. The "padron" is the self-doubled Beatrice passing for Federigo. She has encountered Truffaldino upon entering Venice and hired him to take her luggage to the inn. Impatient of her arrival ("Son stuffo d'aspettar, che no posso più. Co sto me patron se magna poco" [I'm so fed up with waiting, I can't stand it any longer. One doesn't eat much with this master] [23]), he hires on also with her lover Florindo, just arrived in the city in search of her. Florindo's luggage too must go by way of Truffaldino to Brighella's inn. Both lovers send the servant of two masters to the post office; he picks up, mixes, reseals, conceals their letters. To cover his game, Truffaldino doubles himself into a phantom "other," Pasquale. As the Menaechmian errors of the comedy heighten in frequency, Truffaldino's frenzy is given a choral counterpoint of diabolic imagery reminscent of his original's origins: "Vada al inferno questo sicario [assassin]; (47); "Oh, diavolo" (49, 52). This comes to a point as Truffaldino serves two meals for his two masters, so agile in his harried confusion that a fellow servant observes, "Salta di qua, salta di là; è un diavolo costui" (He jumps here, jumps there; that one's a devil [58]). Of course; and having survived the ballet, this particular dramatic daemon returns to his appetitive origin and his embodiment of doubling: "Ho servido a tavola do padroni, e un non ha savudo dell'altro. Ma se ho servido per do, adess voio andar a magnar per quattro" (I have waited table for two masters, and neither one has known about the other. But if I have served two, now I want to go to eat for four [59]).

This double meal develops into the *lazzo* of the trunks of the twin lover-protagonists, brought by Truffaldino to the inn and confused. From the trunks emerge clothing which fuses and confuses the lovers until an unexpected portrait in a pocket reveals to them their mutual presence when each had thought the other lost. Or *almost* reveals it. For when Florindo discovers the picture, Truffaldino extemporizes a tale of his other master's death which drives the young man to despair and a promise of suicide. Beatrice immediately enters and Truffaldino tells her an equally dreadful tale of Florindo's death; she too runs to her room in order to join her lost one in, as she cries, the tomb. The two emerge from their rooms with daggers in hand ready for self-destruction. A farce of physical prevention and gradual revelation follows, as the putative dead are revived, and death becomes only an old tale told by "the little dark man" from Hell, Truffaldino. The happy parody is doubled as the Venetian lover Silvio is revived by news that Clarice's rival suitor has been Beatrice, woman in disguise: as he declares to Pantalone upon this news, "Oh cielo. Voi mu ritornate da morte a vita" (Oh, heavens, You bring me back from death to life [73]).

As in the beginning of modern drama with the commedia troupes, the inamorati are crossed but saved, revived by the daemonic servant. And appropriately, if with superficial inadvertence, since Arlecchino / Truffaldino's undifferentiating appetite doubles for the eternally repetitive sexual appetite of faceless young love in the comic paradigm.

But this is Venice in the eighteenth century, and as we earlier commented, the inamorati have a cool eye on the main chance. Pantalone and Dottore Lombardi, Beatrice and Florindo, have as economic a vision of beatitude as has always been attributed to the critical tradition's Truffaldino. It is the Venetian society of *La Putta onorata*, of *i Rusteghi*, of Franco Fido's recent judicious overview of the interweaving of game and gain in Goldoni's world.[33] Goldoni accepted the pieties of this world in some very real sense and yet questioned it with a comic sense of things which went as deep as the origins of his genius, origins shared by Settle or Garrick as, in another place, they sensed the persistent audacity of the theater and its double.

Truffaldino boasts that he has waited on two masters without their knowing, and he later boasts again: "Ho magnà ben, ho disnà ben, e sta sera cenerò meio, e fin che posso voî servir do padroni, tanto almanco che podesse tirar do salari" (I have eaten well, dined well, and will eat better tonight; and as long as I can serve two masters, I can at least draw double wages [65]).

It was an invitation to remember and have trust in the psychic function of comedy even in a Christian society sunk once again into the righteous clutches of satire. That was an eighteenth-century mode from which neither Garrick nor Goldoni would refrain. That was the surface stuff of Hogarth and of *Il Servitore di due padroni* or *La putta onorata*. The meals, the trunks with their gaudy and mistaken costumes are meant to question an older and profounder Christian assertion: "Therefore I say unto you, take no thought for your life, what ye shall eat, or what ye shall drink; nor yet for your body what ye shall put on" (Matt. 6:25). So had said the evangelist in his Gospel. But, as always in comedic doubling, Truffaldino had doubted, then demonstratively refuted the moralist by gaining a double wage. He had resurrected and restored the lovers, but he had profited from the belly god. "Niuno può servire a due padroni. . . . Voi non potete servire a Dio ed a Mammona." "No man can serve two masters: for either he will hate the one, and love the other; or else he will hold to the one, and despise the other. Ye cannot serve God and mammon" (Matt. 6:24). But the old daemon Harlequin can and did, breaking through the surface of social comedy in the eighteenth century to flash signals of recognition across places and time to remind that comedy really pays the psyche double wages. It is order restored by chaos rampant.

CHAPTER 8

Carlo Goldoni:
Beyond *La Civiltà Veneziana*

This final essay seems to demand a personal and historical headnote, for its first version embodies in part the genesis of my oblique way of thinking about drama as a genre characterized by its antiformal, antigeneric dialectic with its own alleged rules.

Once upon a long time ago I was living in isolation in a village above Florence with a library of English dramatists and Florentine Platonists, making up a book about the connections I imagined between them and that connection's ultimate impact upon the drama. At that point I discovered a great dramatist and his city. It was a little late in the game, you might say, but not really improbably late for an English-speaking reader, even one who should have known better. When I began to translate my excitement into investigation, I discovered that Italianists had a litany of sophisticated praise for Goldoni as a Venetian dramatist, as a chronicler of Venetian society. Just as this was happening, the Cini Foundation on San Giorgio issued a reprint of the rare first book of Goldoni's great editor.[1] It had come in tandem with a commercial collection of essays by Ortolani which I had read. With the temerity of youth and a calling which I couldn't seem to avoid, I asked the Cini people for a review copy, read the critics, and used my faculty position at The Johns Hopkins University as well as Charles Singleton's kind trust to publish an essay on Ortolani, on the critics—and on how I (brash American and dilettante) felt they had misread Goldoni's intent, disserved his reputation as one of the great international dramatists.

At the time it seemed a learner's isolated homage to another culture. I didn't know that I would later understand my argument with sociological critics and with what I perceived as their (with the Venetians, literal) provincialism to be a mode of understanding, of arguing about the nature of modern drama itself. But it was, and it has given what shape there is to these essays. There are no provinces privileged against theater, no societies which can use the stage as mirror, because there are no enduring dramatists whose view of society is not enhanced by their struggle with generic prescriptions, with mimetic limitations.

In the preceding essay Harlequin was the hero, or antihero, who did the job of arguing reality—or dramatic realism—back into something like myth. He reappears in passing here. But the job of undermining ("pioneering" was the Renaissance word for a military land-mining maneuver) the generic and social expectations is carried primarily by Bettina in La putta onorata *and by Orazio, Goldoni's own avatar, in* Il teatro comico. *And being Goldoni's avatar, this figure draws us back again to the beginning—or end—of this group of dramatic speculations, offering an analogue to the conscious metamorphoses of self into staged presence epitomized in the careers of Ruzante and Grimaldi.*

I

The energy with which he collated, commented on, edited, and reedited the thousands of pages of Goldoni's canon throughout his extraordinarily long career made the late Giuseppe Ortolani one of those rare scholarly legends in his own lifetime: a man who knew his chosen matter better than anyone who comes after him ever will know it, better, undoubtedly, than the author himself knew it. And yet he was a legendary figure peculiarly diffused, one whose views were dispersed by fortune into hundreds of essays thrown up as both adjunct and substance in the course of almost sixty years devoted to his interlocking editions of Goldoni's *opere* which, with a happy grace granted to few first begetters of staggeringly ambitious scholarly projects, he managed to bring to virtual completion just as his life ended. Continuously commenting, Ortolani never wrote his book, that book which Sign. Damerini describes in the elegant and affectionate biography of Ortolani prefacing the collected essays on *La riforma del teatro* as "un piano orgoglioso e grandioso . . . il piano inteso a rifondere in una organica trattazione senza lacune, come in un immenso affresco, lo spettacolo animato e variopinto della civiltà veneziana fra gli albori del secolo XVIII ed il suo tragica crepuscolo" (an overweening and grandiose plan . . . a plan intended to refound in an organic treatment without lacunae, as in an immense fresco, the animated and varicolored spectacle of Venetian civilization between the dawning of the eighteenth century and its tragic twilight).[2]

Setting to work in 1894 under the guidance of Guido Mazzoni upon what his teacher must have conceived as a cleanly circumscribed project for an original *tesi di laurea* on Chiari, Ortolani mined the archives of the Veneto for a decade, read indefatigably in the ephemeral letters, the occasional comedies, the abortive gazettes, passed beyond Venice to embrace all Italy, and beyond that to coordinate the interrelations of literary and pseudoliterary genres in Italy and in France.

As the decades passed, the parade of volumes for both the Municipio and the Mondadori editions[3] was accompanied by the roughly two hundred essays which were now editorial by-products, the pieces of Venetian literary and theatrical history that Ortolani provided as bedrock support for reading the Goldoni corpus. He became a scholarly Pygmalion, dreaming into life the beauty of la Serenissima as he caught glimpses of it along the crumbling *calli* of modern Venice, as he felt history with chauvinistic nostalgia in the walls of the old house at San Toma, which he almost singlehandedly restored as the Casa Goldoni now housing the active Centro Nazionale degli Studi sul Teatro. What he sought in restoring this lost world is perhaps nowhere so poignantly epitomized as in a promise (typically redeemed by the detailed essay which it concludes) to the patient reader of Goldoni's *melodrammi:*

> Rivedrà il sorriso del Goldoni; evocherà mille scene del teatro e della vita di quell'età, buffe, bizzarre, suggestive; gli parrà di assistere a un'ultima mascherata nella fantastica piazza di San Marco; crederà di udire le note improvvise del cembalo e dei violini che scherzano e folleggiano in un tripudio di risa e di trilli, e dileguano malinconicamente nel passato sempre più lontano.[4]

> (One will see again the smile of Goldoni, will invoke again a thousand scenes of the theater and life of that age, absurd, bizarre, suggestive; it will seem that he attends a last [night's] masked festival in the fantastic Piazza San Marco; he will believe he hears the improvised notes of the tambourine and of the violins that joke and crowd in an ecstasy of laughter and ringing, and dissolve into the melancholy of a past always more distant.)

But there is Ortolani the literary critic whose most extended analyses of Goldoni are also gathered in *La riforma del teatro.*[5] The criticism is a coherent corollary to the historical method, and an inevitable development. It has also been as negatively authoritative as the historical aspect of Ortolani's work has been positive. Perhaps it was the attractive force of the latter crossed with the seductive power of consistency wherever it is found, but in fact, twentieth-century Goldoni criticism has been a long commentary refining the position from which Ortolani viewed the playwright and his contemporaries. If one examines the "history" of Goldonian studies essayed by Petronio,[6] it is true that Ortolani's name appears no more often than that of his near contemporary Attilio Momigliano, whose Goldoni essays, also recently collected and reissued under the auspices of the Fondazione Giorgio Cini,[7] now arouse only the ambivalent reactions of almost all turn-of-the-century explication: attractive in direction and yet primitive for want of models. The historical problem is further complicated by the programmatic insistence upon a lyric Goldoni by Croce's heirs, a Goldoni even more insistently abstracted from theatricality than the Goldoni of the historicists.[8] And yet it remains true that Goldoni occupied a relatively small place in the field of vision of Momigliano, Croce, or Apollonio, while his name has been identified with that of Ortolani throughout the twentieth century, his texts read in Ortolani's versions surrounded with Ortolani's commentary and historically placed by Ortolani's authoritative essays on *la civiltà veneziana*. It was inevitable that Ortolani's position should spread by osmosis and should in time become almost immovably bulwarked by repetition. It was also inevitable that, given the historicism of this position with its emphasis upon the importance of the picturesque Venetian middle and working classes, its entrenchment should have been reinforced by Marxist criticism. (I have in mind, of course, primarily Givelegov, but even the wide general influence of Lukacs has encouraged conservatism in respect to Goldoni.)

Ortolani's view is, quite simply, that Goldoni is the master of that realism which his contemporaries believed they saw reflected in his works, looking through the spectacles provided by Goldoni's own occasional insistence. An instructive epitome is the section of a 1940 study of Carlo Gozzi in which Ortolani interposes an internal critical dialogue upon his long summary of Gozzi's own anti-Goldonian dialogue of 1758 entitled *Il teatro comico all'osteria del pellegrin*.

> "Io ti chimerò riformatore, quando avrai riformati i cervelli" (impresa difficile, caro Gozzi, per un misero mortale!) "e ridotti ad aver piacer delle Commedie buone, ordinate, sane" (proprio di questo s'accontentò il Goldoni); "ma sino che cerchi d'appagare solamente il popolo, come fai, con dialoghi sfasciati raccolti per le vie . . . non ripurgandoli . . . dal costume corrotto" (ma ciò è falso, caro conte).[9]

> ("I will call you a reformer when you have reformed their brains" [a difficult task, dear Gozzi, for a miserable mortal!]s "and corrected them to take pleasure in good, ordered, healthy comedies" [exactly by this was Goldoni satisfied]; "but as long as you seek to satisfy only the populace, as you do, with loose dialogues gathered through the streets . . . not correcting them . . . of corrupt manners" [but this is untrue, dear Count].

Ortolani's interlocutor is simply a Gozzian with inverted values. Gozzi finds it debasing, Ortolani bracing, that Goldoni utilizes the actual dialogue and dialect of the streets and canals, but the basic premise is agreed upon: Goldoni's achievement lies fundamentally in presenting a realistic picture of Venetian class structure. Aside from Gozzi's flourishes, neither critic anatomizes the theatrical dialectic of the plays, being sure that they are dealing with social (antisocial, Gozzi would say) mirrors whose play of lights and shadows can be meaningfully evaluated only by subjecting the reflected source to a socioethical examination.

From the beginning Ortolani's position was clearly fixed. The commedia dell'arte represented all that was reprehensible in taste. This was the remora, retarding the early settecento quest for a new drama, because its slapstick lazzi and tired types were playing in an historical Punch-and-Judy booth into which the lifegiving breath of the lagoons and campielli could not penetrate.[10] This rejection of the troupes still shuffling the old scenarii reflected the historicist identification Ortolani was trying to establish between himself and Goldoni's Venice, because it echoed (as Ortolani conscientiously pointed out) not only that explicit stratum of Goldoni's attitudes which the historian was able to recognize, but manifest attacks by Muratori and Chiari upon these same players.[11] Once the premise that the traditional commedianti are the debased coin of the dramatic realm is historically authorized in this fashion, the richer currency of "realism" will be defined and evaluated in direct proportion to its incompatibility with the commedia form. But this particular critical operation presupposes the prior descriptive establishment of that form. And the description which Ortolani inherited was, in Muratori's words, that of a comedy "in cui non troviamo un briciolo di quel Verisimile, che è tanto necessario alla Favola," (in which we do not find a crumb of that verisimilitude, which is so necessary to the Fable) but rather "il far de gli atteggiamenti giocosi, delle beffe, de' travestimenti, e somiglianti buffonerie, Lazzi da loro nominate, le quali non rade volte son fredde, scipite, e troppo note" (the making of grotesque poses, of practical jokes, of disguises, and similar buffooneries, called by them lazzi, which not seldom are cold, insipid, and too familiar), lazzi which incorporate in their dialogue "Equivochi laidi, e poco onesti" (obscene and dishonorable equivocations).[12] The reformed drama which Ortolani will measure against this commedia has predictable outlines: it will be convincingly mimetic of a quotidian behavior in thought and action and portray a group, a class, simple and honest in reaction, whose very commonness will therefore have the charm and sanction of freshness and moral stability. Nostalgic primitivism coupled with the shock of contemporary recognition: this is the impossible dramatic monster which Ortolani supposed had been cultivated in the garden of Goldoni's genius. And it is little wonder that his amiable primitivist delineating the happy natives in the gondole and locande was not recognizable to Goldoni's contemporaries. Primitivism is incompatible by definition with a local present, with the quotidian. For Ortolani's novecento historicist purposes, the words were adequate, but what should a Gozzi make of it were he to hear that only Athens, Paris, and Venice had created comedy: "Ma solo a Venezia, e solo nel Settecento, fu possibile, per merito di Goldoni, la creazione della vera commedia, della commedia pura, senza satira, senza farsa, senza caricatura, senza sottintesi, tutta di riso schietto, che rallegra e rende l'anima più indulgente e più buona" (But only in Venice, and only in the eighteenth century, owing to Goldoni, was the creation of true comedy possible, of a pure comedy, without satire, without farce, without caricature, without double entendres, wholly [made up] of open-hearted laughter which gladdens and renders the soul more indulgent and good).[13]

The paradox permeating Ortolani's Goldonian *criticism*, then, is that his historical mission leads him to accept the eighteenth-century portrait of Goldoni but to invert all the value tones in restoring it. Let us look at a particular extended instance of the effect. In the third volume of his *Lettere scelte*, written at the close of 1751, l'abate Chiari attacked Goldoni's reform as fraudulent, his "realism" as a bad copy of pernicious manners. He cited a catalogue of dubious activities in Goldoni's recent comedies, including those of Bettina in *La putta onorata*, "un fanciulla onorata, che fa tutto il di la civetta dalle finestre, e va prender aria nottetempo col cicisbeo" (an honorable girl, who flirts all day from her window, and goes to take the night air with her cicisbeo).[14] Carlo Gozzi came to the same, if not a harsher, conclusion on the Goldonian "realism" in his *Memorie inutili*: if one could, indeed, find in it "molte immagini comiche, della verità, della naturalezza" (many comic images, of truth, of naturalness), it was nevertheless "la natura copiata materialmente, non imitata; le virtù e i vizi spesso mal collocati, sovente il vizio trionfatore; de lordi plebei equivoci, massime nelle commedie sue nazionali" (nature literally copied, not imitated; the virtues and vices often badly placed, vice often triumphing; of gross, vulgar equivocations, especially in the Venetian comedies).[15] These were just the Venetian plays, of course, which Ortolani found to show Goldoni's talent as a realist best revealed because he found them to echo most explicitly the life of that tribe of noble Venetian savages whose primitive wisdom lay like an indestructible foundation beneath the heaving corruption of the last *carnevali*. For Gozzi, on the other hand, just this carefully elaborated portraiture was the irritant. In *La putta onorata*, for instance, Goldoni had kept within the bounds of his talent, an "abilità indicibile d'innestare tutti i dialoghi in dialetto veneziano, che ricopiava con immensa fatica manuale nelle famiglie del basso popolo, nelle taverne, nelle biscacie, a' tragitti, ne' caffè" (an inexpressible ability to graft [to the fable] all the dialogues in Venetian dialect which he copied down with immense manual effort in the families of the lower class, in taverns, in gambling houses, in the gondola ferries, in the coffee-houses). But Gozzi believed himself to have demonstrated (in the allegorical *Teatro comico*) that "la sua *Putta onorata* non era onorata, e una filza d'altri consimili sbagli suoi; ch'egli aveva adulato il vizio allettando e predicata la virtù seccando" (his *Putta onorata* was not honorable, and a string of his other similar mistakes; that he had adulated alluring vice and proclaimed virtue boring).[16]

Ortolani might be responding to this very passage when he laments how

Altri critici si meravigliavano che il Goldoni creasse le sue commedie ricopiando i discorsi e le scene dalla classe più umili [*sic*] del popolo, portando sulle tavole del teatro quello che ogni giorno si svolge proprio sotto i nostri occhi, nelle nostre case, sulle piazze, senza peripezie, senza filosofie, creando spesso l'azione per virtù del dialogo. Ohimè! non s'avvedevano costoro di muovere all'offesa del realismo goldoniano, di quella ch'è la massima gloria di Carlo Goldoni.[17]

(Other critics marvelled that Goldoni should have created his comedies by copying the discourses and the scenes from the most humble class of people, carrying onto the platform of the theater that which every day unfolds right under our eyes, in our houses, on the piazzas, without peripeties, without philosophies, often creating the action by virtue of the dialogue. Alas, they did not perceive that they displaced, to the detriment of Goldonian realism, that which is the greatest glory of Carlo Goldoni.)

Let us then see how he rescues *La putta onorata* from the obloquy of contemporaries. Immediately Ortolani makes explicit his standpoint, in language suggestive of his historicist's revivifying aim: "Ma tutta la commedia è un inno all'antica Venezia" (But the whole comedy is a hymn to ancient Venezia [*La riforma del teatro*, 143]). It is an imperfect drama, an aesthetic regression in some mechanical sense, with its disguises, preposterous recognitions, with "tutto il ciarpame romanzesco che ammorbava la commedia dell'Arte" (all the romantic junk that corrupted the commedia dell'arte [145]). But it is nonetheless a triumph of Venetian bourgeois virtue eternized: "Il minuetto si rompe, il carnevale sparisce, ma Bettina resta fra le più belle creazioni femminili del Goldoni e del teatro comico" (The minuet is broken, the carnival disappears, but Bettina remains among the loveliest feminine creations of Goldoni and of the comic theater [145]). "È teatro questo?" he rhetorically demands. And as the cultural restorer of a place and time he is justified in answering: "Non so bene: certo è vita" (I don't really know: certainly it is life). Then the process begins, the review of

Bettina's fresh joy in the springtime, of her struggle to maintain virtue against the pressure of a society which would force her to commercialize love, and of her inner chaos of response to Pasqualino. "Per bocca di Bettina," says Ortolani, "[Goldoni] difende le *putte* veneziane dalla nota maldicenza dei forestieri" (through the mouth of Bettina Goldoni defends the Venetian girls from the well-known slander of foreigners [146]). He cites at length a series of episodes, culminating with a paean of praise to the high-water mark of Goldonian realism, the dialogue of the gondoliers. The play may be replete with defects, yet it is "la primavera della commedia popolare del Goldoni" (the springtime of Goldoni's popular comedy) because these structural defects are eccentric to the main design, which is that of "life," not plot. And further, it is a life of bourgeois Venetian benevolence: "È compito della commedia, secondo Molière, 'di rappresentare in generale tutti i difetti degli uomini.' Nella *putta onorata* il Goldoni si propose per la prima volta di commuovere i veneziani con l'esempio d'una passione virtuosa. Bettina è una creatura primitiva, ma sana, ricca di cuore e de buon senso. . . . Questa è arte grande e sublime" (It is the task of comedy, according to Moliere, 'to represent in general all the defects of men.' In the *putta onorata* Goldoni proposes for the first time to touch the hearts of Venetians with an example of virtuous passion. Bettina is a primitive creature, but sound, rich of heart and good sense. . . . This is great and sublime art [154]). If Ortolani has begun his essay by maintaining that *La putta onorata* is life, whether it is drama or not, he closes by affirming its aesthetic greatness. This is not cavalier negligence, I think, but an identification of art with the representation of that quotidian primitivism we first arrived at through watching Ortolani's method and now confront again in his explicit admiration for Goldoni's "creatura primitiva, ma sana, ricca di cuore." The creature is not simply Bettina. As Ortolani describes her, she stands as symbol for the whole art of *La putta onorata*, for the whole of what Ortolani would recognize as the art of Goldoni.

II

Two forces have interacted to press Goldoni's matter into the extraordinarily static descriptive mold which seems the inescapable heritage of mid-century critics. Most obvious is the pressure of Ortolani's determined commitment to a historicist's reconstruction of the social profile of *settecento* Venice, one in which the historical would be not only defined but relived. There is no more obvious source for such ambitions to feed upon than the testimony of drama, that form of chronologically limitless dialogue in which words function to cue into movement multiple modalities of action, among which the verbal is permanent but merely potential catalyst. And then to have the temptation of Goldoni's plenty, too. Second, there has been the paradoxical pressure of Goldoni's self-acknowledged role as a man of the theater, one whose two books of *mondo* and *teatro* were more heavily annotated with the marginalia and underlinings of the actors and the occasional demands of particular theaters than is the case with any major playwright after Molière. These somewhat extraordinary external pressures from the accidents of his theater intensified in his work a "theatricality" of structuring, a persistent thinking in scenic blocks or tailored "character" parts (Medebach, after all, hired the Pisan lawyer to provide services for his *company*). In Goldoni's *capolavori*, of course, the pieces dovetail into a whole transcending the origins and nature of any parts, but the principle of construction made it inordinately easy for the critic (and the historian) to extricate with no immediately apparent damage those scenes and characters in which illusion aims at verisimilitude in mirroring society, the picturesque *campielli* of Ortolani, the Venetian merchant of Fido's Pantalone. And after they had been extracted, their individual bearings sheared away, it was the triumph of Ortolani's powerfully synthesizing imagination to re-fuse them into a convincing new whole as the expression of *settecento* Venice. It was a safe historical maneuver, because the mass of subliterary materials from which he so meticulously worked provided his guidelines for selecting those voices in Goldoni's fictions which spoke most vividly of the city Ortolani had already unearthed, voices which gave a dimension of immediacy to his archaeology.

But it is the nature of theatricality also to perform an antisocial function, and in ignoring this aspect of Goldoni's structure, Ortolani and his successors became violently disoriented in their approach to the dramatist. Because it is a mimetic form, dependent for both its stuff and its effect upon society's recognition of its own image, drama must distinguish itself by denying, even destroying, its daily roots (as must primitivism, to look back toward another formulation of Ortolani's impasse). The lines of survival are drawn simply and clearly in terms of formal control, however much the human "stuff" may overlap: either society imposes its form upon drama to make it at once servilely mimetic and propaedeutic, or drama must impose its laws upon society and make the world not only a theater but theatrical. Insofar as Ortolani was satisfied to play the historian and mine the "stuff" of Venetian society from its dramatic reflection, he was eminently successful; but when he reimposed the merely human rules of that society upon drama, he failed.

Let us now convert this paper currency of high generalization into the commonest of local coin as a beginning toward testing its value. In his *Settecento* (489–93), Ortolani notices with condescension Chiari's autobiographical defense of himself against Goldoni in *Il poeta comico*, a play produced (and set) in Modena when both Chiari and Medebach had deserted the Venetian wars for the provinces.[18] Nothing would seem more engaged, topical, and therefore mimetic and derivative than a minor dramatist's attack upon a great rival, and it is as such an ephemeral attack that Ortolani dismisses the play. But the dramatic form itself induced Chiari to be more sophisticated about the relationships at issue.

Zanetto-Chiari secretly writes a play ("L'irresoluto") in which the central figure is modeled upon his irresolute and dramaphobic patron Fabrizio. From a tangle of confusions and discoveries, Zanetto's entire future, marital and financial, comes to hinge upon Fabrizio's reaction to the play. The actress Fiammetta, fiercely eager to promote Zanetto's hopes, makes a complaint after rehearsal, however, about the protagonist: "Non sono persuasa, / Che in Natura si trovi" (I am not convinced, / That he is found in nature).[19] This shocks Zanetto, of course, because the realism lies just in this figure: "Ghe n'ho el modello in casa / . . . E la Commedia ho fatta su quell' original" (I have his model at home / . . . And I have made the comedy on that original). There is a double irony here which provides a caveat for the critics we have been reviewing. First, Chiari is being characteristically snide about Goldoni's realistic sources for dialect and milieu, although the claimant to verisimilitude is his own dramatic avatar. But the second irony emerges only later when Fabrizio attends the comedy, recognizes himself, and is enthusiastic in his reactions:

> L'Irresoluto sono io.
> Certo che mi ci ha posto; ma mi fa far figura.
> Oh se veduto aveste, siccome vidi anch'io,
> Che stupendo carattere dipinge in scena il mio!
> Generoso, benefico, con tutti, a tutte l'ore,
> De Poeti, e Filosofi, amico e prottettore.
> Che pensa, e non resolve, che cangia di presenza:
> Ma per grandezza ei pensa; e cangia per prudenza.

> (4.3; p. 55)

> (I am the Irresolute.
> Certainly he has placed me here; but he makes me look good.
> Oh, if you had seen, as I saw.
> How stupendous a character mine is as he paints it on stage!
> Generous, beneficent with all, at all hours.

Friend and protector of poets and philosophers.
One who thinks, and does not resolve; who changes aspect;
But who thinks through greatness and changes through prudence)

For now we realize that Fiammetta was right, that the characterization was not verisimilar; it was, rather, a theatrical attack upon the limits of the "imitated." The model who sat for the portrait finds himself remodeled in his own reflected, slightly deflected, image. The concept of "realism" has itself become an illusion in a double sense: Once, as the stuff of that topical mimesis which draws into the play dozens of allusions to Goldoni's shibboleths, to the recent *Istruzioni per il teatro comico* attacking Chiari's reforms, to that contemporary Modena in which interwoven plays are staged by Zanetto and Chiari. And again, "realism" proves illusion since it is that aesthetic aim which the circular relation of Fabrizio to the theater demonstrates to be unattainable. It should be clear in even such a modest case as *Il poeta comico* that the topical atoms of material borrowed from society retain their independent historical validity while losing all of that interpretive significance now passed on to the theatrical form which, in rearranging them, gives a new value to each. And we have circled back to the reverse of the historian's prerogative: he selects monads of aesthetic experience to piece out a social form, while the artist selects monads of social experience to piece out a supra- and (the term should be clearer now) antisocial form.

III

To suggest that a rather casual effort by Chiari has been even more casually read is obviously a different matter than attempting to cast doubt on the relevance of "realism" for the theater of Goldoni. In the immense canon of this writer even the most programmatic critics have found plays too obviously flagrant in passing beyond the limits of realism to be conveyed into categorical sanctuaries. I suppose one might with little fear of contest cite as examples *Il Servitore di due padroni* at the end of Goldoni's range nearest the *commedia improvvisa* and *Il bugiardo* with its obsessed Lelio at that closest to psychological portraiture. But the middle plays, the *inni veneziani*, have seemed safe ground for the historicists, the chronologically central member of this group being *La putta onorata*.

As in dealing with Chiari's *Il poeta comico*, the first formal observation to make is that *La putta onorata* embodies itself as a part of the action. Goldoni's play is overtly about the Bettina who—in spite of the passionate approaches of her *prottettore*, old Pantalone, of the philandering marchese Ottavio, of her inamorato Pasqualino—manages to remain *onorata*: it is, at one level, a socially instructive comedy. And within the action, when the marchesa Beatrice is directing Bettina out of the maze of masculine intrigues, the instrument of liberation is itself attendance at such a comedy. "Oh," cries Bettina, "la me perdona, no ghe son mai stada. Le pute no le va a la comedia" (Pardon me, I've never been there. Girls don't go to the comedy).[20] But Beatrice hastens to clarify that she means a Goldonian comedy of reform: "Le putte non devono andare alle commedie scandalose; ma alle buone commedie, oneste e castigate, vi possono, anzi vi devono andare; e se verrete meco sentirete una certa commedia che forse vi aporterà del profitto" (Girls ought not go to scandalous comedies; but they can go to good, honest, and chaste comedies, in fact, they should; and if you'll come with me you will hear a certain comedy that perhaps will bring you some profit). Persuaded, Bettina is taken to a theater-within-the-theater under cover of a *carnevale* mask, even as so many ladies in Goldoni's first-night *carnevale* audience had been brought to see her performance. Her double role as actress in and spectator attending an "honest" Venetian comedy, thus fusing inner and enveloping audiences, is so developed that it recalls the technique of Bernini's spectacular mirror play of a century before, because Goldoni's spectators hear Bettina and the others within the "inner" theater clap and shout their approval of the other (or is it, perhaps, the same?) play. But where Bernini's effort aimed at glorifying his mechanical artifice, Goldoni's theatrical mirror seems to reflect a more lambent design. Even while one audience listens to the other applaud, the actor-gondoliers who await their clients outside Bettina's theater preen themselves on the weight of their critical judgments in society at large: "Co la [commedia] piase ai barcarioi, la sarà bona. Nualtri semo queli che fa la fortuna dei comedianti" (When the comedy pleases the gondoliers, it will be a good one. We are those who make the fortune of the players [3.14]). But these same gondoliers have just admitted that their famous dialect fliting over traffic rights on the canals was predicated upon the value of bluff, of the face-saving surface which is flimsily adjusted to real attitudes: "Bisogna de la volte criar per reputazion, siben che no se ghe n'ha vogia" (It's necessary sometimes to shout for reputation's sake, although one has no desire to [3.12]). When Bettina does draw the unexpected profit of escaping Ottavio's bullies by redisguising herself in the theater, it seems difficult to miss the ironic analogy suggested by a Goldoni who points out his own reputation as a didactic reformer. The profit lies in disguising one's business in the theater, as in the gondola, "per reputazion." And it is this mocking dialectic between assertions and actions which defines the form and function of *La putta onorata*.

If a chauvinistic sentimentality betrays us into endorsing the local-color ritual of the gondoliers' quarrel over professional honor, their later revelation that this is empty gesturing undercuts the endorsement. And if their own explicit endorsement of the "buone commedie, oneste e castigate" within *La putta onorata* is undercut by our distrust of their superficial conception of honor as well as by the ironic action which bears out the promise of profit offered Bettina, the skepticism should lend a color of caution to our understanding of that reformed, reforming comedy, *La putta onorata* itself. And since, from the title to the *sonetto* in epilogue, the ordering assertion has been the primacy of *onore*, our most instructive test should be to set this word against the action which glosses its content.

The first version is broadly and obviously ironic, as the play opens upon Ottavio's wife badgering him unsuccessfully to accompany her to a *conversazione*. It is not the lack of his company that she regrets, but the loss of reputation which will accompany her in his absence: "È nota la mia prudenza . . . si sa la mia delicatezza . . . son una donna d'onore" (My prudence is well-known . . . my delicacy is known . . . I am a lady of honor [1.1]). We are unable to evaluate with certainty the tone of the following scenes, in which we hear the marchese's servant-confidant tell him upon Beatrice's exit that his lust for Bettina is vain "perche l'e una puta troppo da ben" (because she is too good a girl [1.3]). This is an opinion reflected in her own first appearance with the whining inamorato Pasqualino, who is denied entrance to her house because "le pute da ben no le receve in casa i morosi" (good girls don't receive suitors at home); because, being "una puta da ben, onorata," asserts Bettina, "Ve vogio ben . . . ma me preme la mia reputazion sora tuto" (I love you . . . but I prize my reputation above all [1.6]). Pasqualino is privately delighted: "Brava, cussì me piase. Se vede che la xe una puta ben. Ho faro per provarla. . . . So anca mi come che la va co le pute, e so che quando le averze la porta, la reputazion facilmente la va drente e fuora" (Brava, this pleases me. One sees that she is a good girl. I did it to test her. . . . I know too how it goes with the girls, and I know that when she opens the door, reputation easily flies in and out [1.7]). But our doubts are scarcely set at rest by this ambiguous moral comfort drawn from Bettina's behavior by a bumptious misfit who functions as butt for the drama's sadistic vein.

With the first interview between the aging, shrewd, and lusting Pantalone (which is not to deny that he is also benevolent) and his protégée Bettina, the idea of *onore* takes on another ambiguity. Bettina's sister, the money-eyed Catte, had already (1.7) suggested that marriage was a matter of snatching the main chance, and Bettina—then scornful—now admits as much. If Pantalone assures her that "una puta onorata pol esser sposada da chi se sia" (an honorable girl can marry whomever she wants), Bettina ruefully points out to him that such idealism is a function of his age, an anachronism not constructed on contemporary lines: "Me recordo che . . . ai so ziorni se stimava più una puta da ben, che una puta rica. . . . Ma adesso se vede tuto el contrario. Una povera puta da ben, anca che la sia bela, nissun la varda" (I remember that . . . in your days a good girl was valued more than a rich one. . . . But now one sees the complete contrary. A poor honest girl, even if she is beautiful, no one looks at her [1.10]). Pantalone is struck so remorseful over his own lust by her steadfast and yet incisive morality that he renounces his ungainly passion. Bettina's conviction that honor is a word, a trim reckoning in a world turned commercial, seems countered by this reassuring conduct on Pantalone's part until we discover that his preservation of her virtue is mere prelude to possession, a selfish fattening of the sacrificial babe. With all women, he asserts, conquest is a matter of the right time . . . and price. "A le pute bisogna farghe dei regali" (You have to give girls gifts), Catte reminds him, and Pantalone, left to contemplation, admits that

> Pur troppo la xe la verità. A sto mondo tuti opera per interesse, e le done principalmente le xe pezo de la sansughe. . . . Me spendo volentiera, acioché Bettina se conserva una bona puta, e co la speranze che un zorno la me diga de sì. Chi sa? Le done le gh'ha certi momenti, certi ponti de stela, che no por dir de no, anca che le bogia. (2.18)[21]

> (Unfortunately she is right. In this world everything works by interest, and especially women—they are the worst of bloodsuckers. . . . I spend gladly, so that Bettina saves herself as a good girl, and with the hope that one day she will say yes to me. Who knows? Women have certain moments, certain crossings of their stars, so that they cannot say no, even should they wish.)

Both champions of *onore* in woman, then, Bettina and her protector, see that it is a value intimately related in the modern world to money. While Pantalone publicly pretends that honor is above price, yet privately admits that it can be bought, Bettina immediately admits general corruptibility, but denies that it applies in her particular case. There is a corrective warning scene, however, when Ottavio invades her privacy and is rebuffed by an angry lecture on how he, like all foreigners, mistakenly expects Venetian women to be easy marks, a lecture which she concludes with a popular poem:

Le pute veneziane xe un tesoro,
Che no se acquista cussi facilmente,
Perché le xe onorate come l'oro . . .

(1.13)

(Venetian girls are a treasure,
Which is not gotten so easily,
Because they are honored like gold.)

"Come l'oro": that is precisely the version of honor in Venice articulated by Bettina, by Pantalone, by Catte. It is the assumption motivating the philandering Ottavio. And when Ottavio asks Pasqualino in regard to Bettina, "È giovine da bene e onorata?" Pasqualino replies with an innocent but ironically loaded cliche: "Come l'oro" (1.17).

Even the conduct of Pasqualino himself comes to reinforce the insistence that honor is a commodity in Venice when his supposed father, Menego, opens his eyes to Ottavio's intention of cornering Bettina by marrying her to Pasqualino and giving him employment and a dowry. Pasqualino, after all, is as interested in avoiding the rigors of the oar as he is in Bettina. The opportunity is too good, and while admitting that he understands what the older man means in speaking of "dolor de testa e de la reputazion," (pain of head and of reputation), he prefers to believe that the wife will somehow turn out less vulnerable to temptation than he is showing himself to be: "Mi digo che una mugier onorata pol star anca in mezo d'una armada" (I say that an honorable wife is able to stand [fast] even in the middle of an army [1.18]).

Pasqualino's aphoristic hope closes act 1 by casting a climactic doubt across that honor which is the theme of so many tongues. Problem play or satire? we have been encouraged to ask. But from this point onward the doubts are dissolved as the form progressively reveals itself to be farce.

Lelio, a Plautine prodigal believed on all hands to be son to Pantalone, returns to Venice. Ottavio recognizes him as a likely *sicario* and hires him to beat Pantalone, now recognized as rival for Bettina. Lelio finds his intended victim, feels moved by his age ("Povero vecchio, mi fa compassione. . . . Se lo bastono così all'improvviso, ho paura che caschi morto" [Poor old man, he makes me sorry. . . . If I beat him so suddenly, I'm afraid he may fall dead]), and so approaches him politely—with the news of his duty. Seeing Lelio so outrageously genteel in his violence, Pantalone suggests that a small bribe and a *buon viaggio* might be sufficient intercourse. "Oh, questo poi no; son un uomo d'onore. Ho promesso, voglio mantener la parola; ma senta, io non intendo di volerle romper l'ossa. Quattro solo bastonate; vossignoria caschi in terra, ed io me ne vado" (Oh, this, then, no; I am a man of honor. I have promised, I want to keep my word; but listen, I don't intend [to want] to break your bones. Just four blows; your excellence falls down, and I go away [2.8]).

At the beginning of act 3 we meet the marchesa Beatrice with a usurer, pawning her jewels to pay gambling debts: "Mio marito non me li vuol dare; ed io, che sono una dama d'onore, voglio in ogni forma pagare" (My husband doesn't want to give it to me; and I, who am a lady of honor, want in every way to pay [3.1]). Ottavio surprises her in the arrangements, discovers all, and berates her on the extravagance of paying usury, but Beatrice with a stiff pride which, again, can only be called outrageous, looks down her nose with firm conviction at such irrelevant reprimands: "Quando la cosa è fatta, è fatta. La riputazione vuole che io paghi" (When the thing's done, it's done. Reputation demands that I pay [3.2]). In short, there is honor among thieves—rambling, gambling men and women whose means of support is corruption and vice. And *onore* for these types with their context of farcical situations and attitudinizings is just what it has been for Bettina, Pantalone, and the others: *reputazione*. In these incidents the relation between action and assertion is no longer ambiguous; it is a flat contradiction. We have been moving gradually from the shades of realistic complexity toward the simplicity of farce. But that simplicity is itself made complex by being set in formal dialectic with the "realism" (a word that seems safe enough to use without courting misinterpretation by this stage in the argument). And having reached one pole, Goldoni now begins to move its effects back to overlay the other as the "realistic" plot of Bettina's dilemma as "una putta onorata" reemerges.

Pasqualino surprises Bettina alone in her bedroom, at which she alternately tries to drive him out and to make him understand that he can't elope with her to Ottavio's palace, both for the same reason: "No vogio perder per causa vostra la mia reputazion" (I don't want to lose my reputation because of you [2.10]). Then suddenly the worst happens when Menego finds them together in these compromising circumstances and angrily questions his craven son while Bettina shouts "son una puta da ben e onorata" and Pasqualino himself skulks off crying like a child. Under the skeptical cross-fire of Menego's uncomplimentary similes, Bettina can only keep hurling back the assertion ("son una puta onorata . . . cerchemo onoraramente de maridarse . . . avè da far con una puta da ben" [I'm an honorable girl . . . we tried to marry honorably . . . you are dealing with a good girl]) and watering it with tears. When assertion and action seem in conflict, the unreason of a world in which surface is substance becomes most apparent. Bettina's weeping for reputation redirects Menego's reactions from head to heart: "Poverazza! Adesso adesso pianzo anca mi" (Poor thing! Now I'm crying too). But as the tears reach this flood stage, the heart itself is revealed in a light of satire rather than sentimentalism, for Menego admits, in an inevitable nautical metaphor, that he, too, is falling in love with Bettina (2.12). And this slapstick, satiric commentary upon the insubstantiality of honor—or of any other principle but appetite and self-seeking—is absorbed into the absurdity of farce when we recall that it has rounded out a ridiculously mechanical and improbable circular pattern: as before, the true if not yet recognized father-and-son pair of Pantalone and Pasqualino have been rivals for Bettina's love, now the false but supposed true father-and-son pair of Menego and Pasqualino are in rivalry.

Farce winds to a high pitch as Bettina, kidnapped, is discovered in Ottavio's house by Beatrice. "Ghe zuro," pleads Bettina, "da puta da ben" (I swear . . . as a good girl) and proceeds to explain all. Beatrice believes her, and the "putta onorata" is saved by the unfailing Renaissance mechanism of an exchange of wife and mistress in the darkened bedroom where Ottavio appears to claim his victim—but it is a creaking old mechanism heightened in absurdity by the long trialogue during which Beatrice whispers to Bettina that which Bettina passes on to the panting Ottavio. As a result, Bettina escapes and goes to the theater with the marchesa, who would like to deliver her generously into the hands of Pasqualino. But now Bettina refuses to go with him because she remembers as always that "son una puta onorata." This time the absurdity of her moral pose is commented upon from the stage. Why, asks the marchesa, should honor be involved? Because, Bettina cautiously advises, "lu me vol ben a mi; mi ghe vôi ben a elo, no so cossa che possa succeder" (he loves me, I love him; I don't know what may happen). "Siete troppo rigorosa" (you're too rigorous), suggests Beatrice. "Son una putta onorata," responds Bettina for the hundredth time. "Costei è rara" (those are rare), concludes Beatrice, with a simile which reduces the attitudinizing to the impossible by way of the unsavory proverb, "come la mosca bianca" (like the white fly [3.18]). It is at this moment that Ottavio's bullies unwittingly accomplish what Beatrice cannot, and hand Bettina over to Pasqualino in their confusion. But even now, she cannot accept destiny's delights. Listening to Pasqualino bemoan her supposed kidnapping, she being yet disguised (and by this time the familiar inamorato type has been debased as a fool, parasite, and coward), Bettina can only weep beneath her mask and stand upon a punctilio yet more absurdly comic in its irrelevance than her last: "Demascherarme? No certo. Do morosi de note soli?" (Unmask myself? No, certainly. Two lovers alone at night? [3.20]). Meanwhile, Ottavio has brought home his wife, thinking her to be Bettina, and is willing to defend her "reputation" so violently as to destroy meaning altogether. With Swiftian calm he addresses his veiled proposal to the disguised woman: "Via, la mia cara Bettina . . .

conosco la vostra modestia; mi è nota la vostra onoratezza. So che sdegnate di amoreggiare un ammogliato. . . . Non dubitate. . . . Mia moglie ha una certa imperfezione, per cui morirà quanto prima" (Go on, my dear Bettina . . . I know your modesty; I know very well your honorableness. I know your scorn of making love to a married man. . . . Don't doubt though. . . . My wife has a certain imperfection, through which she will die very, very soon). This is too much for Beatrice, who throws off her mask and attacks Ottavio bitterly: "Uomo perfido. . . . Desiderar la morte di vostra moglie, e forse procurarla per non avere chi vi rimproveri d'un amor disonesto" (Perfidious man. . . . To desire the death of your wife, and perhaps procure it in order not to have someone around who may reproach you for a dishonest love).

Ottavio's conception of honor, like Bettina's own, is wholly verbal: he has gone to this unthinkable extreme so that neither may hear the union spoken of as "disonesto." As I suggested, farce is doubling back upon realism, and the meeting point here makes the farce as fierce as that of Marlowe's *Jew of Malta*. But the more "real," because more socially oriented, psychologism simultaneously begins to shift the direction back to order and control. Ottavio is stunned by Beatrice's accusation, and the harmonious dénouement begins with his immediate repentance. But it is a repentance which recalls all which we have heard about the Venetian commerce in honor. "Veramente io son un gran pazzo; far tanti stenti per una donna" (Truly, I'm a great madman; to make such efforts for a woman), he realizes. Then the qualifying proviso brings us full circle: "in tempo che le donne son così a buon mercato" (at a time when women are so cheap [3.25]).

Immediately afterward, the marchesa leads Bettina once again into the darkened room and—unknown to either of the inamorati—brings in Pasqualino for a last test. While Pasqualino gropes and complains about a Bettina who would not let him enter her house "per paura de perder la reputazion" (for fear of losing her reputation), Bettina controls her impulses until she again bursts into the familiar tears. He hears, grasps her, and the marchesa enters with lights. Discovering her, Pasqualino cries out to Bettina pleadingly, "Mo perché no parlar?" (Why don't you speak?) and receives the answer which brings the farce of puritan pretense to a crescendo. The words are now inevitable as she finally breaks silence: "Perche son una puta onorata" (Because I'm an honorable girl). "Veramente ora conosco che siete tale" (Truly, now I know you are such a one), admits the marchesa, but at this very moment of convinced capitulation to an inhumanly pure virtue, she and we are disillusioned by an echo of the commercialized honor noticed early in the play. Bettina does not embrace Pasqualino. Instead she fends him off with a warning query about the dowry that now seems lost: "Senza dota, come faremo?" (Without a dowry, what will we do?). In another moment all is well: the others enter, the tangled identities are sorted out, the pairings made, the dowry promised. Bettina swoons and is revived by a suggestively symbolic act when the gay Lelio snips some hair from Pasqualino and singes it under her nose, explaining what *he* thinks of all puritan pretensions: "L'odor de l'omo fa revegnir la donna" (The smell of a man makes a woman come to). And when Pasqualino swears that Bettina is sufficient nourishment for his life, Lelio adds his skepticism about romance: "Da qui a una settimana non direte così" (A week from now you won't say so [3.26–30]).

This is not to survey the whole tapestry of interweaving action and linguistic structures which brings into relief the moods of *La putta onorata*, of course. I have said nothing, for instance, of the exaggerated reactions, pro and con, of the two younger men toward the gondola, serving as a *reductio ad absurdum* of the traditional Renaissance insistence upon the natural gravitational force of an inherent, blooded gentility. I hope I have said enough, however, to demonstrate that neither Gozzi nor Ortolani saw the point of *La putta onorata* to be precisely similar to that of *L'amore delle tre melarance*: form is being used to expose not only the mechanisms of jerry-built theatrical romances, but the sentiments which these mechanisms had incorporated as an essential part of their tired predictability and falseness. When the theater laughs so consciously at its own reforming pretensions, as in the escape of Bettina and Beatrice from the theater-within-the-theater, it is making it as impossible to take seriously the gaily ridiculous repetition of "son una puta onorata" throughout the play as do the sharply acrid comments on love and honor made by Lelio at the close.

But we cannot stop here, I think, and leave Goldoni's reputed hymn to a lyric Venetian primitivism simply revaluated as a satire. There is something else which has been missed because we have spoken so consistently of Goldoni's realism, something which is less an attitude than an entire dimension of his best drama—ultimately, perhaps, its most important, most dramatic dimension. I have mentioned a farcical pole toward which *La putta onorata* gravitates after act 1 and have suggested that it sometimes draws out a sadistic brutality in its fun. Let us recall now that even in *La putta onorata* there is one mask from the commedia dell'arte repertoire untouched by psychological refinement. That is Arlecchino, the irresponsible master of misrule who leaps disruptively upon the stage from a dark, long history as a daemonic ritual figure. His powers are so diminished that he seems a mere supernumerary when we think back to his genius in *Il Servitore di due padroni*. But, indeed, that makes the test more revealing, because even here where he has no plot role, Arlecchino serves a significant theatrical function. He masquerades as the husband of Catte, the host of Bettina. But he is really *appetite*, the naked force which all the others mask. The first time we see him he comes in to scoff at Bettina for refusing gifts from Ottavio, meanwhile eating and drinking all which has been brought in homage to her by the would-be seducer. He will hear nothing of *onore*: "Verdè se sì mata! Recusar el caffè, recusar i regali" (See the mad woman! To refuse coffee, refuse gifts [1.15]). The other time he returns home to learn of the secret betrothal of Bettina and Pasqualino under the direction of Catte and shouts joyously for a party: "Se magna?" (One eats?). But, alas, there can be no celebration while all must be kept in secrecy, and Arlecchino so warned simply bursts toward the door screaming with outrage: no food, no secrecy. Bettina pleads with him to use his good judgment, but Arlecchino has Arlecchino's age-old answer: "Co no se magna, no gh'è giudizio che tegna" (When one doesn't eat, one has no judgment). Nothing can silence him—except Pasqualino's last ducat. With that bribe, he leaves as gaily as he has come: "Zitto, zitto, zitto. Se paron, comodeve, e fe pulito" (Shut up, shut up, shut up. Esteemed patron, accommodate yourself, and [you are] well conned [2.15]). And with this ironic gibe, he turns over his house—and society—to Pasqualino and the rest.

This touch of Arlecchino helps define the function of the farce, to see how Goldoni goes beyond satire. His dramas stand above those of his contemporaries because they are *theatrical* in the sense that they never allow the theater to remain merely three-dimensional: inevitably they import a psychic disorientation which peers around the edges, steps for a moment to the center of the stage, disappears to arrive again in new guise. Now it is character, now it is action, but always it is contradiction. And then, too (and we may now be reminded of our earlier purely theoretical hypothesis on the function of theater), Goldoni's plays refuse to allow life to remain merely three-dimensional because the theatricality of the theater is always explicitly tending to impinge upon the "realism" of the stage and to equate for the audience Goldoni's two books in which he read the secret of chaos, of that energy for disorder which dissolves the protocol of his *teatro e mondo*.

Society for Goldoni is an order, a rhythm, which tries to impose itself upon the chaotic energies of things. But as the older *maschere* had developed, so the new ones of Goldoni developed, into surrealistic images of the hyperbolic, improbable nature of man. It is indeed paradoxical that Goldoni's realism should have been defined in contradistinction to the techniques of the commedia dell'arte by his most admiring critics, for nowhere has the daemonic origin of Arlecchino been more starkly apparent than against the backdrop of Goldoni's "real" Venice.

Bettina, Arlecchino—these set in conjunction with the gondolieri in a Venice staged before Venetians comprised one mode of simultaneously displaying and denying social comedy, a genre we traditionally label the comedy of manners.

Franco Fido, the most perceptive of contemporary *Goldonisti*, through a brilliant equation of gambling and theatricality both in the *Mémoires* and in a persistent strain of scenes and metaphors in the plays, has shown the interaction of *teatro e mondo* at the edges of another dramatic extremism, one different from farce or daemonism, but closely analogous. Fido defines it as the necessity of domesticating "the symptoms of a mental disorder,"[22] that is, the socializing of *"amour propre"* as an element of "game" or "play." It is in his play about plays that Goldoni may have most quietly exhibited the implications which are always present when the comic art wryly confronts its own high seriousness.

IV

"Revenons à moi, car je suis le héros de la pièce." Here, a few paragraphs from the beginning of his *Mémoires*, we have Goldoni's epigraph for the Sternian autobiography and for *Il teatro comico* and its tradition. The *Mémoires* are, like those of Casanova and Tristram Shandy, a true cock-and-bull story, a transparently conventional series of fictions substituting for life so dramatically that they permanently suspend belief in anything undramatic, quotidian: the world becomes a theater only because at its center stands this winking, self-lauding, and self-deprecating raconteur and redirector of the nature of things, the equivocator who lies like truth, the hero of the piece, the actor as author.

Il teatro comico is a central document in Goldoni's early triumph with Medebach's company at the Teatro Sant'Angelo in Venice. An item in Goldoni's critical war with the abbot Pietro Chiari, it was rationalized by Goldoni in 1751 as a preface to his reformation of the Italian stage. But to accept this "background" as the basic function of *Il teatro comico* is to miss the dynamics of the original performance, which had to affect the Venetian audience and so complicate the literal presentation of the "new" comic theory of the Goldonian stage by Orazio, the first *amoroso* and director of the company. Horatian moderation, as Orazio sees it, has displaced the rigidities of Aristotelianism and managed to correct (even while temporarily incorporating) the very different conventional rigidities of the commedia dell'arte masks. This is true of the plot action at story level, but that tells us nothing of the real play, the play as acted by a vastly popular troupe before an audience familiar with its repertoire and with its "author," Carlo Goldoni.

Let us remember that Girolamo Medebach, head of the troupe, both plays himself and speaks for Goldoni in what is a "rehearsal" play: the actors have come together to rehearse their author's new play, are interrupted by a poetaster who induces them to try out his flagrantly old-fashioned play also, and the action closes when all go off to dine at the director's expense. The first action is the arrival of the prima donna Placida, who gets in a huff about the lesser actors not having arrived. She is wheedled and soothed into complaisance by Medebach, who gives a running side commentary upon the ease with which he can handle silly actresses. When one recalls that Placida was played by Medebach's wife, it seems certain that the audience would have seen the discussion of old versus new drama as a rather superficial vehicle for the actual drama of the good-natured marital battle of the sexes. This sort of comic effect is doubled when Vittoria Falchi is given the part of the pretentious, old-fashioned diva Eleanora, who is humiliated as she gradually is divested of silly airs of superiority by the troupe members, since it is her husband Francesco Falchi (in the role of *amoroso* Eugenio) who concludes her humbling with the epithet "virtuosa ridicola."

The most significant instance of this inner playing, however, is one which redimensions as problematic the explicit propaganda for a "new" drama being offered by the director Medebach / Orazio. In the 1751 Bettinelli edition of Goldoni's works there is a crucial stage direction which was eliminated a decade later in the Pasquali edition, when *Il teatro comico* had become merely an historical document for the embattled Goldoni, about to leave Venice forever, his "reform" apparently having failed. Viewed as an Horatian critical document rther than as that dramatic action Goldoni originally conceived, *Il teatro comico* is a theatrical cadaver from which the lifeblood has been drained. But the Bettinelli edition, published while the play was fresh on the boards, tells us that "*Pantalone Dottore Brighella Arlecchino*" all play "prima senza Maschera e poi colla Maschera" (first without mask and then with mask).[23] How many layers of complication did such staging offer the mid-eighteenth-century theatergoers when they saw Antonio Mattiuzzi Collalto enter without the characteristic mask and "en habit bourgeois,"[24] to discuss with Medebach / Orazio the dangers and difficulties of playing Pantalone in works by the company's new author Goldoni? Many knew that Cesare D'Arbes, the group's master comic, had triumphed as Pantalone without the mask in *I due gemelli veneziani* numerous times during the 1748–49 seasons, but also that D'Arbes had been a very successful masked Pantalone for years before that. And they also knew that the recently departed D'Arbes had been replaced by another popular Pantalone of reputation among the traveling companies, in which, Goldoni said, "il avoit de bonnes dispositions avec son masque, et étoit encore meilleur à visage découvert" (*Mémoires*, 267). The maskless play *I due gemelli veneziani* was to become so thoroughly identified with Collalto that it would cause a rupture betweem himself and Goldoni and lead Collalto to elaborate a new play in France, *Les trois Jumeaux*. The question which the troupe appears to be confronting during the "rehearsal" which is *Il teatro comico*—the possibility of unmasked, written comedies replacing the improvisations and masks of the traditional commedia dell'arte—had been settled long before. Collalto and the others are replaying an historical moment, with Collalto playing the role of the D'Arbes he had succeeded as the troupe's Pantalone, the D'Arbes who had strongly resisted Goldoni's efforts to unmask the players. And D'Arbes, as acted by his successor in *Il teatro comico*, is a foolish and fearful old-timer out of step with the recent innovations. *Comédie à clef*, satire, and the "smug" triumph of Goldoni are all aspects of *Il teatro comico*. But their interaction and final significance is complicated by the fact that the actors present a masked inner play, a commedia dell'arte script written by the foolish poetaster Lelio, who must be seen as a mocking self-satire by Goldoni.

Carlo Goldoni knew that the dramatic transaction goes much deeper than the "realism" he was espousing, also quite seriously. In *Il teatro comico* he sets knowledge into action. The players playing themselves without masks are no less masked by their theatrical roles than when they play under the literal commedia masks. The actor is always vehicle of a double awareness, a "metaphor" as Ortega y Gasset so happily described him in his *Idea del teatro*, both himself and his role. But the author, too, is double. He is the magical manipulator who makes a new reality with his art of illusion, but also the poor ape of God whose illusion is so transparent as to mock itself. As the former, Goldoni is that victorious innovator for whom Orazio speaks and whom the players fear; as the latter, he is poor Lelio whose efforts the actors mock.

In his little play Goldoni has shown the preposterous unreality of realism to be akin to the transparent unreality of the original commedia dell'arte conventions before a rococo Harlequin went to Persia and the moon on the Parisian stage. But he is further showing through his action the power of both over a spectator who wants to share the double life of the actor and author in the theater, to be both himself and the other role with whom he and the actor alike share vicarious union. And the author-actor stands at the center of the enterprise: "Je suis le héros de la pièce," Goldoni can say of *Il teatro comico*, placing himself within the tradition of mirrored corridors in which art and reality continually reflect one another. It is the tradition in which the commedia dell'arte was born out of such successes as Beolco's re-creation of himself as Ruzante. And it is the tradition which Goldoni's great seventeenth-century predecessor Gian Lorenzo Bernini continued in making not only the author-director but the stage machinery itself protagonists in the metaphysical search which is comedy. Goldoni would have endorsed the truth Bernini articulated so succinctly: "Infatt dov'è naturalezza è artifitio" (In fact, where there is naturalness there is artifice). It is the first rule of the comic theater.

Notes

1. LIVES OF THE DAEMON PLAYERS

1. Richard Findlater, *Joe Grimaldi: His Life and Theatre*, 2d ed. (Cambridge, 1978), 9. All information on Grimaldi's career, except where otherwise noted, is from Findlater, cited hereafter by page number in the text.

2. M. Willson Disher, *Clowns and Pantomimes* (London, 1925), 13–14.

3. George Lupino, cited in Findlater, *Grimaldi*, 36.

4. Findlater, *Grimaldi*, 30–31; Charles Dickens, *Memoirs of Joseph Grimaldi*, ed. Richard Findlater (1838; New York, 1968), 42–43.

5. Cited in Findlater, *Grimaldi*, 43.

6. *Memoirs*, 31–32.

7. *Memoirs*, p. 59.

8. Findlater offers as epigraph to another chapter a citation from Kierkegaard that is equally apt here: "The more one suffers, the more . . . one has a sense for the comic. It is only by the deepest suffering that one acquires . . . an authority which by one word transforms as by magic the reasonable creature into a caricature" (86).

9. Cf. *Memoirs*, 185–86.

10. R. H. Horne, quoted in Findlater, *Grimaldi*, 167.

11. For example, Grimaldi reports repeated injurious falls through broken stage traps in *Memoirs*, 192–93; cf. 211–12, 220–21, 223, 252–53, 255–59.

12. The Grimaldi family heritage is Ibsenite in its dramatic concinnity. Joe's son, well on his way to becoming his father's successor, himself possibly syphilitic, became alcoholic and psychotic, several times being placed under medical surveillance until his death at age thirty. But some weeks before that event actually occurred, his death too was prematurely announced in a lurid newspaper account (Findlater, *Grimaldi*, 218–19).

13. Ibid., 176, cited from Jerrold's life of Cruikshank as an anecdote from the pre-Dickensian version of the *Memoirs*.

14. This is a consistent thread in Findlater's account of Grimaldi. Cf. pp. 64–65, 100, 116, et passim.

15. Disher, *Clowns and Pantomimes*, 85–89.

16. Cf. David Mayer III, *Harlequin in His Element: The English Pantomime, 1806–1836* (Cambridge, Mass., 1969), 60, 262.

17. Disher, *Clowns and Pantomimes*, 104. One should remember that Harlequin in the pantomimes traditionally enacted resurrections as well as transformations with his magic bat: see Mayer, *Harlequin in his Element*, 39 et passim.

18. Cf. *Memoirs*, 175-77.

19. On *Mother Goose* cf. Findlater, *Grimaldi*, 110-22 and *The Reminiscences of Thomas Dibdin* (London, 1827), 1: 396-401.

20. Louis Luigi Riccoboni, *Histoire du Theatre Italien* (Paris, 1728), 55-56; cf. 50-56.

21. This and all information on Beolco's career, except where otherwise noted, is from the introduction and notes to Ruzante, *Teatro*, ed. Ludovico Zorzi (Turin, 1967), hereafter cited as Zorzi: cf. p. ix. All citations of Ruzante's work are from this monumental edition, cited by page number in the text. The birth date (traditionally believed to be 1500) was revised in Paolo Sambin, "Nuove archivistiche per Angelo Beolco e Alvise Cornaro," *Italia medioevale e umanistica* 9 (1966): 266.

22. K. M. Lea, *Italian Popular Comedy* (Oxford, 1934), 1: 231 ff.; Vito Pandolfi, *La commedia dell'arte* (Florence, 1957-61), 1: 24 ff.; Mario Baratto, *Tre saggi sul teatro: Ruzante, Aretino, Goldoni* (Venice, 1964), 27-28.

23. The name changes from time to time in the plays, but the character remains constant even as it develops in maturity. And the name "Ruzante" displaces Beolco in the correspondence and in private written allusions to the author / actor. Ruzante is a not uncommon name in the Veneto at the time, and a definite peasant model for Beolco's remolding has even been suggested (Zorzi, xxiii). However, in *L'Anconitana* Ruzante gives a brief metaphoric account of his own name which carries overtones of sodomy among the isolated shepherds (*Teatro*, 816), and Zorzi comments as well on philological connections with the slurred, defective speech of Padovan peasant dialect (1469-70). Cf. Giorgio Padoan, "Angelo Beolco da Ruzante a Perduoçimo," *Lettere italiane* 20 (1968): 198-99. For the mock eclogue in dialect immediately before Beolco, see Emilio Lovarini, *Antichi testi di letteratura pavana* (Bologna, 1894); cf. also Baratto, *Tre saggi*, 16-19.

24. This is a reflection of the tendency of the best Italian criticism to "place" Ruzante and Beolco both in the regional and class struggles of their time in the Veneto. Emilio Lovarini's sixty-year lifework as editor and interpreter is responsible for much of the biographical and historical context we have for the plays and playwright. The most important results are gathered in Lovarini, *Studi sul Ruzante e la letteratura pavana*, ed. Gianfranco Folena Padua, 1965). The texts constituting the dialect background of a "letteratura pavana" were made available by Lovarini in *Antichi testi di letteratura pavana*, and many of these texts are analyzed and related to Beolco's work in the first thorough critical study of the corpus, Carlo Grabher's *Ruzzante* (Milan and Messina, 1953). As Lovarini and Zorzi continued to make the works more widely available in separate editions of several of the plays, Grabher's study was followed by the penetrating essay (first published in 1956) in Beolco's realism vs. theatrical conventions, provided by Mario Baratto in *Tre saggi*. This study (concentrating on the early works) emphasizes "Ruzante" 's emergence as dominant over Beolco (pp. 25, 30, 54, et passim), but brilliantly and eccentrically places an emphasis upon "appetite" in an historical context of peasant life and energies (pp. 37-39, 42, 50-53). Cf. also pp. 58-59 on "genre" disruption (my terminology). Stimulated by the appearance of Zorzi's edition, Giorgio Padoan produced a painstaking monograph, "Angelo Beolco da Ruzante a Perduoçimo," *Lettere italiane* 20 (1968): 121-200, which extended and corrected Zorzi's historical detail and refocussed certain critical inferences drawn from Beolco's interacting allegiances to the peasantry, to Cornaro and the mainland aristocratic *padovani*, and to Venice. (This and other of Padoan's essays on Ruzante are collected in *Momenti del Rinascimento Veneto* [Padua, 1978]. Padoan's editions of *La Pastoral* and *I Dialoghi* [Padua, 1978, 1981] contain valuable and detailed post-Zorzi commentary.) Padoan's monograph was followed by Mario Prosperi's *Angelo Beolco nominato Ruzante* (Padua, 1970), wherein the same triple allegiance is traced but counterpointed with a thread of comparison with Erasmus's relationship toward the Reformation. Besides Franco Fido's essay cited in n. 25, below, the only English-language treatment of Beolco is Nancy Dersofi's *Arcadia and the Stage: An*

Introduction to the Dramatic Art of Angelo Beolco called Ruzante (Madrid, 1978), an up-dated dissertation with convenient bibliography and summaries. The thesis confusedly attempts to relate the sociohistorical emphasis current from Grabher through Padoan to Beolco's evasion (my inference) in transferring the lost pastoral idyll of the peasant to the manipulable world of the stage. Pages 47-49 and 85-86 of Dersofi's study brush against the context of festive folk forms and *carnevale*, as had Grabher, pp. 50-51, 91, 95, 98. This context is whimsically introduced into the heavy-handed Marxist "stagings" detailed in the essays published together by Fernando Mastropasqua and Cesare Molinari, *Ruzante e Arlecchino: Tre saggi sul teatro popolare del cinquecento* (Parma, [1970]).

25. In the best brief essay on the plays Franco Fido says that "Beolco's whole work lies between two dreams, that related by young Ruzante to the audience in the vernacular prologue of *La Pastoral*, and . . . one told by the same, older, Ruzante to his friend in the late letter to Marco Alvarotto" ("An Introduction to the Theater of Angelo Beolco," in *Renaissance Drama*, 6, ed. A. C. Dessen [Evanston, 1973], 213). This is an important observation, because the dream tradition is central to continuities in Renaissance drama (a point I documented in *The Theater and the Dream: From Metaphor to Form in Renaissance Drama* [Baltimore, 1973]) and because the dream form is so closely analogous to the magic formulae of so many folk and comedic resurrections, not least those throughout Ruzante's work.

26. A disputed interpretation of the phrase: cf. Zorzi, 1297, n. 106.

27. Mikhail Bakhtin, *Rabelais and His World* trans. Helene Iswolsky (1965; Cambridge, Mass., 1968), esp. 145-52, 368-474.

28. On the mariazo and its forms, see Paolo Toschi, *Le origini del teatro italiano* (Turin, 1955), 413-35; Zorzi, xxxvii-xlvi, with special reference to the Veneto with debts to Grabher, Baratto, and others.

29. See Cope, *Theater and the Dream*, 294, for a summary bibliography.

30. Cf. Zorzi, 1291, n. 65, and 1293, n. 84. In the latter discussion, Zorzi picks up Lovarini's suggestion that in *La Pastoral* Beolco may have played Ruzante in mask, accounting for the enlarged head.

31. Cf. Baratto, *Tre saggi*, 25, 30, 54.

32. Much of Italian criticism inevitably focuses upon the dialects of Beolco's plays and the implications for changing relationships among allegiances to the mainland Veneto, Venice, and the literary heritage of Florence. Therefore, Beolco's attitude toward Bembo has been widely explored; but see esp. Padoan, "Da Ruzante a Perduoçimo," 193-96, for particularly apt associations.

33. Cf. a comment in Beolco's "Seconda oratione" on how the times are so wearisome that husband and wife separate from one another, "one goes here, one goes there, according as one may have a better mode of living than the other" (1211).

34. In the following pages I offer an alternative interpretation of Ruzante's career to that given in Fido's "Theater of Angelo Beolco," 212-13: "In the urban setting of these elegant plays, at the same time more 'classical' and more 'middle class' than anything he had written before, there is no room for the character of Ruzante and his *snaturalité*."

35. Cf. Padoan, "Da Ruzante a Perduoçimo," 182-85, for detailed parallels.

36. Lea, *Italian Popular Comedy*, 1: 71-77; Pandolfi, *La commedia dell'arte*, 1: 158-64. Implicit in my discussion is a displacement of Pandolfi's conclusions about the merger of Arlecchino into the Plautine slave / *commedia erudita* servant taking place only late in the sixteenth-century history of the troupes.

37. Your Parasite
Is a most precious thing,   .   .   .

.   .   .   your fine, elegant rascall, that can rise,
And stoope (almost together) like an arrow;

. . . .
And change a visor, swifter, then a thought!
This is the creature, had the art borne with him;
Toiles not to learne it, but doth practice it
Out of most excellent nature.
                    (*Volpone*, 3.1.7-8, 23-24, 29-32)

38. Bakhtin, *Rabelais and His World*, 317. Cf. pp. 325, 349, et passim, on the "mouth."

39. On structural influences see Zorzi, 1462-63; on the dating debate, pp. 1459-60. Padoan ("Da Ruzante a Perduoçimo," 185-98) argues for the very late date of 1534-35.

40. Bakhtin, *Rabelais and His World*, 219. Italics mine.

41. See Baratto, *Tre saggi*, 11 ff.; Zorzi, xiv-xxiv; Padoan, "Da Ruzante a Perduoçimo," 134-35, 170-71, et passim.

42. Zorzi, 1470, n. 28, makes an important and modest observation to be compared with the pertinent discussion in Allardyce Nicoll, *The World of Harlequin: A Critical Study of the Commedia dell'Arte* (Cambridge, 1963), 44-55.

43. "Ritrovatore" would become a popular title for the godlike poet in the later Renaissance aesthetic of Tesauro.

44. The tryst is set for Arqua (875). Dersofi (*Arcadia and the Stage*, 150) points out the ironic implications: this is the burial-place of Petrarch, whose praise of Laura Doralice has mentioned in act 1.

45. Cf. Zorzi's analyses of Ruzante's name, cited in note 23 above.

46. Zorzi, 1473, n. 43, notes the distinctions between court and country styles which Beolco is emphasizing.

2. "THE BEST FOR COMEDY"

1. For the praise of Edwardes see E. K. Chambers, *The Elizabethan Stage* (Oxford, 1923), 3: 309; 4: 233, 246; Leicester Bradner, *The Life and Poems of Richard Edwards*, Yale Studies in English, no. 74 (New Haven, 1927), 1-18, 57-58, et passim. Bradner's study constitutes the only extended examination of Edwardes.

2. The most concerted effort to assign a play to Edwardes' authorship, curiously, has centered upon *Misogonus*: for detailed summaries see R. Warwick Bond, *Early Plays from the Italian* (Oxford, 1911), 166-67; Chambers, *Elizabethan Stage*, 4: 31-32.

3. The quotation is from Alfred Harbage, *Shakespeare and the Rival Traditions* (New York, 1952), 62. Cf. Chambers, *Elizabethan Stage*, 3: 37-41; Madeleine Doran, *Endeavors of Art: A Study of Form in Elizabethan Drama* (Madison, 1954), 103, 263-64, 299-300; Bradbrook, *Growth and Structure of Elizabethan Comedy* (London, 1955), 24. Even abstract interludes were influenced. The victory of Wit over Tediousness in Redford's *Wit and Science*, with its later imitations in *The Marriage of Wit and Science* and *The Marriage of Wit and Wisdom*, were sensationalized as a knight's sanguine decapitation of a giant.

4. *Common Conditions*, ed. Tucker Brooke (New Haven, 1915), lines 1498-99, hereafter cited by line number in the text.

5. *Clyomon and Clamydes*, ed. W. W. Greg, Malone Society Reprints (Oxford, 1913), lines 839-40, hereafter cited by line number in the text.

6. C. H. Herford and Percy Simpson, *Ben Johnson* (Oxford, 1925-52), 10: 221-22, show that Jonson is not alluding necessarily to Wever's plays, but to a proverbial type.

7. *Hickscorner* employed the device very briefly for unregenerate "Imagination" (John S. Farmer, *Anonymous Plays, 1st Series* [London, 1905], 156-57). The oaths are

commonest in *Gammer Gurtons Needle*, where they appear thirty-seven times, but they serve no characterizing function, being placed in the mouths of six of the eight major characters. Preston, like the author of *Hickscorner*, very briefly injects the "gog's" oaths into the Huff, Ruff, and Snuff farce scene in *Cambyses*. The most revealing touchstone, however, is Tom Tosspot in Ulpian Fulwell's *Like Will to Like*, who lays explicit claim to "saying my prayers with wounds, blood, guts, and heart: / Swearing and staring" (*The Dramatic and Miscellaneous Writings of Ulpian Fulwell*, ed. John S. Farmer [London, 1906], 19). In practice, Tom's use of such oaths (pp. 12, 17, 41, 43) is scarcely noticeable and does not at all distinguish him from the equally casual swearers Ralph Roister (pp. 41, 43), Cuthbert Cutpurse, and Pierce Pickpurse (pp. 28, 47).

8. In the first scene the oath recurs ten times in eighty-three lines; in the later scene the tinker-robbers speak thirty-four lines in which the oath is heard seven times.

9. Doran, *Endeavors of Art*, 101. Cf. Chambers, *Elizabethan Stage*, 3: 178; Bernard Spivak, *Shakespeare and the Allegory of Evil* (New York, 1958), 254.

10. My position is antithetical to that developed in Spivak, *Shakespeare and the Allegory of Evil*, 225-26, 291-303. Interested in the genesis of Iago, this critic reads all early Vice figures as types. If they break through conventionality, they are distortions of type, not ambiguous characters.

11. The conclusion is so truncated that Brooke conjectured, quite plausibly, that in an unknown source narrative Conditions carried, not a poison, but a harmless potion.

12. See Sedmond's talk (in the role of Nomides) of "raging storms," etc. (*Conditions*, 760 ff.). This could be simply metaphoric, except that he is now in Phrygia, a land which Conditions had earlier described as "Cleane ouer the sea" (441).

13. Frederick Gard Fleay, *A Biographical Chronicle of the English Drama, 1559-1642* (London, 1891), 2:296.

14. *Apius and Virginia* (1575), ed. W. W. Greg, Malone Society Reprints (Oxford, 1911), lines 922-27, hereafter cited by line number in the text.

15. Willard Farnham praised the play in this direction, but illustrated the point only by indicating Chaucerian borrowings (*The Medieval Heritage of Elizabethan Tragedy* (1936; corr. ed. Oxford, 1956), 251-58). Doran gives similar faint praise in *Endeavors of Art*, 295-96. Spivak sees Haphazard's dominance, but finds the separate actions "otherwise dissociated" (*Shakespeare and the Allegory of Evil*, 272).

16. Conditions says of himself that he is "nere kinde to dame fortune to raise and to let fall" (166). This statement influenced Brooke to describe him as embodying "a philosophic idea . . . a parable of the *common conditions* of life" (Introduction, *Common Conditions*, xiv-xv). But unlike Haphazard, Conditions does not consistently motivate or control action. And his ambivalences are those of character; "Fortune" knows no remorse, fear, or affection. Neither did Haphazard. Spivak, *Shakespeare and the Allegory of Evil*, 294-97, thinks differently.

17. *Damon and Pythias*, ed. Arthur Brown and F. P. Wilson, Malone Society Reprints (Oxford, 1957), lines 6-33, hereafter cited by line number in the text.

18. Cf. Harbage, *Shakespeare and the Rival Traditions*, 343-44.

19. Cf. lines 1847, 1850, 1851-52, 1965-67, 2073, 2207.

20. See W. Y. Durand, "*Palaemon and Arcyte, Progne, Marcus Geminus,* and the Theatre in which They Were Acted, Described by John Bereblock (1566)," *PMLA* 20 (1905): 502-28. Cf. Chambers, *Elizabethan Stage*, 3: 311; Bradner, *Edwards*, 72-82.

21. For instance, the first part of *Palamon and Arcite* concludes with regal preparations for a joust: see Durand, "*Palaemon and Arcyte*," 512.

22. Cf. his "I will go in with a heavye and pensiue hart too. / To think how Pithias this poore gentleman to morow shal die" (1299-1300).

23. Cf. *Common Conditions*, lines 25, 73, 150, 166, 371-73, 439, 460, 478-87, 749-51, 764, 821-23, 1101-6, 1142, 1798; *Sir Clyomon*, lines 7, 388-89, 404-5, 1972-73, 1980,

1984, 1985, 1997, 2037, 2207. Edwardes wrote two poems developing the storm-tossed-ship-as-fortune trope: see "Wanting his desyre he complayneth" and "Of Fortunes Power" in Bradner, *Edwards*, 116–17.

24. W. Y. Durand, "A Local Hit in Edwardes' *Damon and Pithias*," *Modern Language Notes* 22 (1907): 237. Cf. Bradner, *Edwards*, 21.

25. My reconstruction of chronology assumes the fictive axiom that an author's work matures as it progresses, seldom completely true. No reasonable chronology, however, can separate widely the plays I have treated: internal and external evidence agree on that cardinal point.

26. Harbage, *Shakespeare and the Rival Traditions*, 39.

27. Chambers, *Elizabethan Stage*, 2: 34–35; Michael Shapiro, *Children of the Revels* (New York, 1977), 14–16.

3. PEELE'S *OLD WIVES TALE*

1. Laurilyn J. Rockey, "*The Old Wives Tale* as Dramatic Satire," *English Theatre Journal*, 22 (1970): 270, stating a connection first noted by F. G. Gummere, "Critical Essay on *The Old Wives Tale*," in *Representative English Comedies*, ed. Charles Mills Gayley (New York, 1916), 1: 341–42. The most thorough development of this thesis is John Doebler's "The Tone of George Peele's *The Old Wives Tale*," *English Studies* 53 (1972): 412–21.

2. For Professor Sarah Clapp the Huanebango story appeared to be "a consummate illustration of the cleverness, the wit, the humor that were Peele's" because it subverts the natural expectations of poetic justice and romantic fulfillment present in the source legends, since the lady's imperfections do not disappear when the lover attains her. But these details alone "do not signify as much to us as does Peele's cleverness in turning upon itself romantic folk-lore." Almost forty years later (with the added aid of Stith Thompson's indices) Professor Charles Adams concluded that Peele, "consciously utilizing folktales and motifs from oral tradition, . . . has turned the language, the form, and the taletellling situation of the *Märchen* from an essentially serious mode of entertainment into a humorous vehicle of dramatic parody." (Sarah Lewis Carol Clapp, "Peele's Use of Folk-lore in 'The Old Wives' Tale,' " *Texas Studies in English*, no. 6 (1926), 146–56, and Charles S. Adams, "The Tale in Peele's *Old Wives' Tale*," *Midwest Folklore* 13 (1963): 13–20.)

3. Arthur M. Sampley, "Plot Structure in Peele's plays as a Test of Authorship," *PMLA* 51 (1936): 689–701.

4. The facts of Peele's Oxford career as playwright, playboy, and postgraduate master of ceremonial entertainments are gathered in David H. Horne's biography, *The Life and Minor Works of George Peele*, ed. C. T. Prouty (New Haven, 1952), 1: 31–64, esp. 41–46, 57–64.

5. Ibid., 57.

6. Susan T. Viguers, "The Hearth and the Cell: Art in *The Old Wives Tale*," *Studies in English Literature* 21 (1981): 217.

7. John D. Cox, "Homely Matter and Multiple Plots in Peele's *Old Wives Tale*," *Texas Studies in Language and Literature* 20 (1978): 344.

8. Patricia Binnie, ed., *Old Wives Tale* (Manchester and Baltimore, 1980), 3–6.

9. *The Old Wives Tale*, ed. W. W. Greg, Malone Society Reprints (Oxford, 1908), line 120, hereafter cited by line number in the text.

10. It is Sir Andrew Aguecheek's catch of "Thou Knave": see *Twelfth Night*, ed. J. M. Lothian and T. W. Craik, New Arden Shakespeare (London, 1975), app. II, pp. 182–85.

11. Viguers' essay, "The Hearth and the Cell," is admirably persuasive on thematic stage settings for this opposition between Madge's milieu and Sacrapant's.

12. On sleep as renewal see Viguers' observations, ibid., 220-21.

13. Jackson I. Cope, *The Theater and the Dream: From Metaphor to Form in Renaissance Drama* (Baltimore and London, 1973), 170-72, 196-210.

14. C. L. Barber, *Shakespeare's Festive Comedy* (Princeton, 1959), 220.

15. A. P. Rossiter, *English Drama from Early Times to the Elizabethans* (1950; New York, 1967), 20-21.

16. *The Knight of the Burning Pestle*, 1.300-302, ed. Cyrus Hoy, in *The Dramatic Works of the Beaumont and Fletcher Canon*, ed. Fredson Bowers (Cambridge, 1966-), 1:24.

4. MARLOWE'S *DIDO* AND THE TITILLATING CHILDREN

1. John Brinsley, *Ludus Literarius; or, The Grammar Schoole* (1627), ed. E. T. Campagnac (London, 1917), 107, 257.

2. In his copy of Dyce's edition of Marlowe, now in the Folger Shakespeare Library. See *Dido Queen of Carthage* and *The Massacre at Paris*, ed. H. J. Oliver (Cambridge, Mass., 1968), xix. All quotations are from this edition.

3. Harry Levin, *The Overreacher: A Study of Christopher Marlowe* (1952; Boston, 1964), 16-17; Clifford Leech, "Marlowe's Humor," in *Essays on Shakespeare and Elizabethan Drama in Honor of Hardin Craig*, ed. Richard Hosley (Columbia, Mo., 1962), 70-75.

4. Don Cameron Allen, "Marlowe's *Dido* and the Tradition," in Hosley, *Essays*, 68.

5. Too much literal credence has been placed in Jonson's epitaph for Salomon Pavy, who died while a member of the Children of the Queen's Chapel. The poem is an extended conceit on the untimely death of the boy, rather than a literal critique of his ability to enact "Old men so duely, / As, sooth, the *Parcae* thought him one" (*Ben Jonson* [Works], ed. C. H. Herford and P. and E. Simpson [Oxford, 1925-52], 8:77).

6. Turnabout declamations are the principal feature of John Lyly's classical court plays, as of *Euphues*. Jonas Barish, "The Prose Style of John Lyly," *ELH* 23 (1956): 14-35, noted the Euphuistic structure of the plays; Marlowe anticipated Barish in discerning that Lyly had uncovered the ideal vehicle for the talented boy players. This essay takes issue with Wolfgang Clemen's view that the declamations are late "dramatic" revisions of *Dido* (*English Tragedy before Shakespeare* [London, 1961], 161-62). Michael Shapiro, "Children's Troupes: Dramatic Illusion and Acting Style," *Comparative Drama* 3 (1969): 42-53, argues for a variety of styles available to the boys: naturalistic, parodic, and declamatory (pp. 50-51).

7. *Jos. Isaei Caesenatis Notae* to Lactantius' *Div. Inst.* (Migne, *PL*, VI, 896) summarizes opposing interpretations of Ganymede as catamite and soul.

8. Cited in J. B. Steane, *Marlowe: A Critical Study* (Cambridge, 1964), 7, 364.

9. E. K. Chambers, *The Elizabethan Stage* (Oxford, 1923; corr. ed. 1951), 2: 33.

10. Harold N. Hillebrand, *The Child Actors: A Chapter in Elizabethan Stage History* (Urbana, Ill., 1926), 160-63, and Irwin Smith, *Shakespeare's Blackfriars Playhouse: Its History and Its Design* (New York, 1964), 182-85, detail the Clifton affair.

11. Alfred Harbage, *Shakespeare and the Rival Traditions* (New York, 1952), 210-13, pointed out that homosexuality was a staple topic in plays for the boys' private theater. Cf. W. Robertson Davies, *Shakespeare's Boy Actors* (London, 1939), 9-18.

12. Quotations, in order, are from Chambers, *Elizabethan Stage*, 2: 18, 50.

13. Ibid., 4: 217.

14. Ibid., 224.

15. Ibid., 256–57.

16. John Lyly, *Endimion*, 5.3.187–88, in *Works*, ed. R. W. Bond (Oxford, 1902), 3: 76.

17. Hillebrand, *Child Actors*, 148, argues the probability of there being occasional adult performers with the boys, as does Shapiro, "Children's Troupes," 43–44.

18. Oliver, Introduction to *Dido*, xxxiii, comments upon a modern production by boy actors in Southampton in 1964: "When a drama such as *Dido* is acted by boys, it is the parts of the *women* that 'come over' realistically. A schoolboy has no difficulty in conveying the distress of Dido; but a schoolboy Aeneas, perhaps no taller than his Dido and Anna, cannot be much more than a puppetlike figure, no matter how good an actor he may be, and is bound to seem somewhat artifical and even stiff in comparison. Presumably Marlowe knew this."

19. Douglas Cole, *Suffering and Evil in the Plays of Christopher Marlow* (Princeton, 1962), 82, n. 7.

5. *BARTHOLOMEW FAIR* AS BLASPHEMY

1. Ray L. Heffner, Jr., "Unifying Symbols in the Comedy of Ben Jonson," in *English Stage Comedy: English Institute Essays, 1954* (New York, 1955), 96. That Jonson's contemporaries recognized *Bartholomew Fair* as a study in arbitrary authority as the cause of both Puritan and profane social revolts is demonstrated by Richard Brome's *Covent-Garden Weeded* (1632–33). Here the "weeder" is a justice of the peace who invokes "my Reverend Ancestor *Justice Adam Overdoe*" for precedent in hunting out all the "enormities" (*Dramatic Works of Richard Brome* [London, 1873], 2: 2–3). These enormities turn out to be hypocritical puritanism in a young man whose motive was to cross the will of an uncontrollably dominating, whimsical father, and wild carousing on the part of other sons allegedly studying law. There is a hubbub of patented "protestations" among the members of the Philoblathicus roaring club (2: 39–41) which corresponds closely to the "vapouring" contest of *Bartholomew Fair*, and there is the eventual discovery by the twin authorities Crosswill and Cockbrain that their efforts not only have caused, but cannot control, revolt by their progeny. While Brome's play lacks the symbolic structure which broadens Jonson's scope, it nonetheless has been closely studied by one critic who concludes justifiably that "a cautious correlation can be made between the terms of this play and circumstances of Caroline England . . . Brome here approaches in humorous terms the fact that . . . an inflexible and unintelligently restrictive policy on the part of the paternal state can induce a desperate and equally inflexible reaction" (R. J. Kaufmann, *Richard Brome, Caroline Playwright* [New York, 1961], 86–87; cf. 67–87).

2. Ben Jonson, *Bartholomew Fair*, 2.1.42, ed. E. A. Horsman, Revels Plays edition (London, 1960), cited hereafter in the text. It is pertinent to notice that the justice fails in his duty and holds no Pie-powders Court at all on this notable day; see 4.6.64–69.

3. Henry W. Wells, *Elizabethan and Jacobean Playwrights* (New York, 1939), 205.

4. For a fascinating Anglican case history one can turn to that of Henry Burton, preacher at St. Matthew's in London, who from his pulpit stimulated his notorious parishioner John Bastwick; see William Haller, *The Rise of Puritanism* (New York, 1938), 250–59). Cf. the general survey in William P. Holden, *Anti-Puritan Satire, 1952–1642* (New Haven, 1954), 137–41, 151–52.

5. *Ben Jonson*, ed. C. H. Herford and P. and E. Simpson (Oxford, 1925–52), 7:584. For the fullest discussion, see J. Dover Wilson, "Ben Jonson and *Julius Caesar*," *Shakespeare Survey 2*, ed. Allardyce Nicoll (Cambridge, 1949), 38–42.

6. Horsman, *Bartholomew Fair*, pp. xiv–xix.

7. For the modern audience, this legal word's religious aspect might coalesce with the other Old Testament language only in retrospect. But in Jonson's early-seventeenth-century London, the Puritans' specialized adaptation of "covenant" certainly dominated over the secular sense; see Champlin Burrage, *The Early English Dissenters . . . 1550–1641* (Cambridge, 1912), 1: 68 ff., esp. 75n, 76–77.

8. Overdo's topical identification has been much discussed. But for our context, it is worth recalling two points: (1) that "mirror" cannot here be used in the sense of a warning glass and (2) that the word sometimes means "paragon" in the seventeenth century, an ambiguity which allows it to function simultaneously by warning against allegorical reading and by inviting one to read the symbolic identity of Overdo and his Jehovan prototype. See the alternative discussions in Herford and Simpson, *Jonson,* 10:177, and in Horsman, *Bartholomew Fair,* pp. xx–xxi, 12n. My argument below makes apparent on internal rather than historical grounds that Herford and Simpson have implied an incorrect solution to the rhetorical question they raise concerning "profaneness": "Throughout the play Troubleall invariably says 'quit you,' 'multiply you,' 'save you,' 'bless you.' . . . He never prefixed 'God.' Has this prefix been omitted from the text because of the statute against profaning God's name in plays?" (*Jonson,* 10:177–78).

9. Herford and Simpson, *Jonson,* 10:178, gloss from Isaac's blessing to Jacob: "God Almighty bless thee, and make thee fruitful, and multiply thee" (Gen. 28:3). In any case, "multiply" is the most ubiquitous of Old Testament blessings, and its progenitive quality enters into the sexual aspect of *Bartholomew Fair,* which is concerned so largely with fruitfulness vs. sterility, as discussed below. "Quit" is also emphatically pointed at the basic quality of the symbolic action, I believe. This word, like "covenant," bridges the legal and religious vocabularies, and in each offers that forgiveness (or "mercy") which balances strict justice.

10. For Busy, casuistry is the manufacture of masks. As he explains to the Littlewits on the subject of eating pig, it "hath a face of offence with the weak, a great face, a foul face, but that face may have a veil put over it, and be shadowed as it were" (1.6.66–69). This "veil" is a hypocrite's counterpart, of course, to Overdo's "cloud" and Wasp's "vapours."

11. The symbolic stocks are a traditional device borrowed from the morality plays; see T. W. Craik, *The Tudor Interlude* (Leicester, 1962), 92–96.

12. Littlewit, dispenser of the license, and Overdo, dispenser of the warrant, agree in accepting classification under the rubric of "fool." Overdo makes love to the term by adopting the disguise: "They may have seen many a fool in the habit of a Justice; but never till now, a Justice in the habit of a fool" (2.1.7–9); Littlewit is delighted with Win's epithet: "A fool-John she calls me. . . . Pretty littlewit of velvet! A fool-John!" (1.3.52–53; cf. 1.1.27–29).

13. For a detailed history of the commercial origins and emphasis of the fair through Jonson's time, see Henry Morley, *Memoirs of Bartholomew Fair* (London, 1880), 13–141.

14. Alice, beating Mistress Overdo, complains against amateurism: "The poor common whores can ha' no traffic, for the privy rich ones; your caps and hoods of velvet call away our customers, and lick the fat from us" (4.5.68–70).

15. "And they shall make an ark of shittim wood: two cubits and a half shall be the length thereof, and a cubit and a half the breadth thereof" (Exod. 25:10).

16. This episode parallels those in which Overdo, attempting to save Edgworth from bad companions, is first beaten and then stocked, being mistaken for the very thief he is unwittingly attempting to aid (2.6 and 3.5).

17. It is proper to recall at this point L. C. Knights' classic account of piracy and high finance among the Jacobeans in *Drama and Society in the Age of Jonson* (London, 1937).

18. Cf. the interaction of the image of Cokes as a child in the fair with the New Testament warning to "children sitting in the markets" cited in sec. 2 of this chapter.

19. The invitation to the pleasures of Ursula's booth should be recalled when one hears Busy's remark immediately preceding his identification of Ursula as world, flesh, and devil: "Bottle ale is a drink of Satan's . . . devised to puff us up and make us swell in this latter age of vanity, as the smoke of tobacco to keep us in mist and error" (3.6.29–32). Overdo elaborately expands the attack on "froth" and tobacco, claiming that the latter makes "the brain smok'd like the backside of the pigwoman's booth" (2.6.40–41).

20. In the *Masque of Queens* (1609) Jonson employs Ate, or Mischief, as dame of the witches, and in this masque she imprecates: "Exhale Earth's rott'nest vapors; / And strike a blindness, through these blazing tapers / . . . see euery foote be bare" at the height of her attempt to bring hubbub on for the "roaring boys" (Herford and Simpson, *Jonson*, 7:296, 299–300). Cf. Jonson's long note "n" (ibid., 286–87) discussing the iconography and sources of "*Ate*, or *mischeife* (for so I interpret it)," which indicates a different but historically related tradition of development, even while Jonson retains the central images of misty vapors and blindness.

21. Cesare Ripa, *Iconologia* (Padua, 1625), 178; Vicenzo Cartari, *Imagini delli dei de gl'antichi* (Venice, 1674), 197–98). Spenser, splitting *Discordia* into the mother-son combination of Occasion and Furor, adopts the emphatic detail which recurs in Jonson's Ursula scene, as well as the flaming torch: "Her other leg was lame, that she no'te walke" (*Faerie Queene*, II.iv.4). Cf. *Works of Edmund Spenser*, ed. E. Greenlaw et al. (Baltimore, 1932), 2:226–27 (McManaway) on other emblem sources for the legs and speculations on cross-fertilization of iconography.

22. Giovanni Piero Valeriano, *I ieroglifici* (Venice, 1625), 111, 114. There is a further interweaving of these symbolic traditions when Winwife denominates Ursula "Mother o' the Furies, I think, by her firebrand" (2.5.71). The mother of the Furies was variously identified as Night or Darkness, and Boccaccio's explanation is the metaphoric blindness of unreasoning passion: "Le Chiamano figluole d'Acheronte; & della Notte, non per altra ragione (à me pare) che per questa. Quando non succedono secondo il disio i voleri, è forza che la ragione ceda . . . che nasce una perturbatione di mente; laquale non senza giudicio de cecità de mente continua, & per lo continuare, diviene maggiore fino a tanto, che cade nell'effetto: il quale oprato senza ragione, necessariamente conviene parere furioso. Et così le furie nascono di Acheronte, & della Notte." (They are called the daughters of Acheron and Night for no other reason than this (it seems to me). When its objects do not follow according to desire, of necessity the reason surrenders in such fashion that there is born a perturbation of the mind, which blindly continues and, in continuing grows greater until, in effect, it stumbles and falls: this action without reason necessarily has the appearance of fury. And so it is that the furies are born of Acheron and Night). *Della geneologia de gli dei* (Venice, 1627), fol. 44r–v.

The recollection of the Furies draws the Discordia iconography back into tight interaction with the stern justice of Overdo also, inasmuch as they figured as strict purveyors of justice notable for their disregard of mitigating circumstances; and as Boccaccio goes on to elaborate this aspect of tradition, he ironically helps to equate the double chaos created by Ursula and by Overdo with his metaphor of smoke: "Che poi stiano dinanzi a Giove, non è maraviglia; come che egli sia detto benigno, & pio: percioche al pio giudice è bisogno haver per ministri de'vindicatori delle sclerità, de quali se mancano, ò non tengono cura, l'autorità delle leggi, leggiermente và in fumo. Appresso, alle volte per li peccati, de popoli, dalla divinità è conceduto, che negli elementi si congiunga il furore, & che per la discordia di quelli s'infetti l'aere; onde nascano pestilenze mortali, per le cui noi infelici siamo inghiottiti". (That they should have stood before Jove is not to be marveled at, although he is called benign and compassionate, since it is necessary that the charitable judge have ministers of vengeance against evil which, if they are lacking or careless, permit the authority of the laws to dissipate into smoke. Enkindled by the sins of the people, the divine permits fury to mingle in the elements, and for their discord the air is infected; whence are born mortal plagues, by which we, unhappy men, are swallowed up). Ibid.

23. That the infernal denizens of the fair seem the only characters capable of humane compassion is emphasized by the other roaring pimp, Whit, interceding in Cokes's behalf when he is about to be attacked during the puppet show: "No, I pre dee, captain, let him alone. He is a child i' faith, la" (5.4.218-19). But the mercy of hell is strained, since it is Troubleall's champion, Knockem, from whom Whit here must rescue Cokes.

24. Fitting name, we see at last, for a woman who leads all the others into the booth of Discord.

25. We may notice now that Overdo himself implied the analogy in calling the pig booth "the very womb and bed of enormity" (2.2.107).

6. *THE CONSTANT COUPLE*

1. Daniel O'Bryan, *Authentic Memoirs . . . Of the most Celebrated Comedian, Mr. Robert Wilks* (1732), 13, cited in Eric Rothstein's biographical account, *George Farquhar* (New York, 1967), 17.

2. Eugene Nelson James, "The Burlesque of Restoration Comedy in *Love and a Bottle*," *Studies in English Literature, 1500-1900*, 5 (1965); 469-90.

3. *The Constant Couple*, in *The Complete Works of George Farquhar*, ed. Charles Stonehill (London, 1930), 1: 91, cited hereafter by page number in the text. Volume 1 of this edition gives the text of both versions of the play.

4. Introduction to *The Rival Queens*, ed. P. F. Vernon (Lincoln, Neb., 1970), xvi-xix.

5. Colley Cibber, *Apology*, ed. Robert W. Lowe (London, 1869), 1: 105-7.

6. *A Brief Supplement*, in Cibber, *Apology*, 2: 301.

7. Cibber, *Apology*, 1: 205; cf. *The London Stage, 1660-1800* (Carbondale, Ill., 1965), 1: 446. There are indications that this sort of theatrical allusion was in some part a publicity collusion. The comedian Joe Haines was indispensable, and so played in both companies during the 1697-98 season. Among other parts, he played Pamphlet in *Love and a Bottle*, then (write "and") spoke the epilogue to that play as though he were a member of Betterton's company complaining of Drury Lane's recent successes.

8. *A Comparison Between the Two Stages* (1702), ed. Sterling B. Wells (Princeton, 1942), 22. All production details are borrowed from calendars in *The London Stage*.

9. Wildair is infected once (110). Lee mentions the temple to Jupiter Ammon in the dedication to *The Rival Queens*, and Alexander identifies himself with Ammon throughout the play: see *Dramatick Works of Mr. Nathaniel Lee* (London, 1734), 3: 206, 224, 237, 254, 265, 266, 282.

10. Lee, *Works*, 3: 218.

11. Ibid., 249. The coincidence with Wildair's citation suggests that Farquhar may be the author of the prologue to the anonymous play presented at Drury Lane in late February 1698. It was published as a "Prologue: Spoke by Mr. Powell, in answer to a scurrilous one, spoke against him, at *Betterton's* Booth in Little-Lincolns-Inn-Fields," and includes the lines: "Oh! my Statira! Oh, my angry dear, / Lord, what a dismal sound wou'd that make here" (*The Fatal Discovery; or, Love in the Ruines* [London, 1698], sig. A4r).

12. *The Triumphs of Virtue* (London, 1697), 31-32.

13. For dating of the revision see George W. Whiting, "The Date of the Second Edition of *The Constant Couple, Modern Language Notes* 47 (1932): 147-48.

14. Cibber, *Apology*, 1: 135-36.

15. Whiting, "Second Edition of *The Constant Couple*," 147-48. The probability that the Wilkes-Rogers relationship became common knowledge early is strengthened by a jibe at the Drury Lane actresses in *A Comparison Between the Two Stages*: "*Sullen*: Well, then what think you of the *Lurewells* and *Angelicas* of t'other House? *Critic*: To my knowledge there are many *Lurewell's* among 'em, but not one *Angelica*: Many Punks, but not one honest Woman" (13).

16. Cibber, *Apology*, 1: 200.

17. Ibid., 165-68. The anonymous "Satyr on the Players" is, of course, less complimentary: see John Downes, *Roscius Anglicanus*, ed. Montague Summers (London, 1929), 59. Cf. John Harold Wilson, *All the King's Ladies* (Chicago, 1958), 177-81.

18. *Supplement* in Cibber, *Apology*, 2: 313.

19. *Letters of Sir George Etherege*, ed. Frederick Bracher (Berkeley and Los Angeles, 1974), 186.

20. Farquhar adumbrated the dilemma of idealistic sentiments in high society in *Love and a Bottle*: see James, "Burlesque in *Love and a Bottle*," 483-84. There is a slight but clear echo of Lurewell's conduct in Silvia's explanation of her disguise in *The Recruiting Officer*: "Do you think it strange, Cousin, that a Woman should change? But, I hope, you'll excuse a Change that has proceeded from Constancy; I alter'd my Outside, because I was the same within" (Farquhar, *Works*, 2: 198).

21. In this sequel both Wildair and Lurewell have surrendered to the theatrical mores mirrored as well as questioned in *The Constant Couple*. When Angelica, supposed dead, returns, Wildair apologizes for his conduct: "Don't be angry, my Dear, you took me unprovided: had you but sent me Word of coming, I had got three or four Speeches out of *Oroonoko* and the *Mourning Bride* upon this occasion, that wou'd have charm'd your very Heart" (Farquhar, *Works*, 1: 208). Lurewell has already admitted to him that "I hate Love that's impudent. These Poets dress it up so in their Tragedies, that no modest Woman can bear it. Your way is much the more tolerable, I must confess" (189).

7. HARLEQUIN'S REINVASION

1. Claudio Guillen, *Literature as System: Essays toward the Theory of Literary History* (Princeton, 1971), 7-8.

2. Robert Weimann, *Shakespeare and the Popular Tradition in the Theater: Studies in the Social Dimension of Dramatic Form and Function* (Baltimore, 1978), 170-71.

3. Paolo Toschi, *Le origini del teatro italiano* (Turin, 1955), 71-73.

4. Ibid., 437-563 passim; Sesto Fontana, *"Il Maggio"* (Florence, 1964).

5. "Comedie des Chinois, intitulé la Baguette de Vulcain" and "Avantures des Champs Elisées" in [Evaristo Gherardi], *Le theatre italien; ou, Le recueil de . . . le theatre italien* (Anvers, 1696), 464-564.

6. Elizabeth Griffith, *The Times* (London, 1780), sig. [A]3r.

7. Carlo Goldoni, *Mémoires*, in *Tutte le opere di Carlo Goldoni*, ed. Giuseppe Ortolani (Verona, 1935-56), 1: 454. All citations of Goldoni are from this text by volume and page number.

8. [Elkanah Settle], *The Siege of Troy, with a New History of the Trojan Wars* (London, [1728?]), 144. The conjectural date is that attributed to the William Andrews Clark Library copy, which is identical with the "1703" copy in the Huntington Library.

Textual citations are from the Clark Library copy of *The Siege of Troy* (n.p., n.d. [1707?]).

9. Cf. the essay on Farquhar's *The Constant Couple*, Chapter 6 above, and Peter Holland, *The Ornament of Action: Text and Performance in Restoration Comedy* (Cambridge, 1979), 90-92.

10. Elkanah Settle, *The Virgin Prophetess; or, The Fate of Troy* (London, 1701). The twenty-two-foot-high painted scenes for this play are different in many details from those used for *The Siege of Troy* (there is, for instance, a "Palace of Cupid" for the operatic choristers) but closely echoed for the most part in the Bartholomew Fair piece.

11. Sybil Rosenfeld, *The Theatre of the London Fairs in the Eighteenth Century* (Cambridge, 1960), 110.

12. Ibid., 76-77; cf. pp. 54, 80, 84, 86, 94-95, 101.

13. Roger Fiske, *English Theatre Music in the Eighteenth Century* (London, 1973), 7-11.

14. Robert Withington, *English Pageantry: An Historical Outline* (Cambridge, Mass., 1918), 1: 61-62.

15. Dovizi da Bibbiena, *La Calandria*, in *Commedie del cinquecento*, ed. Nino Borsellino (Milan, 1967), 2: 24.

16. George Winchester Stone, Jr., and George M. Kahrl, *David Garrick: A Critical Biography* (Carbondale, 1979), 24; Fiske, *English Theatre Music*, 169-70.

17. Stone and Kahrl, *Garrick*, 220-21; David Garrick, *Plays*, ed. Harry W. Pedicord and Frederick L. Bergmann (Carbondale, 1980-83), 1: 402-8. On the "speaking" pantomime from Garrick to Grimaldi's *Harlequin Mother Goose* see Robert Fahrner, "*The Touchstone* (1779) and the Return of the 'Speaking Pantomime,' " *Theatre Survey* 22 (1981): 191-99.

18. Garrick, *Harlequin's Invasion*, in *Plays*, 1: 206, hereafter cited by page number in the text.

19. "The Dentist," in Flaminio Scala's *Il teatro delle favole rappresentative*, tr. Henry F. Salerno (New York and London, 1967), 85-91; "The Quack Doctor: A Negro Farce," in Gary D. Engle, *This Grotesque Essence: Plays from the American Minstrel Stage* (Baton Rouge, 1978), 28-40.

20. J. G. Robertson, *Lessing's Dramatic Theory* (Cambridge, 1939), 4 ff.; Betsy Aikin-Sneath, *Comedy in Germany in the First Half of the Eighteenth Century* (Oxford, 1936), 7-29, 40-60. Lessing is the *locus classicus* authority who points out that Harlequin returned as Hans Wurst dressed in white instead of the traditional diamonds ("Aber Harlekin hiess bei ihr Haenschen und war ganz weiss anstatt scheckigt gekleidet"). Lessing, *Hamburgische Dramaturgie*, no. 18 (1767), ed. F. Schroeter and R. Thiele (Halle, 1878), 110-11.

The year 1737 was the *annus mirabilis* for attacks upon the popular drama under various guises of a new classicizing return from chaos to rule. The Gottsched-Neuber coalition produced its manifestos in Germany, Ignacio de Luzán's *La poética o reglas de la poesía* was published in Spain, and in England the Licensing Act permitted the ascendency of the patent theaters.

21. "Und in der That hat man aus der Erfahrung gesehen, dass das italienische Theater seit etlichen Jahrhunderten nicht viel kluges hervorgebracht hat. . . . Harlekin und Scaramutz sind die ewigen Hauptpersonen ihrer Schaubuehne . . . sondern machen lauter ungereimte Streiche. "Johann Christoph Gottsched, *Versuch einer critischen Dichtkunst* (Leipzig, 1742), in *Ausgewaehlte Werke* ed. Joachim Birke and Brigitte Birke (Berlin and New York, 1973), 6, pt. 2: 342-43; cf. pp. 358-59 on the French adaptations. All citations are from this edition; translations are my own.

22. *Versuch einer critischen Dichtkunst*, 347-48. See Aiken-Sneath, *Comedy in Germany*, 42-51, on the *Ollapatrida* and Gherardi. Like Beolco, Stranitzky himself

played his peasant creation, Hans Wurst. Cf. Karl Friedrich Floegel, *Geschichte des Gro-tesk-Komischen*, augmented by Max Bauer (1788; Munich, 1914), 1: 312-24.

23. " . . . wie zum Exempel die Harlekinpossen der Italiener: aber darum ist es doch nicht lasterhaft" (348).

24. "Sie haben das Laecherliche nicht in den Sachen, sondern in naerrischen Klei-dungen, Worten und Geberden . . . hat Harlekin und Scaramuz. . . . Diese muessen durch bunte Waemser, wunderliche Posituren und garstige Fratzen, den Poebel zum Ge-laechter reizen" (357).

25. See note 20, above. Lessing cites Moeser's book with basic approval (no. 18 [1767], p. 113). This essay of June 30, 1767, was occasioned by the Hamburg *National-theater* presentation of a Marivaux play and reflects Lessing's strong interest in Goldoni (five of whose comedies were presented a total of twenty times at Hamburg between 1767 and 1769): see Robertson, *Lessing's Dramatic Theory*, 45, 107, 279-80.

26. Justus Moeser, *Harlekin; oder, Vertheidigung des Groteske-Komischen*, aug-mented ed. (Bremen, 1777), hereafter cited by page number in the text. Translations mine.

27. Cf. Luigi Riccoboni, *Histoire du theatre italien* (Paris, 1728), 57, on Cecchini.

28. "Was ich aber billig, als ein Geheimniss meiner Familie, bewahren sollte, ist dieses, dass ich in allen meinen Ausbildungen den Anstand einer Dumheit behalte" (60).

29. Moeser self-consciously coins the word "Misstheile" for the mixing of disparate parts within the character and the genre of harlequinade (he uses the English "disparate" himself). *Harlekin*, 75n.

30. Ortolani in *Tutte le opere*, 2: 1199-1200.

31. "Quelle tentation pour moi! Sacchi étoit un Acteur excellent, la Comédie avoit été ma passion; je sentis renaître dans mon individu l'ancien goût, le même feu, le même enthousiasme; c'étoit *le Valet de deux Maîtres* le sujet qu'on me proposoit." Goldoni, *Mémoires*, pt. 1, ch. 49, in *Tutte le opere*, 1: 223.

32. Ortolani in *Tutte le opere*, 2: 1199-1200.

33. Franco Fido, *Guida a Goldoni: Teatro e società nel Settecento* (Turin, 1977), 89-101; the first version of this study appeared as "Goldoni e il gioco tra 'vraisemblance' e 'vérité' " in *Studi Goldoniani* 2 (Venice, 1970): 179-88.

8. CARLO GOLDONI

1. Giuseppe Ortolani, *Settecento: Per una lettura dell'abate Chiari, studi e note*, Edizione fuori commercio presentata dall'Istituto de Lettere Musica e Teatro della Fon-dazione Giorgio Cini in memoria del suo primo direttore (1905; Venice, 1960).

2. Giuseppe Ortolani, *La riforma del teatro nel settecento e altri scritti*, a cura di Gino Damerini e con bibliografia a cura di Nicola Mangini, Civiltà veneziana, studi 14, Istituto per la collaborazione culturale (Venice and Rome, 1962), xiii.

3. *Opere complete di Carlo Goldoni*, edite dal municipio di Venezia nel II centen-ario della nascita, 39 vols. (Venice, 1907-52), with *Indici* issued uniformly in 1971, and *Tutte le opere di Carlo Goldoni*, ed. Giuseppe Ortolani, 14 vols. (Milan: Mondadori, 1935-56).

4. Ortolani, "Appunti sui melodrammi giocosi del Goldoni" (1934), in *La ri-forma del teatro*, 212.

5. "Intorno alla 'Putta onorata' di Carlo Goldoni" (1937), " 'La buona moglie' di Carlo Goldoni" (1937), " 'Il campiello' " (1939).

6. Giuseppe Petronio, ed., *Goldoni*, Storia della critica, 17 (Palermo, 1958).

7. Attilio Momigliano, *Saggi goldoniani*, Istituto per la collaborazione culturale, Civiltà veneziana, saggi 5 (Venice and Rome, 1959). It is particularly interesting to com-

pare the readings of *Il campiello* by Momigliano (pp. 71-105) and Ortolani (*La riforma del teatro*, 171-82).

8. Croce's own brief but pregnant comments (principally in *La poesia*, Saggi filosofici, 8 [Bari, 1937], 59-61, 139, 250-51), are most elaborately developed in Mario Appolonio, *Storia del teatro italiano* (1940; Florence, 1954), 3: 371-97. Cf. the observations of Petronio, *Goldoni*, 49-55, and the anti-Crocean categorization of certain recent criticism in Franco Fido, "Itinerari e prospettive della critica goldoniana," *Belfagor* 16 (1961): 195-210, esp. 197. Apollonio, 371-73, is particularly useful in identifying the "realist" critics' confusions with aspects of Goldoni's own semiarticulated dualism.

9. Ortolani, *La riforma del teatro*, 302.

10. For Ortolani's repeated assaults upon the commedia dell'arte heritge of the eighteeenth century, see his *Settecento*, 228, 281; *La riforma del teatro*, 8-10, 31, 53-55, 157, 232-33, 261, 275. Soon after the bicentennial year of 1907, the vulgarizing Emilio del Cerro wrote his *Nel regno delle maschere* (Naples, 1914), a slight study of the commedia dell'arte from the beginnings through Gozzi's *fiabe*, which received an unlikely impetus from Croce's laudatory preface. And here one already finds a detailed analogue to Ortolani's view when del Cerro says that "la 'commedia goldoniana' fu ai suoi tempi un vero specchio riflettante la vita d'allora, sopratutto veneziana" (the *commedia goldoniana* was to its own times a true mirror reflecting life then, above all, Venetian [life] [297]), a mirror which owed nothing to the mechanical plot structures and types of the *commedia improvvisa* tradition (351-52). In 1922, Pirandello presented the initial version of his *Teatro nuovo e teatro vecchio* for a conference of historians of the theater in Venice (I cannot determine whether Ortolani was present). On this occasion he gave the authority of his credentials to a Goldoni whose realism was to be defined in the light of its contrast to the commedia dell'arte. Goldoni's style, opined Pirandello, "ci sembra così schietto e aderente alla realtà dei suoi personaggi tolti proprio di peso dalla vita del suo tempo" (seems to us unadorned and adherent to the reality of his characters taken precisely from the measure of the life of his time). But to his contemporaries, "il dialogo di Carlo Goldoni dovette apparire anche ai suoi ammiratori insipido e sofistico, confrontato col linguaggio della commedia dell'arte . . . di frasi stereotipate, di motti e lazzi tipici e tradizionali, di botte e riposte sacramentali, protocollate come in un manuale d'etichetta" (the dialogue of Carlo Goldoni must have appeared, even to his admirers, insipid and sophistic, when compared with the language of the commedia dell'arte . . . [made up] of stereotyped phrases, of typical and traditional sayings and turns, of blows and obligatory responses, recorded as if for a performance). Luigi Pirandello, *Saggi, poesie e scritte varii*, a cura di M. lo Vecchio-Musti (Verona, 1960), 238-40.

11. Ortolani, *Settecento*, 268-69, 424-25; *La riforma del teatro* ("Appunti per la storia della riforma goldoniana"), 41-64 passim.

12. Muratori *Perfetta poesia italiana* (Modena, 1706), 68, cited from Ortolani, *Settecento*, 269.

13. Ortolani, *La riforma del teatro*, 114. And yet there is some evidence that Ortolani must have felt the difficulty of a position which would establish a pure, benign, and yet mimetic comedy in the soil of a society rushing to political decline, a society of *cicisbei* and poseurs, a society culturally dominated by that debilitating feminine audience which we have noticed above. In the earlier *Settecento* Ortolani felt the necessity of explicitly abdicating historical logic in the interest of a mystique of personality: "Se nella letteratura del Settecento, a Venezia, si desiderano invano le vivisezioni degli individui, la satira vigorosa della societa, bisogna accusare l'indole degli autori, fra cui non erano La Bruyère, Moliere, nè il Parini e non farne colpa alle leggi della Reppublica" (If one searches eighteenth-century Venetian literature in vain for incisive examinations of individuals, for vigorous satirization of a society, one must accuse the nature of its au-

thors—among whom there was no La Bruyère, Molière, nor Parini—and not place guilt upon the laws of the Republic [192]). Certainly more than an evaluation of censorship, this is a reflexive reaction to his own value-context paradox.

14. Cited from Ortolani, *Settecento*, 456n. Cf. 454-57.

15. Carlo Gozzi, *Memorie inutili*, a cura di Domenico Bulferetti (Turin, 1923), 1: 200.

16. Ibid., 209. Cf. Gozzi's satiric sonnet on the same subject quoted in Ortolani, *La riforma del teatro*, 144.

17. Ortolani, *La riforma del teatro*, 107. For similar instances one may read particularly pp. 111, 158-59, 162, 168, 176-82, 203, 261, 290, and 304, as well as the essay on *La putta onorata* discussed below; on p. 168, for example: "Il commediografo veneziano fu sopratutto un contemplatore e adoratore della vita, senza veri problemi intellettuali: un adoratore umile, semplice, ingenuo, come certi pittori del Rinascimento, ma per questo superiore a tanti pensatori piu potenti. Egli è a modo suo, un primitivo, un artista puro" (The Venetian comic playwright was above all a contemplator and worshipper of life, without true intellectual problems: an humble adorer, simple and ingenuous, as were certain painters of the Renaissance, but because of that, superior to many more powerful thinkers. In his way, he is a primitive, a pure artist).

18. Pietro Chiari (1711-85) was a Jesuit who dedicated himself to reforming the romance and the drama along lines borrowed from France. He was for several years Goldoni's principal rival at the principal rival theater of Venice. Girolamo Medebach was the director of the Teatro Sant'Angelo in Venice, where Goldoni was playwright-in-residence during the most productive period of his career, 1748-53.

19. *Il poeta comico*, 1.3, in Pietro Chiari, *Commedie in versi* (Bologna, 1760), 3: 17-18; translations mine.

20. Carlo Goldoni, *La putta onorata*, 3.4, in *Tutte le opere*, hereafter cited by act and scene in the text; translations mine.

21. Pantalone's moral stature is further diminished when he swears "da mercante onorato" and Catte comments, "Oh che zuramento che l'ha fato! No digo che no ghe sia dei mercanti onorati, ma . . ." (Oh what an oath he has made! I do not say that there may not be some honorable merchants, but . . . [3.10]) and proceeds to outline a bill of particulars on his sharp practices.

22. Franco Fido, *Guida a Goldoni: Teatro e società nel Settecento* (Turin, 1977), 98; cf. 89-101. This important study is the first major movement by an Italian drama critic out of what one might tag "the Ortolanian circle."

23. *Tutti le opere*, 2:1331.

24. Goldoni, *Mémoires*, ibid., 1:268.

Index

Notes are indexed (by number) when they contain a substantive discussion of a topic relevant to the main text.

Jackson I. Cope is Leo S. Bing Professor of English at the University of Southern California. His other works include *The Metaphoric Structure of "Paradise Lost," The Theater and the Dream*, and *Joyce's Cities*.

THE JOHNS HOPKINS UNIVERSITY PRESS

Dramaturgy of the Daemonic

This book was set in Baskerville text by Oberlin Printing Company from a design by Cynthia W. Hotvedt. It was printed on 55-lb. Booktext and bound in Holliston Kingston Natural cloth by BookCrafters.